Hannah Rothschild is a director and writer. Her feature documentaries, including *The Jazz Baroness,* have been shown on the BBC and HBO. She has written for newspapers and magazines, including *Vanity Fair, Vogue,* the *New York Times,* the *Spectator* and *Harper's Bazaar.* She is vice-president of the Hay Literary Festival, and a Trustee of the National Galley and Waddesdon Manor. *The Baroness* is her first book.

Praise for *The Baroness*

'[A] lovingly compiled memoir about an eccentric member of one of the nineteenth century's richest families who dedicated her life to jazz ... an honest portrait of an extraordinary life. It's a gripping yarn that more than proves that life is stranger than fiction'
Anne Sebba, *Literary Review*

'Richly textured, elegantly told and often as surprising as its subject, Hannah Rothschild's biography of her great-aunt is a moving tribute to a fascinating woman'
Martin Williams, *Country Life*

'Hannah Rothschild tells this story with care, balancing narrative tension with a desire to lay out all the facts so readers can make up their own minds ... wholly gripping'
Rachel Cooke, *Guardian*

'Very moving ... A most beguiling book and tale'
Libby Purves, *Midweek*, Radio 4

'Rothschild's riveting account of her eccentric great-aunt Nica stands out for its nimble writing and brilliant story'
Independent, 50 Best Summer Reads

'Rothschild's unique insider understanding of her family – which she traces back to a Jewish ghetto in Frankfurt in the 1790s – arguably helps her to make better sense than an outsider might. Her empathy and affection inspire her to perhaps delve deeper for an explanation for some of Nica's decisions. What emerges is a colourful, entertaining study of a fearless, fiercely loyal, independent, audacious and slightly bonkers adventuress, who was regarded with

tremendous affection – and bemusement – by those
who knew her in the jazz community'
Alison Kerr, *The Herald*

'Her story . . . is full of interest and warmth.
She was ballsy and kind'
Sam Leith, *Spectator*

'Hannah Rothschild has done a brilliant job of telling the story,
which is by turns moving, shocking and inspiring. Filled with
photographs and startling details, it's utterly absorbing'
Elle

'An eminently readable, well-researched biography'
Helen Davis, *Sunday Times*

'A tale of mystery, intrigue and exoticism'
Simon Yaffe, *Jewish Telegraph*

'A fascinating insight into the struggles of jazz musicians
and the rise of the Rothschild dynasty'
BBC Music magazine

'Hannah Rothschild has done brilliantly to give the
long, sad story of Nica's decline a romantic allure . . .
[An] eloquently written labour of love'
Christopher Hudson, *Daily Mail*

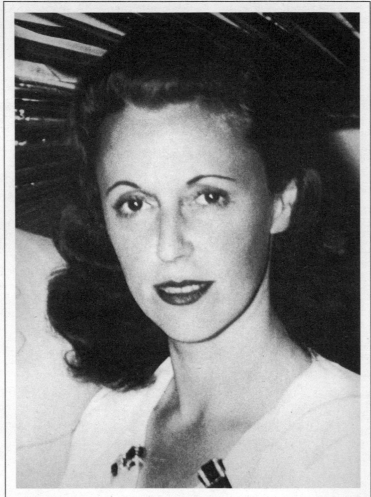

Nica, taken in Mexico, 1947

The Baroness

The Search for Nica, the Rebellious Rothschild

HANNAH ROTHSCHILD

virago

VIRAGO

First published in Great Britain in 2012 by Virago Press
This paperback edition published in 2013 by Virago Press

Family tree drawn by John Gilkes

A CIP catalogue record for this book
is available from the British Library.

ISBN 978-1-84408-605-4

Typeset in Garamond by M Rules
Printed and bound in Great Britain by
Clays Ltd, St Ives plc

Papers used by Virago are from well-managed forests
and other responsible sources.

MIX
Paper from
responsible sources
FSC
www.fsc.org FSC® C104740

Virago Press
An imprint of
Little, Brown Book Group
100 Victoria Embankment
London EC4Y 0DY

An Hachette UK Company
www.hachette.co.uk

www.virago.co.uk

For Jacob and for Serena

Contents

The Rothschilds
Selective family tree

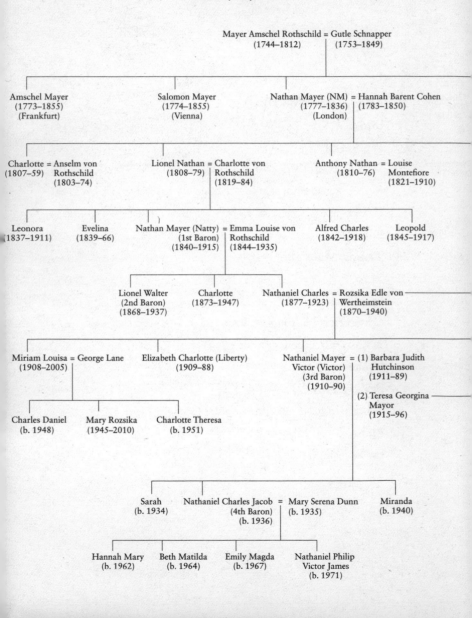

Mayer Amschel Rothschild = Gutle Schnapper
(1744–1812) (1753–1849)

Amschel Mayer
(1773–1855)
(Frankfurt)

Salomon Mayer
(1774–1855)
(Vienna)

Nathan Mayer (NM) = Hannah Barent Cohen
(1777–1836) (1783–1850)
(London)

Charlotte = Anselm von
(1807–59) Rothschild
(1803–74)

Lionel Nathan = Charlotte von
(1808–79) Rothschild
(1819–84)

Anthony Nathan = Louise
(1810–76) Montefiore
(1821–1910)

Leonora
(1837–1911)

Evelina
(1839–66)

Nathan Mayer (Natty) = Emma Louise von
(1st Baron) Rothschild
(1840–1915) (1844–1935)

Alfred Charles
(1842–1918)

Leopold
(1845–1917)

Lionel Walter
(2nd Baron)
(1868–1937)

Charlotte
(1873–1947)

Nathaniel Charles = Rozsika Edle von
(1877–1923) Wertheimstein
(1870–1940)

Miriam Louisa = George Lane
(1908–2005)

Elizabeth Charlotte (Liberty)
(1909–88)

Nathaniel Mayer = (1) Barbara Judith
Victor (Victor) Hutchinson
(3rd Baron) (1911–89)
(1910–90)
(2) Teresa Georgina
Mayor
(1915–96)

Charles Daniel
(b. 1948)

Mary Rozsika
(1945–2010)

Charlotte Theresa
(b. 1951)

Sarah
(b. 1934)

Nathaniel Charles Jacob = Mary Serena Dunn
(4th Baron) (b. 1935)
(b. 1936)

Miranda
(b. 1940)

Hannah Mary
(b. 1962)

Beth Matilda
(b. 1964)

Emily Magda
(b. 1967)

Nathaniel Philip
Victor James
(b. 1971)

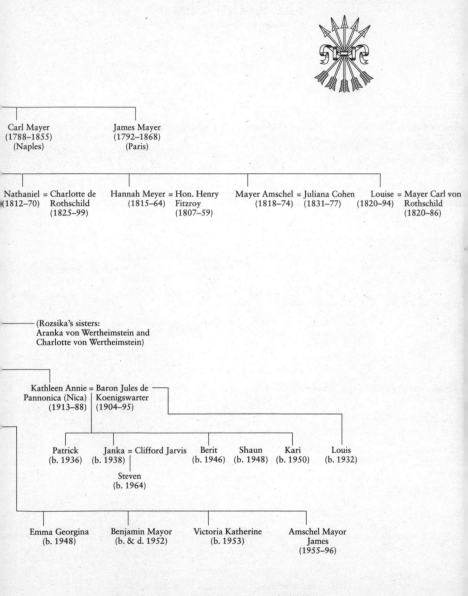

Carl Mayer
(1788–1855)
(Naples)

James Mayer
(1792–1868)
(Paris)

Nathaniel = Charlotte de
(1812–70)   Rothschild
            (1825–99)

Hannah Meyer = Hon. Henry
(1815–64)   Fitzroy
               (1807–59)

Mayer Amschel = Juliana Cohen
(1818–74)   (1831–77)

Louise = Mayer Carl von
(1820–94) Rothschild
           (1820–86)

(Rozsika's sisters:
Aranka von Wertheimstein and
Charlotte von Wertheimstein)

Kathleen Annie = Baron Jules de
Pannonica (Nica) | Koenigswarter
(1913–88)   (1904–95)

Patrick
(b. 1936)

Janka = Clifford Jarvis
(b. 1938)

Steven
(b. 1964)

Berit
(b. 1946)

Shaun
(b. 1948)

Kari
(b. 1950)

Louis
(b. 1932)

Emma Georgina
(b. 1948)

Benjamin Mayor
(b. & d. 1952)

Victoria Katherine
(b. 1953)

Amschel Mayor
James
(1955–96)

I

The Other One

My grandfather Victor was the first person to mention her; he was trying to teach me a simple twelve-bar blues chord but my eleven-year-old hands were leaden and too small.

'You're like my sister,' he said. 'You love jazz but can't be arsed to learn to play it.'

'Which sister? Miriam or Liberty?' I asked, trying to ignore the barb.

'No, the other one.'

What other one?

Later that day I found her in the Rothschild family tree: Pannonica.

'Who is Pannonica?' I asked my father, Jacob, her nephew.

'She is always called Nica but beyond that I don't really know,' he said. 'No one ever talks about her.' Our family is so large and scattered that he did not seem surprised to have mislaid a near relation.

I was not put off. I pestered another great-aunt, Nica's sister Miriam, the renowned scientist, who divulged, 'She lives in New York,' but would not offer any further information. Another relation told me, 'She's a great patron, the Peggy Guggenheim or Medici of jazz.'

Then there were the whispers:

She's known as 'the Jazz Baroness'. She lives with a black man, a pianist. She flew Lancaster bombers in the war. That junkie saxophonist Charlie Parker died in her apartment. She had five children and lived with 306 cats. The family cut her off (no they didn't, someone countered). Twenty songs were written for her (no, it was twenty-four). She raced Miles Davis down Fifth Avenue. Did you hear about the drugs? She went to prison so he wouldn't have to. Who's he? Thelonious Monk. It was a true love story, one of the greatest.

'So what is Nica like?' I asked Miriam again.

'Vulgar. She is vulgar,' Miriam said crossly.

'What does that mean?' I persisted.

Miriam would not elaborate but she did give me her sister's number. When I went to New York for the first time in 1984 I rang Nica within hours of arriving.

'Would you like to meet up?' I asked nervously.

'Wild,' she answered in a decidedly un-great-aunt, seventy-one-year-old kind of way. 'Come to the club downtown after midnight.'

This area had yet to be gentrified and was known for its crack dens and muggings.

'How will I find it?' I asked.

Nica laughed. 'Look out for the car,' and hung up.

The car was impossible to miss. The large, pale-blue Bentley was badly parked and inside it two drunks lolled around on the leather seats.

'It's good they're in there – it means no one will steal the car,' she explained later.

Set back from the street was a small door leading down to a basement. I knocked loudly. Minutes later a hatch opened in the upper door and a dark face appeared behind a grille.

'What?' he said.

'I'm looking for Pannonica,' I said.

'Who?'

'Pannonica!' I repeated in slightly desperate English tones. 'They call her Nica.'

'You mean the Baroness! Why didn't you say so?'

The door swung open to reveal a tiny basement room, shabby, smoky and cramped, where several people sat listening to a pianist.

'She's at *her* table.'

Nica, the only white person, was easy to spot, sitting nearest the stage.

She hardly resembled the woman I had studied in our family photograph albums. That Nica was a ravishing debutante, her raven hair tamed and dressed, her eyebrows plucked into fashionable arches and her mouth painted to form a perfect bee-sting pout. In another portrait, a less soignée Nica, her hair loose and face free of make-up, seemed more like a Hollywood version of a Second World War double agent. The Nica before me looked nothing like her younger self; her astonishing beauty had since waned and now those once-delicate features bordered on the masculine. Her voice will always stay with me, a voice that had been pummelled like a shoreline by waves of whisky, cigarettes and late nights, a voice that was part rumble, part growl, and was frequently punctuated by wheezy bursts of laughter.

Smoking a cigarette in a long black filter, her fur coat draped over the back of a spindly chair, Nica gestured to an empty seat and, picking up a teapot from the table, poured something into two chipped china cups. We toasted each other silently. I'd been expecting tea. Whisky bit into my throat; I choked and my eyes watered. Nica threw back her head and laughed.

'Thanks,' I croaked.

She put her finger to her lips and, nodding at the stage, said, 'Sssh, just listen to the music, Hannah, just listen.'

At the time, I was twenty-two and failing to live up to the expectations, real or imagined, of my distinguished family. I felt inadequate, incapable of making it in my own right, yet unable to

© Victor Rothschild

Nica in 1942.

make the most of the privilege and opportunity available to me. Like Nica, I was barred from working in the family bank; the founding father N. M. Rothschild had decreed that Rothschild women were only allowed to act as bookkeepers or archivists. Caught in a holding pattern between university and employment, I was keen to work at the BBC but was managing only to collect letters of rejection. Although my father, who had followed in the family tradition of banking, found me jobs through various contacts, I was hopeless at running a bookshop, property development or cataloguing artworks. Depressed and disheartened, I was not looking for a role model, but I was looking for options. At the heart of my search was a question. Is it possible to escape from one's past or are we forever trapped in layers of inherited attitudes and ancient expectation?

I glanced across the table at this newly discovered great-aunt and felt a sudden, inexplicable surge of hope. A stranger walking into the club would merely have seen an old lady sucking on a cigarette, listening to a pianist. They might have wondered what this fur-coated, pearl-wearing dame was doing, swaying to the music, nodding appreciatively at a particular solo. I saw a woman who seemed at home and who knew where she belonged. She gave me this piece of advice. 'Remember, there is only one life.'

Shortly after our first meeting I went back to England, where I finally got a job at the BBC and began making documentaries. Again and again my thoughts turned to Nica. In those days, before the Internet and cheap transatlantic airfares, travelling to America and maintaining friendships across continents was difficult. We met at her sister Miriam's house at Ashton Wold in England as well as once more on my next trip to New York. I sent Nica postcards; she sent me records, including one called *Thelonica*: an album by Tommy Flanagan and a musical tribute to her friendship with the jazz pianist Thelonious Monk. One of the album tracks was 'Pannonica'. On the back she'd written: 'To dear Hannah, Lots of love, Pannonica.' I wondered about Thelonious and Pannonica; how had two such strangely named people with disparate pasts ever come to meet? What could they have had in common?

She asked me to play the record to my grandfather Victor, who said that he only quite liked it. 'He didn't really get Monk either,' Nica said. I enjoyed my role as a musical go-between from brother to sister. Another time she asked me to give my grandfather one of the pianist Barry Harris's records. He gave it another duff review. Next time I saw her, I told her. 'I give up,' Nica said dismissively. 'He only likes trad.' Then she roared with laughter.

Nica was fun. She lived in the moment, she was not reflective or didactic, and she did not seek to burden you with her knowledge or her experiences. It was a relief compared to being with her brother Victor or her sister Miriam, where encounters became an intellectual assault course, a mental decathlon in which you were required to show how much you knew and how well you could display your rationale, thinking, knowledge and bravura. When I got into Oxford

University my grandfather called me to ask, 'Which scholarship did you get?' I admitted that I had been lucky to scrape a place. He hung up, disappointed. In her ninety-fourth year Miriam asked how many books I was writing. None yet, I said, but I was making another film. 'I've done too many of those to count,' she said. 'I am writing ten books, including one of Japanese haiku.' Then she hung up.

I did not know anything much about jazz but Nica never made me feel 'uncool' or 'unhip' or care that I had no idea what dig, cat, fly, zoot, tubs, Jack and goof meant. But she was absolutely adamant about one thing: Thelonious Monk was a genius, up there with Beethoven. She called him 'the Einstein of music'. If there were seven wonders in the world, she said, he was the eighth.

When I was planning a trip to New York in December 1988 to do some filming for a documentary about the art world, I set aside three nights to hang out with Nica and had saved up questions to ask her. But then, on 30 November 1988, she died suddenly, following a heart bypass operation. I had missed my opportunity. I missed my great-aunt.

Those unposed questions continued to hover. There were sudden unexpected reminders: a glimpse of the New York skyline in a feature film; a refrain from a Monk song; seeing her daughter Kari; the scent of whisky. While I spent my professional life making filmed portraits of other people, both dead and alive, another plan was percolating. I made films about collectors, artists and outsiders: subjects and themes that were relevant to Nica and her story. Perhaps her untimely death did not mean the end of our relationship; perhaps those questions could be posed posthumously to her surviving friends and relations.

Slowly I started to piece together an outline of her life. She was born in 1913, before the First World War at a time when our family was at the height of its power. She had a cosseted, pampered childhood, living in art-filled mansions. Later she married a handsome baron, by whom she had five children; she had owned a fabulous chateau in France, wore designer frocks and jewels, flew aeroplanes, drove sports cars and rode horses. Part of a glamorous high society, she lived in a cosmopolitan world peopled by tycoons, royalty, the intelligentsia, politicians and playboys. She could get to meet anyone, go anywhere, and she often did. To those who have little or nothing, such an existence must seem like paradise. Yet one day in 1951, without warning, she gave it all up and went to live in New York, where she swapped her upper-class friends for a group of brilliant, itinerant black musicians.

She literally disappeared from British life, only keeping in touch with her children and close family members. The next glimpse most people got of Nica was when her antics were splashed across the newspapers. 'Bop King Dies in Baroness's Boudoir' made headlines on both sides of the Atlantic, as did reports that she was going to prison for possession of narcotics. She reappeared, played by an actress, in Clint Eastwood's biopic *Bird* and then as herself in the documentary *Straight, No Chaser*. The original footage was shot in

© Christian and Michael Blackwood, *Straight, No Chaser*, Warner Bros.

Nica and Thelonious Monk, 1968.

1968 by two brothers, Christian and Michael Blackwood, who, using a hand-held camera, followed Monk from his bed to the concert hall, through airports and backstreets, capturing on celluloid the flotsam and jetsam of his daily life. The footage included scenes with his friend, the Baroness Nica de Koenigswarter, née Rothschild.

In this footage I got my first glimpse of Thelonious Monk. Hovering in the background was my great-aunt.

'Do you know who she is?' the High Priest of Jazz asks the camera crew as he dances around the tiny basement. Weighing over 220 pounds, standing six feet four, the pianist looks both out of scale and graceful as he whirls about in a sharp suit, beads of perspiration glinting on his dark skin. Monk hums as he moves from the sink to the table, his heavy gold rings clunking against a glass of whisky. Suddenly, full of purpose, he turns to the camera.

'I said, do you know who she is?' he barks at the film crew.

No one replies, so Monk points across the room. The camera follows his gaze to settle on a white woman, Nica, who is surrounded by four black men in this kitchen-cum-dressing room, the waiting area between street and performance. The camera takes in the scene; there is not an ounce of glamour in the place with its bare light bulb and stack of unwashed dishes. Nor does the woman look like your usual rock chick or groupie: she is the wrong side of forty; her hair hangs lankly to her shoulders; the stripy T-shirt and jacket do not do much for her comely figure. She certainly does not resemble either an heiress or a femme fatale.

'She's a Rothschild, you know,' Monk persists. 'Her family laid the bread on the King to beat Napoleon.' Then turning back to Nica, he says, 'I tell everyone who you are, I'm proud of you.'

'Don't forget they threw in the Suez Canal for good measure,' she replies, clearly a little drunk. Nica looks at Monk with a mixture of love and admiration before returning to the task of getting a cigarette into her mouth.

'But that was over a year or more ago,' interjects a younger musician.

'Here, have the Suez Canal,' Nica says, clamping the cigarette with her front teeth and holding out an imaginary canal in her hand.

'That's a bitch,' the younger guy comments.

'I tell everyone who you are,' Monk says. For a man whose first language is supposed to be silence he's remarkably voluble. 'You know who she is?' Monk asks again, walking towards the camera just in case anyone isn't concentrating. 'She's a billionaire, a Rothschild.'

I have watched this footage many times, searching for clues about Nica and trying to imagine the reaction of her old friends and extended family. I asked my father Jacob, what did everyone think?

'We didn't talk about her much,' he said.

But when you heard that she had been sent to prison or when the famous saxophonist was found dead in her apartment? I pressed.

My father hesitated. 'I suppose we were all rather bemused and slightly shocked.'

I turned amateur detective. What had taken Nica from the grandest drawing room to the shabbiest cellar? Leaving had real consequences. Divorce, at that time, was a fast track to social ostracism, and the custody of children was rarely given to absconding women. With no qualifications or career, Nica was dependent on her family for support. Was there a terrible secret, some dark reason why she had to be suddenly rushed out of the country and into this foreign environment?

Maybe she was mad. She had made some fairly dotty public statements. Asked by a journalist why her marriage ended, Nica replied, 'My husband liked drum music.' She told the filmmaker Bruce Ricker that the catalyst for her moving to New York was hearing a record. 'I must have played it twenty times in a row and then more. I missed my plane and never went home.'

'She bought Art Blakey a Cadillac and you know what that means,' someone told me.

What exactly are you saying?

'Well, you don't just buy someone a car, do you?' he said knowingly.

There were other rumours about other men. What if I found out that my aunt was nothing more than a dilettante, a permissive woman attracted by a certain lifestyle? Suppose that was all there was? What would I do with this information?

Yet the Nica I knew, who seemed grounded and determined, was not some crazy harpy. She did lose custody of her younger children but she never abandoned them: indeed, her eldest daughter Janka came with her to New York when she was sixteen. Nica never wanted to leave the people she loved; she wanted to escape from a life she described as a 'jewel-encrusted cage'.

'Do you realise what you're doing? A lot of people aren't going to like this,' advised Nica's old friend, the trombonist Curtis Fuller, when he heard I was investigating Nica's life. 'You're going to catch some serious shit.'

Naively, I had not realised that many people, particularly those in the family, wanted Nica to remain a mere footnote in other people's stories.

I should not have been surprised: obsessive secrecy is a family trait and secrets have, on many occasions, served us well. Secrets kept us alive in the Frankfurt Ghetto in the eighteenth century, through various pogroms and, with a few exceptions, during the Holocaust. Secrets were the source of our fortune on Wellington's battlefields, in the oil wells of Baku and, latterly, they saw us through the mire of volatile financial markets.

Many Rothschild women, including those I knew well, stonewalled my questions or refused to take my calls. I received two unpleasant, threatening letters. This, I found out, had happened before, to Nica's sister Miriam, when she wrote a biography of her uncle, *Dear Lord Rothschild*. It contained stories of family suicides. Although one had already been reported in the national press, Miriam's 'crime' was to break ranks and speak about it publicly. She was castigated by a female relation: 'However salacious you think it necessary to capture the attention of the public, I never could imagine that you could soil your own nest in this way by making a story out of it.'

Nica's children were initially enthusiastic about my research but changed their minds, arguing that their mother would have hated any form of biography. I cared about what they thought and, mindful of their feelings, I dropped the project for a few years. Later they published a biographical essay together with a collection of her private photographs and interviews, titled *The Musicians and Their Three Wishes*, which offered a unique insight into her life. Every musician Nica met was asked to tell her three things they really wanted. Their answers are brief but revelatory. Monk says, 'To have a wonderful friend like you.' Miles Davis says, 'To be white.' Louis Armstrong, 'That I live for a hundred years.' Nica had tried to publish this book during her lifetime as a tribute to her friends, but every publisher turned it down. Then her children added their mother's photographs to the manuscript, and the images brought the text alive. Few of the pictures are composed, the lighting is haphazard and their condition is variable, but none of that matters: together they offer an extraordinarily evocative glimpse into a lost world.

I met the great saxophonist, Nica's friend Sonny Rollins, and told him about my abandoned project. 'You have to carry on,' he insisted. 'Her story is our story. It has to be told.' I started work again and continued my research. Wherever my job or holidays took me, I went armed with a video camera and notebook just in case there was someone who remembered something. I've conducted scores of interviews, collected piles of news clippings, album sleeves, documentaries, photographs, letters, emails, tapes and assorted memoirs. It was an adventure that started at one of the Rothschild family homes in Ashton Wold, Peterborough, with Miriam, and criss-crossed the globe from Harlem to Holland, from Mexico to Manhattan and from Spain to San Francisco.

I made a radio programme and then a documentary feature film about her, both called *The Jazz Baroness*. The latter was shown on the BBC and HBO, and it still tours festivals worldwide. Storytelling on film is one form of biography; the written portrait offers other possibilities. I was keen to explore them all, to mine every seam. Why? Mainly because hers is such an extraordinary story, a musical odyssey spanning both a century and the globe with all the ingredients of a melodrama: the heiress and the suffering artist; the butterfly and the blues; love, madness, war and death.

But there are other, personal reasons. Though we were born half a century apart, in different circumstances, with dissimilar characters, investigating Nica's life has helped me to understand my own. She has taught me to look for the similarities rather than the differences, to value choice over convention and, above all, to be more courageous. Why has this project taken me nearly twenty-five years to complete? There is part of me that wonders if I could make it last a little longer. Again and again I asked, who are you, Nica? Heroine or lush? Freedom fighter or dilettante? Rebel or victim?

2

Queen of the Fleas

'Why are you doing this, Hannah? Is it just about self-publicity?' Miriam demanded.

'There are many easier ways to get publicity,' I answered defensively.

'Can't you think of anything else to do? Why does it have to be about the family?'

'You wrote a whole biography of your uncle Walter,' I countered.

'But that was different.'

'Why?'

'Because it was about science. Science matters.'

'Music matters to many.'

But Miriam was not entertaining that thought.

'Shall I stop coming?' I asked.

'Oh, I suppose you'd better not,' she said.

Invariably if I did not go and see her for a while, my telephone would ring. 'When are you coming? I'll be dead soon.' Then she would hang up.

To the outside world, my great-aunt Miriam was a distinguished entomologist but to her relations she was a formidable, exacting and inspirational matriarch who extended her benevolent if capricious hand to those in need. Until her death in 2005, she spent most of her ninety-six years at the Rothschild family house, Ashton Wold. The place was always a safe haven for family and friends, including, at times, Nica, her children and me. Miriam was an expert on family history, an endless source of information about and analysis of our forebears. She was the quintessence of her generation and utterly indispensable to my project. What's more, she knew it.

Many times over the next few years, I went to see Miriam, driving up the A1, through north London and out into the heartland of middle England. It is a beautiful part of the country if one likes flat landscape and vast agricultural tracts. Personally, I found it a relief to turn off a busy road, leave behind the gentle orange glow of the town of Oundle and enter Miriam's natural wonderland.

Nica and Miriam's father Charles, an amateur entomologist, fell

Miriam Rothschild in her wildlife garden at Ashton Wold.

in love with the estate when he realised it would make an ideal conservation ground for butterflies and dragonflies. He tried to buy the land, but the local estate agent told him the owners would never agree to sell – they did not need to. By coincidence, it turned out that Charles's father Nathan Rothschild already owned it. In 1900, work started on building a large three-storey house and laying the foundations for formal gardens, greenhouses, ponds and a park.

Although Nica's brother Victor, as the son and heir, inherited the bulk of the family's possessions and all the estates, in 1937 he gave Ashton to his sister Miriam. In an attempt to save money on heating, Miriam sliced off the whole top floor, lowering the once imposing three-storey façade. Then, declining to prune any plant, she let nature take its course. Soon every wall and many windows were covered with climbers and creepers, while a riot of ivies, roses, honeysuckles, wisteria and other species were allowed to grow unchecked. In the height of summer Ashton Wold looked more like a buzzing, rustling mound of greenery than a house. Surrounded by a 190-acre park teeming with deer that Miriam flatly refused to cull, the land is ringed with the wild-flower meadows that she became so famous for promoting.

Visiting Miriam was always an adventure. My spirits would quicken with excitement as I drove through her local village with its pub, the Chequered Skipper, named, of course, after a butterfly. A gatehouse heralded the start of the long dilapidated drive that wound through arable fields and meadows. After a mile, one would pass the long, high, brick-walled kitchen garden that once contained several acres of plant beds and greenhouses that in the 1920s were capable of producing flowers all year round for the house, and vegetables for the entire estate. In Miriam's time, the structures collapsed, leaving only their foundations and shards of window glass. A few were kept up to house a pet owl, as a butterfly house and to grow exotic crops.

In the garden, the vestiges of formal ponds, clipped yew hedges, summerhouses and beds were still visible but only just. Forty years

The greenhouses at Ashton Wold, Peterborough, in 2004.

of laissez-faire gardening had allowed weeds to choke waterways, paths to close up and trees to fight for space. Nature thrived in those conditions. In early summer the undergrowth teemed with grass snakes. Wild buddleia and flower meadows encouraged a huge variety of insects and butterflies.

'Welcome to Liberty Hall!' Miriam would shout out to arriving guests. 'Do whatever you like here.'

At any one time you might sit down with visiting professors, relations, the odd duchess, the philosopher Isaiah Berlin, the academic John Sparrow plus an assortment of the (mainly male) acquaintances that Miriam met on her various travels. Tea was set out permanently on a long table in the drawing room so that anyone, including the house's enormous population of mice, could help themselves at random. I once pointed out that there were a couple of four-legged 'visitors' scuttling around near the Victoria sponge. 'Well, just be glad they are mice as it means there aren't rats near by. Mice and rats don't cohabit, you know,' said Miriam in her matter-of-fact way.

Lunch was always served with a minor Rothschild wine and the table was laid for at least ten lest any unexpected visitors appeared.

Like Nica, Miriam loved the company of animals; Nica loved cats, while Miriam preferred dogs and even had, for a time, a pet fox. Both Miriam and Victor kept owls. When Miriam's died, it was stuffed and put back on the bookshelf where it had liked to perch. The long entrance hall at Ashton Wold was lined with box files containing Miriam's scientific experiments, and the walls of the downstairs loo were covered in the rosettes won by her champion cows. The room where I slept was so overrun by mice that the floor was often covered in their excrement. There was no point in complaining, as Miriam would never have understood the fuss.

Towards the end of her life Miriam moved her bedroom to a large room on the ground floor, mainly taken up with a workbench, microscopes, papers and family photographs. 'I keep the fleas there in plastic bags by my bed,' she was fond of saying. 'It was a habit that started when the children were small to stop them from disturbing the insects.'

The whole family was mad about insects; I found out that Nica was actually named after one. One day an American friend sent me a bootleg version of the song 'Pannonica' that Monk had written for Nica. Recorded at the Five Spot Café, it is accompanied throughout by the chatter of the crowd and the clinking of glasses. Nica was in the audience, and made the recording, as she so often did. Monk, who rarely spoke, cleared his throat to get attention. 'Good evening, ladies and gentlemen,' he said in his gentle way. 'Here is a little tune I wrote for this beautiful lady here. I think her father gave her that name after a butterfly he tried to catch. Don't think he caught the butterfly.'

I asked Miriam about the butterfly Nica was named after.

'Butterfly!' Miriam roared dismissively and then zoomed out of the room in her high-speed electric wheelchair. My heart sank – what had I done to upset her?

Yet Monk's dedication did seem to provide various clues about Nica and her own mythology. She presented herself as an exotic, elusive creature. It was an intriguing analogy: trying to capture Nica was not unlike glimpsing a butterfly as it flits, dances, bobs and soars over a garden, buffeted by uncertain breezes, drawn by delicate aromas, with the sun momentarily catching its luminescent colours. Suddenly the butterfly will disappear into the neck of a plant or close its wings and, thus camouflaged, become a leaf or a petal.

I decided to find out whether the butterfly *pannonica* was to be found in the entomological collections of either her father Charles or her uncle Walter. Both men had amassed enormous holdings during their lifetimes and after their deaths most of them were given to the nation; more than six million were left to London's Natural History Museum, forming the bulk of its entire collection of bugs and butterflies. I did not set my hopes high: surely there was little chance of finding one butterfly among so many others. I wrote with low expectations and was astonished to receive an invitation to visit the museum's vaults to view the species *pannonica*. Our ancestors were not only great collectors but obsessive documentarians; everything was so carefully catalogued and cross-referenced that little got lost.

One dreary November morning in 2007, I went to the Natural History Museum to see the entomologist Gaden Robinson. We met under the enormous dinosaur skeleton in the main hall and walked down tiled passages, past weird and wonderful creatures, to the storerooms. Robinson led me through huge metal stacks. There I saw the now stuffed giant tortoise that Charles and his daughters used to ride on in the great park at Tring. That poor animal had died of unrequited sexual desire (not for Nica or her, Miriam assured me). The vaults are enormous: long rows of cabinets, filled with beautifully made mahogany specimen trays. 'We're in roughly the right area,' Robinson said, striding down the middle. How did he know what to look for? 'Butterflies on the right, moths on the left. Here's the subgenus, *Eublemma*.'

To my astonishment he turned left, not right, and strode down an aisle.

'But this is the moth section,' I said.

'*Pannonica* is a moth.'

Walter Rothschild riding on a giant tortoise.

'A moth. Are you sure?'

'Quite sure. Here we are.' And he started to pull open the glass-backed drawers.

'But she told everyone she was a butterfly,' I said to Robinson. 'There is even a song written for her called "My Little Butterfly", and endless references to the derivation of her name.'

Robinson turned to me and said quite crossly, 'Butterflies are just moths with go-faster stripes. People think they are terribly, terribly different but butterflies are just three out of many dozens of families of moths that have adopted a high-flying lifestyle; because they are flying in the daylight they tend to exhibit brighter colours than moths. With all due respect to people who find butterflies incredibly sexy, they are just suit-cut moths.'

'Why are butterflies less interesting?' I asked.

'I am not saying they are less interesting, but I am putting them in their proper place. People tend to consider butterflies to be nice but see moths as nasty, which is just public perception. It is erroneous; butterflies are moths with better public relations.'

Once located, *pannonica* turned out to be a humble little insect, the size of a small fingernail and hardly a head turner. We carried the tray of *pannonica*s back to Robinson's office. Each specimen had been carefully mounted on a pin and individually labelled by hand in beautiful Victorian lettering. Using a magnifying glass, we could make out the words. First came 'NC Rothschild' (Nica's father Charles), then the date, August 1913, and finally the place where it was found: Nagyvárad, Bihor, the place where Nica's mother was born. It was in this village Charles met Rozsika and it was here that the family would return every summer to see their relations until the war intervened.

There were about ten little *pannonica*s caught between 1910 and 1914. I looked at the last, aware of the poignancy of the date; it was the last time Charles would go moth hunting as by then his health had begun to deteriorate. Holding this specimen up to the light, I saw that, far from being a dowdy little moth, it was rather beautiful, its lemon-yellow wings with tips the colour of a fine Château Lafite wine. I laughed, realising that being named after a creature of the night was entirely appropriate: Nica came alive after dark.

'Did Nica know she was actually named after a moth?' I asked Miriam a few weeks later.

'Of course,' she said as if I were a total simpleton. 'Pannonica means "of Hungary" and it's also a name given to a mollusc and a vetch. If only you bothered to look in the *Lepidoptera* catalogues, you'd have seen it: *Eublemma pannonica*. It was identified first by Freyer in 1840.'

'Why did Nica say that she was named after a butterfly?'

Miriam rolled her eyes, harrumphed and then left the room. I should have run after her to ask what that harrumph meant, but I did not really need to. Miriam – the eldest sister, the one who stayed behind, who took care of business, who carried on her father's work, who looked after her extended family – was clearly exasperated by aspects of her youngest sister's behaviour.

As the daughter and sister of entomologists, Nica would have known exactly what kind of creature she was named after. I wondered why she preferred mythology to the truth. Did it suit her to stay in the shadows, not to tell the whole story, not to give the complete picture?

Though proud of her heritage and dependent on her inheritance, she remained aloof, preferring to live on another continent, pursuing different interests and deciding to jettison her maiden name even after her divorce. What, I wondered, had made Nica so different from Miriam and Victor who remained steeped in Rothschild life? As my research continued, I realised that Nica felt ambivalent about both her name and her family of origin. She knew that, to the Rothschilds, her birth had been a disappointment. They had wanted a boy.

3

The Rose of Hungary

In 1913, the year of Nica's birth, the Rothschild family were facing two crises. One was entirely of their own making; the other was beyond their control. They had, over the previous century, built a massive global empire but the world in which it operated was crumbling. The inexorable decline of the Austro-Hungarian Empire, in parallel with the expansionist policies of her neighbours Germany, France and Great Britain, meant the balance of power in Europe was in flux.

In war and in peace the Rothschilds were bankers to governments and monarchs, underwriting the dreams and fears of European states. As the financiers of armies and industry, it was said that no one went to war or considered peace without first consulting the Rothschilds. During the Franco-Polish crisis of 1836, a Rothschild matriarch claimed, 'There will be no war because my sons won't provide the money for it.' It was not an idle boast: her offspring owned and controlled a multinational banking corporation that exercised unrivalled power over the international markets. Their empire spread from the oilfields of Baku to the railway network stretching from France to Belgium and from Spain across

Austria into Italy. From commodities to arbitrage, and from mines to commerce, the Rothschilds' reach extended from South Africa to Burma and from Montana to the Caucasus and beyond.

Prosperous financial empires depend on stable political situations. While the family could influence the leaders of countries and their policies, even the Rothschilds lacked the power to hold a continent steady; the family watched in dismay as Europe drifted towards war.

Internally they faced an even greater problem: the lack of male heirs. The family business was founded and administered on the principle that only Rothschild men could inherit and run the business. It was a principle enshrined in his will by the founding father, Mayer Amschel, in 1812 and it is still upheld today.

> My daughters and sons-in-law and their heirs have no share in the trading business existing under the firm of Mayer Amschel Rothschild and sons . . . and [it] belongs to my sons exclusively. None of my daughters, sons-in-law and their heirs is therefore entitled to demand sight of business transactions. I would never be able to forgive any of my children if contrary to these my paternal wishes it should be allowed to happen that my sons were upset in the peaceful possession and prosecution of their business interests.

Furthermore, if any of the partners were to die, their widows and their children had no automatic right of inheritance; ownership of shares reverted to the surviving fathers, brothers or sons. Daughters were expected to marry within the Jewish faith and possibly even within the family. James, writing to his brother in 1824 about his new wife who was also his niece Betty, said, 'One's wife . . . is an essential part of the furniture.'

Originally there had been five capable sons to run the five European branches but, over the final decades of the nineteenth century, fate and luck had denuded them; this dearth of men had led directly to the closure of the Frankfurt branch in 1901. The two heirs, Mayer Carl and Wilhelm Carl, had ten daughters between them but no male issue. The Naples branch closed in 1863 as Adolph Rothschild had also failed to produce a son to take over. By the turn of the century, the English branch was running dangerously low in Y chromosomes. Although few Rothschilds would admit it, their absolute reliance on males was as undermining to their business as were the vicissitudes of war and the vagaries of taxation.

So it was unsurprising that, in December 1913, members of the family waited anxiously for news of the birth of a child to their cousin Charles and his wife Rozsika. It would be their fourth. The couple had already produced an heir, Victor, in 1910 but they needed a spare. So far they'd managed only girls: Miriam in 1908 and Liberty in 1909.

Men ran the bank; women stayed within the family and ruled the homes. Waiting for the baby at Tring Park in Hertfordshire (as it was then) were the unborn baby's grandparents, Nathan (Natty) and Emma. Both were born Rothschilds, married Rothschilds and produced Rothschilds. Natty Rothschild was the first non-Christian to take a seat in the House of Lords and the first to be invited to stay with Queen Victoria at Windsor Castle (she instructed her chefs to serve him a special ham-less pie). He became head of the British branch of the Rothschild bank in 1879. An international financier, Natty made loans to the governments of America, Austria and Russia; funded Cecil Rhodes in South Africa and the De Beers diamond conglomerate; and put together the financing of the Suez Canal. Natty advised his own government through successive administrations: his closest association was with Disraeli; Randolph Churchill and Balfour depended on his counsel. At the outbreak of hostilities in 1914, Lloyd George called a meeting of leading bankers, businessmen and economists to discuss the financing of the war: although the future Prime Minister and the Jewish peer had had many disagreements in the past, Lloyd George remarked afterwards that 'only the old Jew made any sense'.

His business acumen was matched by a philanthropic zeal. Appalled by the pogroms in Russia, Natty refused a lucrative business deal with the Russian government on principle. He donated large amounts of money and campaigned for public support against the persecution of Jews in Romania, Morocco, Russia and elsewhere. Closer to home, he rebuilt all the public housing around Tring, providing 400 new, modernised homes, and created and chaired the Four Per Cent Industrial Dwellings Company, a combination of business and philanthropy to create 6,500 new homes. The problem for Natty's offspring was that he was so capable, so demanding and so critical that it would have taken many ordinary sons to maintain his exacting standards. Instead, he had produced three children, and the two boys were not showing much promise. Now seventy-three and in frail health, Natty, like the rest of the family, was looking in hope towards the next generation.

Natty's wife Emma was born in 1844 and was to live until the age of ninety-one. Arriving from Frankfurt in 1867 to marry her cousin, Emma was told that a house had already been chosen for her, Tring Park, which lay in the Rothschild heartland of the Vale of Aylesbury. To make life easier, the family extended the local railway to its door. Emma saw the house for the first time on the day after her marriage, a typically generous if presumptuous gift.

Like many of the Rothschild women, Emma was indomitable and forthright. She thought nothing of summoning the Prime Minister Benjamin Disraeli to criticise his novels, telling him that while they were quite well written, he did not understand women. She spoke three languages, all with a slight German accent, and laughed differently in each. Perhaps her longevity was due to her taking vigorous daily exercise or her regular habit of having a cold bath every morning.

Charles's brother Walter, Lord Rothschild – her eldest son, the heir apparent – was also waiting. A child of delicate health, he was educated at home. He grew into a huge stuttering bear of a man, weighing over twenty stone and, according to his nieces, he could

keep the whole house awake with his snores. He never married although he did have two mistresses; one bore him an illegitimate daughter; the other blackmailed him for most of his life, threatening to tell his mother about their relationship. His two great loves were his mother Emma and animals, dead or alive. As Lord Rothschild, he was the recipient of the famous Balfour declaration, the letter written in 1917 by the British government, acknowledging that it viewed with favour the establishment of a national home for the Jewish people in Palestine. This letter paved the way for the creation of the State of Israel. But although interested in Judaism

*Walter Rothschild driving
his team of zebras. Hidden
from view is the fourth
animal, a pony, essential to
keep the untameable zebras
on the road.*

and Palestine to an extent, nothing really got in the way of Walter's
first passion, the study of animals and insects.

Walter had not inherited the family's aptitude for making
money. For years he had a desk at the bank but while he pretended
be working on financial matters he was actually using his personal
inherited fortune to create the greatest collection of animals ever
assembled by one man. These included over two million specimens
of butterflies and moths, 144 giant tortoises, 200,000 birds' eggs,
300,00 bird skins and other rare and fabulous specimens, ranging
from starfish to giraffes, which today form an important part of the

collections of the natural history museums in London and in the United States. What made his collection so extraordinary was not just its size and reach but the meticulous way it was catalogued. Every tiny creature was labelled, logged and cross-referenced.

Walter employed agents the world over to forage and gather on his behalf. There was Meek, who looked for birds in the Louisiade Archipelago and in Queensland; Captain Gifford on the Gold Coast; Dr Doherty in the Sula Islands; Mr Everett in Timor; two Japanese men in Guam; and Mr Waterstrade in Lirung. This was only a few of the bird seekers. What he couldn't catch, he bought. A compulsive shopper, Walter combed auction rooms and private sales for treasures to augment his collection. Among the animals named in Walter's honour are a giraffe, an elephant, a porcupine, a rock wallaby, a hare, a fish, a lizard, a cassowary, a rhea, a bird of paradise, a Galapagos finch and an improbable fly whose female sex has eyes on the end of large stalks. Walter, in turn, named some of his discoveries after people he admired, including Queen Victoria and Princess Alexandra, whom he visited at Buckingham Palace in his zebra-drawn carriage.

He built a private museum at Tring Park to house his collection. During wet weather his nieces and nephew played hide-and-seek among the racks of stuffed creatures. I also went there as a child and have since taken my own daughters on visits to wonder at it all. On special occasions we go behind the scenes, into the vaults that hold the birds' eggs and even the bird skins, including those found by Darwin on his voyage on the *Beagle*. In one case there is a skeleton of the now extinct dodo and in another a pair of fully dressed fleas, once performers in a Mexican circus.

Looking at the huge collection amassed by Walter in his museum and by other relations in their houses, I wondered where this impulse to aquire comes from and why so many members of my family seem to share it. Part of it is a form of hoarding, one-upmanship and conspicuous display. But concurrent with this ostentation is the collector's desire to create a perfect, ordered world over which they have some control, a sense of power and security; perhaps at the heart of collecting is the simple need to create external order out of internal chaos.

Walter, like everyone else, longed for his brother and sister-in-law to produce another son. He knew that he had failed to live up to the family's expectations, and that his financial incompetence had dashed so many dreams.

Charles – the father in waiting – was an extremely handsome man with a delicate mental constitution. He had from an early age been susceptible to disorders of mood. Charles also loved animals but his misfortune was to be just good enough at banking. Had he, like Walter, been allowed to indulge solely in a manic passion for naturalism, Charles's life might have turned out differently. Instead, all the expectations of his father and relations were projected on to him, an intolerable weight for any person.

Sent to prep school aged eight, Charles wrote pathetically to his mother that he loved home '10,000,000,000,000 times better than anything'. The hint of homesickness was not taken and, aged thirteen, Charles was sent from prep school to Harrow, where his fellow pupils included future dukes, generals, bishops and politicians such as Winston Churchill. It was hoped that introducing Charles early on to England's movers and shakers would enhance his professional life. Later he wrote, 'If I ever have a son, he will be instructed in boxing and jiu-jitsu before he enters school, as "Jew hunts" such as I experienced are a very one-sided amusement and there is apt to be a lack of sympathy between the hunters and the hunted.' While at Harrow, Charles was regularly released like a fox and told to run for his life while his fellow students, baying like hounds, tried to catch him. Once tracked down, he was beaten till he bled. The teachers turned a blind eye. The hunters didn't record their memories but a fellow pupil, the historian George Trevelyan, confirmed his friend's intense unhappiness and his lasting memory was of Charles mounting small animal skins or setting butterflies.

I imagine poor Charles hunched over his collection of Swallowtail butterflies, piercing them with a sharp pin, rubbing formaldehyde down their delicate bodies and then carefully, in his precise hand, writing their details on a tiny card. He bequeathed these butterflies to the school in the hope that other young men would find comfort in their study. The Jew hunts partially explain why Charles refused to send his daughters away to school but does not answer why he decided to send his son, my grandfather Victor, to Harrow, his hated alma mater. Perhaps he thought his butterflies would protect him.

Recently, Harrow decided to auction off this legacy and just before the hammer came down, I went there to see Charles's collection. In a damp basement under the science lab, behind a pile of old computers, broken lights and other educational detritus, I found Charles's butterflies, a lepidopterist's dream: the most complete collection of Swallowtails remaining in private hands, rivalled only by three major museums. Over 3,500 specimens comprising 300 different subspecies are stored in glass drawers in handsome mahogany cases.

Swallowtails are the Goliaths of the butterfly world. The Birdwing, from Papua New Guinea, is the largest known butterfly and was caught, or literally blasted out of the forest, by collectors using shotguns. But the real thrill of the Swallowtail is not its size but its looks. Nothing man-made, no painting by Ingres or Velázquez, none of the jewels of Catherine the Great or the intricacies of Mogul art can come close to the shocking beauty of these creatures. Each species of Swallowtail is noticeably different, distinguished by its shape and by its hues. A butterfly's wing is made up thousands of tiny, loosely attached pigmented scales which individually catch the light but together create a depth of colour and iridescence unmatched elsewhere in nature.* A contemporary pupil told me how 'gutted' he was that the collection was going, but admitted that he was one of the few who appreciated this cache.

Walking away from the school, I saw hundreds of boys, all dressed as Charles would have been in blue jackets and flat straw boaters, rushing through the streets towards their next lesson. A sudden sharp gust of wind blew, sweeping hats from heads high into the air. I stood and watched as the boaters floated and twisted down to earth like a mass of pale yellow butterflies and was reminded about my gentle great-grandfather and the comfort he found in nature.

Charles was at his happiest acting as assistant to his brother Walter or conducting his own field research. Aged nineteen, in 1896 he was allowed one fleeting fortnight of independence, and chose a collecting expedition along the Nile. His letters home comment on the strange and wonderful sights he witnessed en route. 'The Cattle in Shendi are very interesting beasts.' Or 'I have been trying very hard to get a turtle for Walter.'

On his return to England, Charles went to the office diligently but his investment ideas were met with a polite but resounding rebuttal. No one thought that there was enough future in copper to justify building a smelting factory; few agreed with him that opening a branch in Japan had prospects; and in the view of his fellow bankers a recent invention in which Charles wanted to invest, the gramophone record, would be a failure.

Kept under his mother's thumb at home and in the shadow of his forebears at work, Charles made a great strike for independence in marrying a beautiful Hungarian Jewess whom he met while hunting butterflies and rare fleas in the Carpathian Mountains. Writing to a friend who also suffered from mood disorders, Charles said, 'I am so glad that you really are better and that the "blues" are getting less. Marry as I have done and you won't have any at all.' Rozsika von Wertheimstein was the only woman he ever loved.

Rozsika von Wertheimstein came from an eminent but poor family. She was known as the Rose of Hungary on account of her looks; her dark-brown, purple-ringed irises caught the light like butterfly wings. Nica later admitted that everyone was 'absolutely

*Charles Rothschild in 1907 with his wife, Rozsika,
taken outside her family home at Csételek in Hungary.*

terrified' of Rozsika. Even so, Miriam, when asked if she could have
anything, any dream in the whole world, replied, 'I would like to
have just one more hour with my mother again.'

Born in 1870 in Nagyvárad, Hungary (now the Romanian city
of Oradea), Rozsika was the daughter of a retired army officer.
When she met Charles in 1907, she was already thirty-four and
many assumed her best prospect was to become postmistress in the
village. According to Miriam, 'She was brought up in a country
where anti-Semitism was perfectly open. Only a very small per-
centage of Jews were allowed to go to the university. In Hungary,
if you were Jewish, it really was a way of life. You were completely

Rozsika Edle von Wertheimstein, Nica's mother,
a great beauty, was known as the Rose of Hungary.

separated.' Denied a formal education, Rozsika was self-educated and could read Hungarian, German, French and English.

Rozsika was considered rather 'fast'. Her days were filled with waltzing on the ice in the winter and tennis parties in the summer. She smoked openly and liked to challenge the boys to barrel jumping on the ice. She was the first woman in Europe to serve a tennis ball overarm, a rather daring movement as it exposed the shape of the breast. Rozsika was summoned to Vienna to demonstrate the move to the Archduchess, when the news of this latest exploit got out.

Marrying a Rothschild was considered a stroke not just of good luck but a huge achievement, akin to winning the Derby, and the engagement was reported across Europe. The couple's wedding vows were 'solemnised' in Vienna in a simple ceremony for which the temple was decorated in white and evergreen, while the bride wore ivory-coloured satin. Arriving back in England from their honeymoon in Venice, Rozsika saw her new home for the first time and was informed that she would spend her married life there, bringing up her children alongside her mother-in-law, Emma, and her husband's brother, Walter. She is listed as attending various state balls at Buckingham Palace and at court, but Miss von Wertheimstein had been erased: she had become Mrs Charles Rothschild.

Perhaps the strain of getting pregnant four times in five years tamed Rozsika, or perhaps her new life stunned her into some form of submission, but there are no reports of her barrel jumping in England. She was constantly surprised by the formality that existed

Nica and her sisters with their nannies on Queen Alexandra Rose Day.

in her new family's household: although she and Emma lived under the same roof for twenty-five years, they never kissed or hugged. Rozsika knew what was expected of her.

Hence, the birth at the Rothschild family home in London of Kathleen Annie Pannonica on 10 December 1913 was a terrible blow. The baby girl, swaddled tightly, was immediately dispatched into the care of two nurses. The following day, the infant, still in the sole charge of her nannies, was transported by private train and taken to live with her siblings on the Tring estate of her grand-mother Emma.

For the next seventeen years, Nica, as she was known, would live between the Rothschild houses, playing with other Rothschild children and hunting with the Rothschild hounds. Cousins were by far the most frequent guests at family houses. Even today, although these estates have gone, the closeness continues. All families fight and fall out, but we still meet up for significant birthdays, anniversaries and celebrations. As Nica said in Yiddish slang, 'Maybe I come from a weird *mishpacha* but we're a close family, believe it or not.'

4

Fight, Flee, Flounder

Nica described her childhood wearily: 'I was moved from one great country house to another in the germless community of reserved Pullman coaches while being guarded night and day by a regiment of nurses, governesses, tutors, footmen, valets, chauffeurs and grooms.' The children's lives were regimented to suit other people's timetables. No expense was spared but neither was any allowance made for individual needs or personal idiosyncrasies.

The pre-war routine never changed. The children slept in a room with their nurse, who woke them at seven every morning. After a bath, the girls were encased in a tight bodice, followed by an immaculately ironed petticoat and finally a starched white dress. Each daughter had a different-coloured ribbon tied around her waist. Miriam's was always blue, Liberty's pink and Nica's red. Their hair would be brushed with one hundred strokes and fixed in place with tortoiseshell slides. Victor, the son and heir, was away at boarding school and only saw his sisters in the holidays. Contact with their parents was limited but when Rozsika was at home the girls would be taken to her boudoir, where they would kneel on the floor, put their hands together and pray for 'God to make me a good little girl, Amen'. Their mother did not observe Jewish customs. Wherever the children slept, they tried to stay awake long enough to hear their father return at weekends, and hear the telltale sound of horses' hooves crunching on the gravel, and the steady progress of the gas-lit carriage making its way up the drive.

The children took their lunch in the nursery and were only allowed to eat dinner with their parents once they had reached the age of sixteen. The food was of the highest quality and prepared by a renowned French chef who spent £5,000 per year on fish alone. Their menu never varied. On Mondays, breakfast consisted of boiled fish; Tuesday was a boiled egg; Wednesday was boiled egg; Thursday was boiled fish, and so forth. The food and daily routine at Tring was, according to Miriam, 'immaculate, incessant and monotonously boring'.

Their routine was as repetitive as the menus. Every morning at exactly the same time, the children were taken on a walk around the park. Running and hiding were forbidden in case the girls soiled their white dresses or got lost. Unlike the children, animals were allowed to roam free in the park, and their enclosure, behind a high fence, was a man-made paradise. There were fallow deer, kangaroos, giant tortoises, emus, rheas and cassowaries, collected by Uncle Walter. The emus terrified the children; they made a curious drumming sound with their feet and followed the prams hoping for food. Miriam remembers the giant birds leaning into her pram with 'nasty gimlet-like eyes and long beaks'.

The winter months were spent at Tring but during the summer the children – along with their servants and animals – decamped to Ashton Wold, some sixty miles away. That house, mothballed during the winter, would have had its dustcovers swept away, the stables prepared and the drive raked to receive Charles and his family. Though informal in comparison to Tring, Ashton had twenty permanent servants and their number swelled to accommodate additional needs.

When Charles was home the children would help him catch and

Victor, Miriam, Liberty and Nica Rothschild.

mount butterflies and other insects. Routine and convention would be temporarily abandoned. To his children, who adored him, Charles was 'absolutely the ideal father'. Victor, Miriam and Nica all told me that he was a great joker. Miriam said, 'My father was a very humorous man with puns and jokes. He'd ask, what's the difference between a sheep and a deer? Mutton is cheap and venison is dear. And everyone would roar with laughter.' Nica, Miriam and Victor told me different versions of this story. 'Occasionally he came to see us in the nursery where he used to tell jokes, which I couldn't understand, but which kept the nursemaids in hysterics.' Charles kept a gold bar in his office and promised that the child who could lift it up with one hand could keep it. Nica and her siblings struggled and strained but none ever managed it. When I was growing up, my grandfather, her brother Victor, repeated the same trick when we went to visit him at the bank.

Music became intrinsically linked to Nica's happy memories of her father. On his return from work Charles let his children crank up the phonograph and helped them choose a record. His tastes ranged from classical masters to contemporary innovators such as Stravinsky and Debussy, but he was also captivated by the new sounds coming out of America and liked listening to a young ragtime player by the name of Scott Joplin. Following the Great War, more records were being produced and Charles brought home Bix Beiderbecke, Louis Armstrong's first outings with the Fletcher Henderson band and George Gershwin's *Rhapsody in Blue*, all of which would echo around the house.

Although Victor was sent to Harrow, Nica's parents disapproved of formal education for women and loathed teachers on principle. 'They thought,' Nica said, 'it was all like *David Copperfield*,' and crushed the individuality out of a child.

The girls' governesses were brought to the house by pony trap each day but taught little beyond sewing and the piano. The three daughters were not even prepared for menstruation and had no

Tring Park, Hertfordshire. Nica's childhood home –
and some of the other occupants.

idea that such a thing as a penis existed. Occasionally their
Rothschild cousins came to stay but other children were usually
only fleetingly glimpsed from a car or carriage window. 'There were
aristocratic families near by but they didn't invite Jewish children
to play or if they did it was to large events,' Miriam said. Nica and
her sisters were confined to the class known as 'Yids' or 'not one of
us'.

Victor left a paper trail of his achievements during his school
years but it was impossible to find any record of Nica's classroom
reports, let alone essays or books. Miriam told me, 'The lessons
were in the day with a lot of intervals for games play. And then at
five o'clock the pony trap would appear and take the governesses
off to their homes outside the house. When I was asked at sixteen
or seventeen what I had been taught in history, I said, "Well, we
never got beyond the Romans."'

Visiting the family archive in London, still based at the bank in St Swithin's Lane, I scoured the records for any mention of Nica. The search was made harder by the family's mania for destroying all personal records. Only the more public documents were kept and there were hardly any references to the children. I can still remember the thrill of a rare sighting of Nica's name in one of the family visitors' books: there in 1928, sandwiched between her sisters, a duke, a minister and a foreign prince, was her signature, 'Pannonica Rothschild', in large, curly writing.

Finding her photograph album at Ashton was another exciting moment. Miriam's bookshelves were crammed with books and objects. Photographs of relations and dignitaries were interspersed with her own publications and books written by friends. Pushed to the back of a lower shelf, I found, by chance, a dark-blue leather photograph album with *Pannonica* etched in gold on the front. Untouched for years, it smelled of neglect and damp. Mice droppings were scattered around it like confetti, but this book, luckily, had not caught their fancy. There, within the heavy, time-stained pages, I saw pictures of a pretty little Nica, who grew, with each page, into an exquisitely beautiful teenager. These were formal photographs and the clothes, apart from their size, never changed: Nica always wore a white lace dress, her hair was neatly tied back with ribbons and her socks were exactly the same length. Yet despite the formality of the pose, her expression crackled with intensity, as if she were taking on the camera lens, challenging the photographer to really capture the essence of her personality, making the period details and the props redundant.

Gradually I pieced together a picture of Nica's upbringing. Besides having few friends, Rothschild children had no privacy. More than thirty people worked in the house and at least another sixty were employed on the farm, in the stables and gardens. The children slept with nurses, ate with footmen standing behind their chairs, rode out with grooms, took baths overseen by maids and walked with their governesses. In addition to the normal retinue of the butler, head housekeeper, chefs, footmen, scullery maids, nurses, grooms, gardeners and chauffeurs, there were members of staff with titles I had never heard of, let alone imagined. A lad was employed to iron top hats but the 'groom of the chambers' had nothing to do with horses; he looked after works of art. The 'odd man' checked the fire buckets; there were separate employees to wind clocks, set alarms, exterminate vermin and polish the grates.

'I knew nothing else; I thought that was how the world was made. I assumed it would always go on like that as there was a real sense of finality about it like the sun rising and setting,' Miriam said, reflecting on her childhood. 'It really was a cage; freedom didn't exist. That was the trouble; it was all perfection, but as far as the children were concerned, it was boring and repetitive.'

Nica, Miriam and Liberty with their mother Rozsika.

Nica aged eleven.

Like many in society, the lives of the senior members of the Rothschild family were well documented in *The Times* Court Circular, which acted like a *Hello!* magazine of its day. Information as anodyne as 'Lady Rothschild has left London for Tring Park' or 'Mrs Rothschild will take tea with Princess Alexandra' was reported and at grand society parties every single invitee would be solemnly listed. When Emma was younger and before Charles started to withdraw, there were huge parties at Tring, sit-down lunches and dinners for several hundred, with bands, fêtes and shows. Nica remembered Albert Einstein coming to some event and performing magic tricks for the children, one of which was to take off his shirt without removing his jacket.

Marrying Rozsika had only temporarily banished Charles's blues. Soon after Nica's birth in 1913, he became more withdrawn, sometimes failing to speak for days on end. At first the family dealt with it by pretending it was not happening. Charles still appeared at mealtimes but sat there in total silence before returning to his room and staring disconsolately out of the window or down the barrel of his microscope.

As the Great War progressed, Charles's apathy increased until finally the family could no longer ignore his behaviour. After 1916, he and his wife were never listed at any social functions; later that year he was sent to a sanatorium in Switzerland in search of help. Although it was supposed to be a period of convalescence Charles was bombarded with requests from the bank: there were pension problems to be dealt with for employees; changes to the manufacturing of gold bars; the payment of Cousin Alfred's death duties; the sale of Rio Tinto shares, to mention but a few. At the same time, he initiated his dream of setting up a nature reserve: private letters show that he was trying to buy land in Essex to start a wildlife park.

Charles remained in Switzerland for two years but although his return was greeted with tremendous hope and optimism, it was clear the 'cure' had not worked. For the family it was a devastating disappointment. For Nica, living in that atmosphere, alongside the constant spectre of mental instability, became normality.

Lonely and isolated, she was left more and more to her own devices, while her parents spent most of their time in London. Her two elder sisters, who were great friends, did not particularly want little Nica messing up their games. Victor was away at school. Uncle Walter lived in a parallel universe of his private museum. Their ageing grandmother Emma had no time for children. Later, when Nica said, 'My only friends were horses,' she was telling the truth. Her childhood was one of physical luxury combined with personal neglect. A Rothschild cousin who knew Nica as a child said that she became increasingly wild. If there was a tree to climb, she would go up it; if there was a higher fence to jump, Nica would aim her horse at it.

This sealed-off, slightly rarefied existence was what Nica, Miriam and Liberty were expected to inhabit until they came of age. Many of Nica's female cousins never left Rothschild homes, choosing to remain spinsters or to marry relations. The result was that, despite their astonishing material advantages and cosmopolitan backgrounds, their horizons were as limited as those of many less fortunate women. They were confined by expectation as well as opportunity; their adult wings clipped, they were as trapped as many of the specimens in Walter's collection. Without independent means, and without access to capital, living on an allowance set by the iron whims of their fathers, Rothschild women were left in a state of comfortable dependence and anonymity. In the family records, only the daughters of the first sons are recorded; their husbands and children were unrecognised.

Rothschild men were equally trapped: they grew up knowing they had no choice but to go into the family business. For both sexes, the weight of expectation was either too heavy or too light. Miriam, Liberty and Nica were not submissive types, nor were they cut out for domesticity. Cushioned by luxury and privilege but given no outlet for their creativity, no vehicle for their talents, the outlook for the three sisters seemed unbearably narrow. They had three choices: to fight, to flee or to flounder. Each of the sisters would choose one of these options.

5

Long, Dark Prison

'**D**o you know anything about anything?'
Miriam was furious when she found out how little I knew
about our Rothschild forebears. We were having lunch alone at
Ashton Wold. My mistake had been to try to bluff my way through
family history. Attempting to get anything past Miriam was a bad
idea.

'I was never terribly interested,' I confessed, before adding the
pathetic postscript, 'until now.'

'Not interested! Until now! Are you aware that a person's life is
shaped long before they are born? We don't appear from thin air.
Do you understand anything about genetics or chromosomes?
Even the Bible teaches us that the sins of the fathers are visited on
at least four generations,' she said, glaring at me. I felt foolish and
defensive. Family history, I reasoned, was something to explore in
one's dotage, along with God and gardening. Besides, Nica was a
twentieth-century figure. Running out of excuses for delving into
the past, I booked a flight to Frankfurt, where the Rothschild story
had begun.

*

I arrived in Germany one wet winter's morning armed with an address and a camera. I had gone in search of the birthplace of the Rothschild family but found only a mass of concrete and tarmac where it had once stood. The only feature that the Allies had not flattened during the raids of 1944 is a small section of wall. The autobahn covers most of the tiny street where the founding father of the Rothschild dynasty, Mayer Amschel, was born in 1744. In the Rothschild museum and archives, I began to piece together our history.

In 1458 the Emperor Frederick III proclaimed that Jews were allowed to remain in Frankfurt only if they paid to live in this cramped, gated street on the north-eastern edge of town. Jews Lane, a narrow thoroughfare only a few hundred feet long, was meant originally to be home to about one hundred people. By the fifteenth century more than five hundred families lived there. By the eighteenth century, a staggering three thousand people somehow squeezed into the Judengasse. Efforts were made to restrict the population by allowing no more than twelve weddings a year and only if bride and groom had reached the age of twenty-five. With Jews being forbidden from owning land, from farming, from entering public parks, inns or coffee houses, or from going within a hundred feet of the town's cathedral, the options for any Jew seeking a profession beyond usury and certain forms of trade were negligible.

As national law didn't or wouldn't offer them protection, Jewish communities created their own systems of justice, medicine, prayer, education and custom. In effect they created states within states, which alienated them further from a suspicious and uncomprehending Gentile community. Moneylending was one of the few professions that Jews were allowed to practise. There is nothing shameful in the Jewish scriptures about handling or even making money; indeed, it's incumbent on Jews to better themselves for the sake of their community and every Jew is expected to give at least 10 per cent of their annual income to charity.

Until the eighteenth century Jews were allowed out of the Judengasse only if they wore garments with two yellow rings on their jackets, while the women had to be veiled. If a Gentile passed by, the Jew had to take off his cap, avert his eyes and stand with his back to the nearest wall. Near the entrance to the Rothschild home was a graffito called 'The Jew's Sow' that showed two rabbis sucking at a cow's teat while the third copulated with the dumb animal. At the top was depicted a small boy covered with stab wounds, supposedly Simeon, aged two, who was 'killed by the Jews', a reference to the popular belief that Jews needed the blood of innocent Gentile children to make their unleavened bread.

The more I read, the more chastened I felt. Miriam's anger was well founded: I had taken my family's history for granted, never bothering to investigate their earlier struggle. What made their achievements still more staggering was reading about the lane that the Rothschilds had come from – a place of such indescribable squalor that Europeans, including George Eliot, made it a 'must-see' attraction as part of their grand tour. Goethe wrote, 'The lack of space, the dirt, the throng of people, the disagreeable accents of the voice, altogether it made the most unpleasant impression, even upon the passer-by who merely looked through the gate.' Apparently when Goethe finally summoned up the courage to enter Judengasse, he was surprised to find that the

© The Granger Collection/Topfoto

The first House of Rothschild, Jews Lane, Frankfurt.

inhabitants were 'human beings after all, industrious and obliging, and one could not help but admire even the obstinacy with which they adhered to their traditional ways'. Another traveller who witnessed this hell-hole was less complimentary: 'Even those who are in the blooming years of their life, look like the walking dead. Their deathly pale appearance sets them apart from all other inhabitants in the most depressing way.' It was hardly surprising that the life expectancy of a Jew in the ghetto was 58 per cent lower than that of a Gentile living a mere street away.

The original patriarch, Mayer Amschel, was orphaned in 1756 aged twelve when a plague swept through Jews Lane. He married well, to Gutle Schnapper, the daughter of a court agent to the Prince of Saxe-Meiningen, and he used his wife's dowry to set up a small coin business. By his mid-forties Mayer Amschel had become the eleventh richest man in the Judengasse, able to buy a comparatively grand house, all of fourteen feet wide but six floors high. The couple had nineteen children, ten of whom survived childhood. Their name Rothschild, or 'zum Rotten schild' – 'At the Red Shield' – was derived from the house-name of a sixteenth-century ancestor.

While Gutle and Mayer Amschel were still on Jews Lane and trying to raise a family, the German poet Ludwig Börne wrote the following description of the place:

> Long dark prison, into which the highly celebrated light of the eighteenth century has not yet been able to penetrate . . . stretching ahead of us lay an immeasurably long street, near us just enough room to reassure us that we could not turn around as soon as the wish overcame us. Over us no longer sky, which the sun needs in order to expand in his breadth; one doesn't see the sky, one sees only sunlight. An evil smell rises everywhere around us, and the cloth that is supposed to shield us from infections serves also to catch the tear of compassion or to hide the smile of malice from the gaze of the watching Jews.

*The five sons of Mayer Amschel were sent to five capitals
of Europe in the late eighteenth century.* © akg-images

I wondered whether Gutle and Mayer Amschel were watching
Börne as he made his way through their midst. Were they perhaps
speculating whether there was any way out, and whether their children had any chance of a life beyond these narrow confines? It
must have seemed like a hopeless dream, given the lives of those
earlier generations, other desperate and talented Jews had been
unable to escape. Perhaps it was some Rothschild offspring that the
poet writes about next, maybe even Nathan Mayer, who went on
to found the London branch of the Rothschild bank:

Trumping laboriously through the filth slows our pace down
enough to permit us the leisure for observation. We set our feet
down skittishly and carefully so that we don't step on any children. These swim about in the gutter, creep about in the filth
innumerable as vermin hatched by the sun from the dung heap.
Who would not indulge those little boys in their small desires? If

one were to consider play in childhood as the model for the reality of life, then the existence of these children must be the grave of every encouragement, every exuberance, every friendship, and every joy of life. Are you afraid that these towering houses will collapse over us? O fear nothing! They are thoroughly reinforced, the cages of clipped birds, resting on the cornerstone of ill will.

'If you had been born there, you would want to escape,' Miriam observed phlegmatically.

I took out our family tree and laid it on the floor. Nine generations separate the founding father from the youngest family member today. I am seven generations away from life in the Judengasse, Nica only five. She was born a century after Mayer Amschel but had a direct link to that time via her grandmother Emma, who was born in Frankfurt in 1844 and often visited her great-grandmother Gutle, who lived in Jews Lane until her death in 1849. I could

Gutle Schnapper, born in 1753.
Nica's great-great-great-grandmother.

imagine young Nica sitting at Emma's feet, listening to the stories, and, in turn, imagine Emma listening to Gutle's. Generation after generation handed down memories, making sure that no one forgot.

Gutle Rothschild, strong and proud, refused to move away from that cramped ghetto even after her husband, sons and grandsons had made a fortune. Another cousin, Ferdinand, wrote about visiting the old lady, who received them in a 'small dingy dwelling' where she rested 'on a couch in her dark little sitting room, folded in a thick white shawl, her deeply lined face enclosed in a full and heavily ribboned white cap'. Gutle outlived her husband by thirty-seven years but despite her longevity and independence, like many Rothschild women after her, her life was governed by the terms of her husband's will.

A highly superstitious woman, Gutle believed that if she left Jews Lane, the memory of where the family had come from would recede. She understood that the fear of returning to the Judengasse created the best incentive for her children to succeed and it was fear that underscored the family's ambitions. Only money and power would protect them from anti-Semitism and a return to that early life of misery. Centuries of persecution had made the Rothschilds secretive and inward facing; they were unable to trust outsiders and did not expect others to understand what they had endured. Their talent for making money, combined with a mania for secrecy, made them the perfect bankers. They offered their clients a unique service: great financial acumen and total discretion.

It wasn't until the 1790s – when the French shelled Frankfurt and Jews Lane was destroyed, leaving two thousand homeless – that the Rothschilds were finally allowed to leave the confines of that one narrow street and mix with outsiders. By then, the family business had expanded from coins into cotton and grain. With the onset of the Industrial Revolution, plus advances in both travel and technology, the Rothschilds started to import cheaper and better cotton from the mills of northern England. Mayer Amschel understood that the most valuable asset for any business was a skilled, informed and trustworthy network of employees. He didn't have to go out and find them; he bred them. Of his ten surviving children, five were boys. Amschel, Nathan Mayer, Karl, Salomon and James shared a room in their modest family home and remained close for the rest of their lives.

Liberation from the Judengasse and a modicum of success gave Mayer Amschel the courage to take the next step. He sent his five sons to the five major capitals of Europe to set up the first international partnership of its kind. Between the 1820s and the 1860s they established themselves in Europe. In Frankfurt, the business was run after Mayer Amschel's death by his eldest son, Amschel; the Paris office was set up by the youngest, James; Carl took Naples, Salomon ran Vienna and Nathan Mayer (known thereafter as NM) founded the London branch.

'What they did, you see,' Miriam explained to me, 'was to set up the first form of a European Union. Though there were quarrels, as there are in any family, [the brothers] spread out and worked together towards a common purpose.' The historian Niall Ferguson, in his definitive biography of the Rothschilds, attests that 'Between 1815 and 1914, it was easily the biggest bank in the world. The twentieth century has no equivalent, not even the biggest of today's international banking corporations enjoys the relative supremacy enjoyed by the Rothschilds in their heyday.' The largest part of their colossal fortune, he explains, was made by lending and speculating in government bonds.

Their first major breakthrough was a contract to supply cash to Wellington's army in 1814. Using a risky combination of deals in exchange-rate transactions, bond-price speculations and commissions, the family made huge profits. Records show that in 1818 they commanded capital of £500,000; by 1828 the value of their stock had risen to £4,330,333, about fourteen times greater than their nearest competitor, Baring Brothers. Unlike many of their fellow bankers, the

Nathan Mayer (NM), Nica's great-great-grandfather.
Founder of the British branch of the Rothschild bank.

Rothschilds reinvested their profits back into their own businesses. For regimes seeking stable financing and secure loans, the Rothschilds were the one-stop shop. Leaving anti-Semitism at the door, kings and rulers expediently visited the bank in St Swithin's Lane.

The Rothschilds invented a web of credits and debits that freed both individuals and states from traditional forms of income. Previously all transactions had relied on ownership – of goods, land, metals, property and so forth – but a bond doesn't have to be shackled to a physical possession; it can be linked to a mere promise of repayment. 'Not only,' Ferguson writes, 'had the Rothschilds replaced the old aristocracy; they also represented a new materialistic religion.'

Thus five young Jewish men, treated for most of their lives as pariahs, were able to establish themselves in foreign countries, without contacts or language, and win the trust of world leaders. My grandfather Victor believed that it came down to character and determination, and that of them all, Nathan Mayer Rothschild, in particular, was possessed of these vital attributes.

NM towers over the history of English Rothschilds to this day.

His portrait hangs in our hallways and his name is still invoked with awe and respect. He was the fourth child of Gutle and Mayer Amschel to be born in Jews Lane. When, in 1799, at the age of twenty-two, he arrived in Manchester, NM had no formal education and spoke no English. He did, however, have a scheme. Realising that none of the cloth merchants talked to one another, he persuaded them to join forces in order to negotiate better prices. His brothers replicated this business model across Europe.

Like his relations, NM had a talent for discretion. When a journalist asked him, 'How did you become so successful?' NM replied acerbically, 'By minding my own business.' On one occasion he left his portmanteau on the Manchester stagecoach and was very keen to get his clothing returned but the only description he was prepared to give to identify his possessions was 'dark hat and coat'.

On 22 October 1806 he married Hannah Barent Cohen, the eldest daughter of Levi Barent Cohen, a leading London financier, and immediately NM was linked by marriage to the leading Jewry, the Montefiores, Salomons and Goldschmidts. Nica's love of music was not inherited from her distinguished ancestor; when asked if he liked that particular art form, NM put his hand in his pocket, jingled some coins and replied, 'This is the only music I like.'

The family's meteoric rise fuelled speculation. From where had these people suddenly sprung? What was their secret? What tricks and skulduggery were involved? It seemed inexplicable that in one generation a family from nowhere had begun advising and financing governments. They even wrote to each other in an indecipherable language, Judendeutsch, an idiosyncratic hybrid of Hebrew and German.

Although they were now free, the Rothschilds still faced animosity. In 1891 the pamphleteer Max Bauer wrote: 'The house of Rothschild is a structureless, parasitical something or other that proliferates across the earth from Frankfurt to Paris to London like a twisted telephone wire.' Edouard Drumont's anti-Semitic rant *La France juive*, published in 1886, was so popular that it was reprinted more than two hundred times. 'The Rothschilds, despite their billions, have the air of second-hand clothes dealers,' he wrote. Later he added, 'The God Rothschild has none of the responsibilities of power and all of the advantages; he disposes over all the government forces, all the resources of France for his private purposes.' William Makepeace Thackeray, a guest at Tring and Waddesdon, added that 'NM Rothschild Esq. play[ed] with new kings as young misses with dolls'.

The retrospective reporting of NM's conduct following the British victory at Waterloo in 1815 perfectly illustrates the wild rumours and conspiracy theories surrounding the family's modus operandi. Some said the banker went on to the battlefield with a pair of racing pigeons that he released when the outcome was sure. The birds flew straight back to his agents at the Stock Exchange, carrying in their pouches the message 'Buy British stocks, sell everything French.'

The French journalist, Georges Mathieu-Dairnvaell reported that NM was in London when the pigeons arrived. Coming on to the floor of the London Stock Exchange, he pretended to be ruined and put on a bravura performance as a broken-hearted bankrupt. Watching the erstwhile omnipotent King of the Jews prostrate himself caused such a vicarious crisis of confidence that everyone sold their stock; meanwhile crafty old NM snuck round the back and bought it all back at knock-down prices. Others accused him of bribing generals and stirring up massive speculation in the bank's favour.

The real story of NM at Waterloo was researched and published by Victor, who proved that NM was in London at the time and that he received news of the British victory from his brother's employees. Once NM had informed the Prime Minister, Lord Liverpool, he went to the Stock Exchange and bought depressed stock. His profit was £1 million, the equivalent today of well over £200 million.

The British government was soon relying on the family for

credit. When Prime Minister Benjamin Disraeli wanted to finance the building of the Suez Canal, he approached his friend Nathan Rothschild.

'How much?' asked Nathan.

'Four million pounds,' answered Disraeli.

'When?'

'Tomorrow.'

'What is your security?'

'The British government.'

'You shall have it.'

Some Jewish families changed their faith to avoid racism. The Rothschilds remained Jews and were proud and respectful of their religion, although few British Rothschilds actually practised their faith. Nica was never instructed in its laws. I wondered whether she found it confusing to be called Rothschild, to be assumed to be Jewish, to endure anti-Semitism, but without any real knowledge of the customs and culture that go with it. The four children of Charles and Rozsika were adrift between the two worlds, understanding neither the Christian nor the Jewish faith. They were caught in a no man's land, between non-Jews who assumed Nica was one thing, and Jews who quickly worked out that the Rothschild children were not one of them either.

Previous Rothschild generations had created perfectly self-contained worlds for their children built on the principles of their religion, as well as the importance of family and ambition. As these imperatives faded, there was increasingly little to keep the various branches together and, in Nica's generation, the family began to disperse.

In Nica's grandparents' generation, fourteen out of a total of nineteen Rothschild marriages were between cousins. Nica's great-grandfather Lionel married his first cousin Charlotte, while her grandfather Natty married another relation, the aforementioned Emma. There were other unions between uncles and nieces. Some commentators assume this intermarriage was to keep the Rothschild fortune intact; others argue that finding suitably eligible Jews was hard. It also seems likely that none of those hard-working men could be bothered or had much time to introduce their daughters to potential suitors outside the family. They worked together and lived together. How else would they meet anyone?

Furthermore, what non-Rothschild could be trusted and who else could possibly understand the shame of their recent past? Rothschild women shared that past as well as their husbands' determination to create a better life for their children, a life free from persecution and penury. Like herds of deer fleeing from predators, they knew that sticking together in packs was the best defence; those who separated made themselves vulnerable. Creating those tight, incestuous communities was an essential part of the recipe for success, but the family units were also building a genetic time bomb.

In the Christian faith, marriage between close cousins had been banned since the sixth century for good reason. Research confirms that interbreeding increases the chances of certain types of mental disorders. Miriam called it the family 'blues'; others put it more bluntly and called it schizophrenia. Past generations' medical records were destroyed; present ones are private, so informed diagnoses are impossible. It is known that there is a biological disposition to disorders of mood and some believe they are hereditary. In the case of schizophrenia, for example, one in a hundred people is likely to develop this illness but the odds shorten to one in ten if a close relation has been affected. Contrary to popular belief, schizophrenia does not mean a split personality. The symptons include disordered thoughts and delusional thinking, sometimes accompanied by hallucinations. It can be triggered by an event, by stress or by drugs. Each case is different and there is no universal panacea. It was an illness that would haunt Nica's life in unexpected ways.

6

Rothschildiana

I decided it was time to pay my respects to NM and set out to find his resting place. I knew, as my father had taught me, that every year descendants must place a stone on the grave of a forebear as a token of respect and remembrance. However, getting access to the cemetery where NM is buried was a laborious process, due to the fear of a resurgence of anti-Semitism and the recent desecration of some Jewish graves across Europe. Early one cold morning in February 2008 a representative of the United Synagogue Burial Authority unlocked for me the iron gates set into a high brick wall in a side road off Whitechapel High Street and tactfully waited out of the wind in the lee of an adjacent block of flats. Were it not for the odd grape hyacinth and cyclamen, or the raised voices of Muslim children at a nearby school, it would have been easy to imagine a place where time had stopped still.

Most of the gravestones, the majority dating from 1761 to 1858, had fallen into disrepair; moss and lichen have obscured the Hebrew inscriptions and foxes have taken up residence in one collapsed sarcophagus. The inscriptions on the headstones act as keys to the social history and aspirations of Jewish settlers at that time.

Some give an address, but only if the place is a long way from Whitechapel, thus proving that the immigrant had risen in this mortal world from slum to suburbia. Trades are also marked on the headstones: a fish indicates a fishmonger and a carpenter is seen felling a tree. At the top of the pecking order are the rabbinical families or Kohanim, with two hands carved at the top of their stone for blessing people, unlike the less important Levites whose emblem is a pitcher of water to wash the hands of their superiors. The graves of NM and his wife Hannah are large, white and simple, with nothing except their names and dates, but on Hannah Rothschild's is the inscription 'I am here. Praise the Lord.'

Gently, I placed a stone on each tomb.

Whitechapel, in the heart of London's East End, has over the centuries been home to wave upon wave of immigrants, with the Huguenots, then the Jews, followed by the Irish and, more recently, a thriving Bangladeshi community finding refuge in its narrow streets. Having moved his business dealings from Manchester to London, in 1809 NM bought a property near by in St Swithin's Lane, still the site of the bank, and he worshipped at Bevis Marks synagogue a few hundred yards away. This area, now known as Banglatown, was his true if adopted home and the birthplace of the bank's British operations. Although he died suddenly in Germany in 1836, aged only fifty-eight, it was NM's express wish that his body be returned to England and buried in the community he had grown to love, near the many charities he had founded, in the heart of the financial city where he had made such a huge impression.

For most of his life N. M. Rothschild lived modestly in a small suburban house and remained involved in the minutiae of his bank's financial transactions until his death. Like many members of the family, before and after, he insisted that his personal papers be burned, but in the business ledgers held in the Rothschild Archive are his last instructions: sell exchequer bills, ship one hundred thousand sovereigns to Paris, purchase two hundred Danube shares, send one hundred bottles of lavender water and a chest of good oranges, and do not allow the gardener to do as he pleases.

The founding father of the Rothschild dynasty, Mayer Amschel, was against conspicuous consumption, arguing that ostentation encouraged envy. When he made a bit of money, he bought a garden, believing that land could be safely enjoyed without attracting unwelcome attention. The next generation had no intention of keeping such a low profile: they had made money, so they were going to use it and enjoy it. They also realised that business wasn't confined to the boardrooms; real power and politics were exercised in drawing rooms and on hunting fields. In England, a seamless line connected the Houses of Parliament and the country house party. To get ahead and stay ahead, the Rothschilds needed to be able to entertain the great and the good, and they now had the financial muscle to do this on a remarkably lavish scale.

Determined to stick together, the family built houses near each other. In London they bought city mansions on Piccadilly and in the country they settled on land in the Vale of Aylesbury, a short train journey away from the city. Here they had constructed the great Buckinghamshire mansions of Mentmore, Halton, Aston Clinton, Hulcott and Bierton. In 1883 the Rothschild family rented the estate at Tring and later bought it for NM's son and daughter-in-law, Natty and Emma. The cousins liked to claim that if they stood on the rooftops of their mansions on a clear winter's day they could wave to each other across the valley. Their houses were gloriously vulgar statements of self-importance: huge, three-dimensional calling cards announcing their arrival.

Like many newly rich, the Rothschilds had more money than taste; they wanted the trappings of wealth and they wanted them immediately. One story, probably apocryphal but far too good to omit, tells of Nica's French cousin James, who was so keen to impress the King of France that he organised a pheasant shoot and had parrots trained to fly among the game, squawking, '*Vive le roi, vive le roi.*'

Of course, the Rothschilds were just the latest in a long line to erect shrines to their own success. The fabulous palaces of Blenheim, Houghton, Castle Howard and Wentworth Woodhouse were all monuments to military victory, mercantile brilliance or political astuteness, and at the time of their creation they caused shock and consternation. Successive generations have distressed the shiny surfaces of new wealth and added the patina of age and respectability.

In 1874 Baron Ferdinand de Rothschild employed the French architect Destailleur to create a nineteenth-century version of an eighteenth-century chateau on top of a large hill at Waddesdon. Percheron horses were imported from France to help transport a mass of building material up the steep incline, which included seven miles of copper piping, quantities of fully grown trees, hundreds of tons of brick and lead, and thousands of yards of iron balustrade, all stamped with the distinctive five-arrow crest, the family's coat of arms, symbolising the five brothers sent like arrows to the capitals of Europe. The panelled interiors and French furniture were acquired en masse from French *hôtels particuliers* such as the Richelieu and the Beaumarchais following Haussmann's remodelling of Paris.

By buying up the assets of grand, well-established families, the Rothschilds were, in effect, tying their history and their provenance to a more illustrious past. The cousins drove up prices in the art market to giddy heights, buying hundreds of paintings, including works by Greuze, Romney, Reynolds, Gainsborough and Cuyp, for their walls. Their rooms were furnished with priceless carpets and furniture. Even if they could only trace their ancestry back one hundred years to Jews Lane, they could now, at least, form strong links via their possessions to the greatest aristocratic and royal families of Europe. By acquiring the panelling of Bourbon kings, the

*Mentmore Towers, late 19th century, designed by Joseph Paxton for Baron
Mayer Amschel de Rothschild. His daughter Hannah lived there with her
husband Lord Rosebery, British Prime Minister. Now uninhabited.*

*Ascott House was enlarged by Leopold de Rothschild in 1874.
It was given to the National Trust in 1947 but is still lived in
by Sir Evelyn de Rothschild and his family.*

Waddesdon Manor was designed by French architect Destailleur in 1874 for Baron Ferdinand de Rothschild. It was given to the National Trust in 1958 but is still run by Nica's nephew Jacob, Lord Rothschild.

Halton House was built between 1880 and 1883 for Alfred de Rothschild. Given to the nation during the war, it is still used as the officers' mess for RAF Halton.

furniture of Louis XV and the paintings of Catherine the Great, plus Gobelin tapestries, Sèvres porcelain and Fabergé eggs, the Rothschilds connected themselves to prestigious dynasties of the past. Their side tables were covered with signed royal photographs and their commissioned self-portraits showed them in ceremonial garb. The French writer Edouard Drumont described one Rothschild house as a place 'without a past', filled with magnificent jewels of French culture stuffed into the huge palace like so much bric-a-brac.

The family wanted to show that they were no longer stateless, banned from owning land and property, or living at the discretion of others. By building those vast houses and amassing huge collections, by owning horses and hounds, banks and bonds, the Rothschilds were not just conspicuously displaying wealth; they were putting down roots and staking a claim to belong, to be part of something. Having matter made them feel that they did matter.

They were hospitable on an unrivalled scale. NM and his sons were small; their forebears had grown up without enough to eat and the effects of malnutrition stunted the next few generations. The Rothschilds resolved that their children, guests and dependants would never go hungry, so Rothschild tables groaned with food. Guests were offered the choice of Ceylon, Souchong or Assam early-morning tea in bed with a choice of longhorn, shorthorn or dairy milk. There were over fifty greenhouses guaranteeing a year-round supply of flowers (the parterre was permanently in bloom), fruits and vegetables. 'In some Rothschild houses,' Nica told me, 'no one bothered to pick the cherries. It was seen as far more elegant to have the gardeners carry the actual trees around the table.'

The visitors' book at Tring Park shows that every day during the summer months between 1890 and 1932 there were lunch parties for up to one hundred glittering guests. The names and addresses of every visitor were written into leather-bound ledgers in an immaculate hand. In the chef's book, the meals were recorded in detail to avoid the social catastrophe of a returning guest having to consume the same dish twice. The Rothschild women organised these events down to the last detail. Excluded from the boardroom, they knew exactly who would be useful to invite to further their husbands' business interests. The family's international connections meant that the guest list was never parochial. The Rothschilds understood the importance of selecting their visitors to create a heady mix of rich and rarefied, artists and royalty, beauty and brains. Indian maharajas, the Shah of Persia, Cecil Rhodes (whom Natty financed in South Africa), Queen Victoria (who insisted on having lunch separately in another room) mixed freely with George V, Edward VII and a smattering of family, including, later, one Miss Pannonica Rothschild.

The family employed world-class chefs, served the finest wine, organised fêtes, concerts and balls. When Nica's cousin Alfred Rothschild built a house at Halton he included a private circus ring, a bowling alley, an ice-skating rink, an indoor swimming pool and an Indian pavilion, so that his visitors could sample every imaginable pleasure. One of the few Rothschilds to show an interest in music, Alfred wrote six piano pieces called *Boutons des Roses* and had his own orchestra, which he conducted dressed in a top hat, blue frock coat and wielding a diamond-studded boxwood baton. Guests were not necessarily appreciative. 'The showiness! The sense of lavish wealth, thrust up your nose,' wrote Gladstone's secretary Edward Hamilton, adding that 'the decorations are sadly overdone and one's eyes long to rest on something which is not all gilt and gold'. Another of Alfred's visitors, the novelist David Lindsay, observed that 'the number of Jews in this palace was past belief. I have studied the anti-Semite question with some attention always hoping to stem an ignoble movement [but] feel some sympathy with [others who say] the Jew is the tapeworm of civilization.'

In France, James de Rothschild was pilloried by Emile Zola in a thinly disguised description of his sometime host: 'Everywhere its mission of ferocious conquest [is] to lie in wait for its prey, suck the blood out of everyone and grow fat on the life of others.' Another regular visitor was Anthony Trollope, who repaid the family's hospitality in 1885 by publishing a social satire that was clearly inspired by the Rothschilds. Few who read *The Way We Live Now* doubted that the character of Melmotte was based on Nica's great-grandfather, Lionel, whose 'horrid, big rich scoundrel . . . a vile city ruffian' came from abroad to make a killing on the stock market. Not everyone was so critical. Benjamin Disraeli, himself a Jew by birth, wrote, 'I have always been of the opinion that there can't be too many Rothschilds.'

Gradually the family insinuated themselves into British life. Alfred became the first Jewish director of the Bank of England in 1869, aged twenty-six, a post he held for twenty years until 1889. He himself never received the longed-for acceptance by society but his illegitimate daughter Almina went on to marry the Earl of Carnarvon; it was her inheritance that funded the British exploration in Egypt and the discovery of the tomb of Tutankahmun. Nica's great-grandfather Lionel, her cousin Jimmy and her grandfather Natty became Members of Parliament. Emma, Nica's grandmother, became firm friends with Disraeli; Herbert Asquith was a frequent guest at Waddesdon. Winston Churchill stayed with the family many times and attended Nica's coming-out ball. Another Hannah Rothschild married Lord Rosebery, a leading Tory and the future prime minister. (No male Rothschilds attended the wedding as Hannah had married out of their religion.)

Even so, Queen Victoria turned down recommendations for Nica's great-grandfather Lionel to be ennobled. 'To make a Jew a peer is a step *she* could not consent to,' she wrote, even though Lionel had financed housing projects in poor areas, loaned the government money, underwritten the US Bond Issue and set up relief funds during the Irish famine. He had also frequently underwritten Her Majesty's government's expenses. The family had to wait another generation for Lionel's son Natty, Nica's grandfather, to become the first Jew to enter the House of Lords.

*

The Nica I knew in America had chosen a completely different kind of life. She loved live music, an art form that evaporates the moment it comes into existence. She owned thousands of records and hundreds of hours of bootleg recordings, but it was clear that it was the performance that mattered to her and, above all, it was about being there, not owning it.

Her house was modest and contained nothing of great value. Instead of works by Rubens, Reynolds, Van Dyck, Guardi and Boucher hanging on her walls, Nica had stuck album covers randomly to the plaster, and in place of back stairs for servants to pass unnoticed, there were cat flaps and walkways for cats. The curtains were tatty and the furniture, apart from the grand Steinway piano, was strictly functional. The only real hint of her European past – the family's enormous fortune and vastly different way of life – was her title, her monogrammed notepaper, her Bentley, her fur coat and her strings of perfect pearls.

Nica's guests were unlikely to be offered food although drink flowed freely. Asked once by the documentarian Bruce Ricker whether the family sent her cases of Rothschild wine, Nica snorted crossly, 'Better believe they don't,' before adding, 'Just try and get a buck from them.' To a casual observer, Nica had made a complete break with the past.

While she might not have bought objects, there was one tradition that Nica maintained. Her family, particularly the women, were assiduous in helping those less fortunate and doing good works in the local community. In London's Whitechapel, for example, the Rothschilds funded synagogues, schools and modern housing. When they realised the importance of having a good pair of shoes at a job interview, they made sure every pupil and graduate of a Rothschild free school was fitted for a new pair of boots annually. These charitable works were not acts of remote munificence: Emma and her granddaughters became personally involved with many cases.

Employees at Tring were the first in the country to enjoy free health care. Long before grand establishments had mod cons, every house on a Rothschild estate had indoor plumbing and mains drainage. Emma, Nica's grandmother, made lists of some four hundred causes that she supported, ranging from building repairs to paying for the passage of a pet lamb to Canada for a poor Jewish emigrant family. Local causes included needlework guilds, choral societies, convalescent homes, lying-in societies and the Tring Band of United Hope. Her daughter-in-law Rozsika and her grand-daughters were all expected to get involved. On royal public holidays the Tring children would receive a commemorative mug filled with sweets plus a bright new shilling. Their families could apply to Emma's coal club in winter or for unemployment bene-fit. For a small subscription all locals could qualify for free health care and nursing. Every family had access to an allotment. In the words of one employee, 'To work at Tring Park was insurance from cradle to grave.'

Nica took this tradition to New York; if she saw a person or an animal in need, she would try to help them. While her grand-mother Emma was systematic in her acts of charity, Nica was largely reactive. Thelonious Monk's son Toot, who as a boy spent a lot of time with Nica, marvelled at her generosity. 'I can't tell you how many mercy missions to save musicians' lives in every way she made,' he told me. 'Whether we were going to a pawn shop to retrieve a guy's instrument or going to buy groceries because some-one didn't have food or going to a rent office to pay somebody's rent because they were about to be thrown on the street or going to the hospital to visit somebody because they didn't have anybody else to visit them. Or going to help somebody get some food, because their girlfriend just had a baby. Every aspect of human ex-istence that I saw musicians deal with, I saw them lean on Nica and I saw Nica respond: she was like Santa Claus and Mother Teresa all rolled up in one.'

Nica did not see her own behaviour as heroic or part of a family tradition. She told me, 'I just saw that a lot of help was needed.'

Her attempts to do good sometimes misfired. 'I even became a manager,' she told Max Gordon, owner of the Village Vanguard club. 'I undertook the job of managing a jazz band, believe it or not, Art Blakey and the Jazz Messengers. Imagine! I thought I could help him and his men become more employable. Me! A manager! It was a disaster.' Remembering perhaps her grandmother's policy of buying children new shoes or giving a man seeking employment something decent to wear for an interview, Nica went out and acquired the Messengers six matching blue tuxedos. 'I thought that would help them get jobs. I was out of my mind.'

By the time of Nica's birth, cracks were appearing in the façade of the House of Rothschild and tensions between the cousins increased. The overriding drive to make money had receded. Instead the family wanted wider experiences, to assimilate further into British society and to enjoy the spoils of their success. The role of the Rothschild women became less defined; in the eighteenth and nineteenth centuries they had been silent, indispensable partners, but with the dawn of the twentieth century they had been so successful in integrating their fathers and sons into the fabric of British society that their importance subtly diminished. The younger generation of men, such as Walter or his brother Charles, were not necessarily born to be bankers. For several generations, there would not be a British Rothschild with significant business acumen. The imperative to succeed in the world of business would lie dormant for many decades.

Less than a year after Nica's birth, the First World War was declared. Many of the servants and estate workers were called up, only to perish on foreign soil. The Rothschild men, swept up by the patriotic mood, enlisted. Nica's cousins joined the Bucks Light Infantry; Evelyn was killed in February 1917 during a cavalry charge against the Turks. His brother Anthony fought at Gallipoli but survived. Fortuitously, the British cousins never had to fight their

French or Austrian relations. Charles was turned down for military service: physically he was fit, but there were doubts about his mental constitution.

The death of Nica's grandfather Natty on 31 March 1915 marked the end of an era. Hundreds of onlookers watched as his funeral cortège made its way from Hyde Park to Willesden, with a carriage drawn by four black-plumed horses. At Tring Park, his widow Emma tried to maintain the previous standards for her grandchildren. For a time she was successful: kept in splendid isolation, Nica and her siblings were largely unaffected by the tumultuous events outside the nursery wing. Their world, however, would be torn apart in a few years' time by the sudden, inexplicable death of their beloved father Charles.

7

The Butterfly and the Blues

One afternoon in the early spring of 1998 at Ashton, Nica's sister Miriam talked to me about their father's depression. She was categorical about its cause. She had, she claimed, the scientific evidence to prove that it was the family's tradition of inbreeding that had damaged their mental health. It was a degenerative illness, Miriam explained, and as Charles got older, the intervals between his recurring bouts of depression grew shorter.

Their father disappeared for many months at a time to a sanatorium in Switzerland. When the war ended it was followed by an outbreak of Spanish flu, which claimed another fifty million lives. Charles was infected but fought off the virus; it left him physically debilitated and even less able to cope with life. Once again he was sent away to recuperate.

No stone was left unturned in the family's desperate search for a way to help Charles. For all their incredible influence and acumen, they were lost. The Rothschilds finally occupied a position of wealth and power, but they had no weapons in the battle against this faceless enemy. When news of a 'talking cure' reached them, promoted by a man named Freud in Vienna, Austrian cousins were dispatched to the psychiatrist to seek his counsel. Other relations and advisors suggested different drugs or sanatoriums; seeking help in Switzerland was not unusual: T. S. Eliot and Max Linder were among those who went there in search of help for depression and nervous breakdowns. In the family archive I found a letter written by Charles's companion Mr Jordan, sent from from Fusio on 25 July 1917; so it seems likely that Charles, along with German writer Herman Hesse, was being treated by Carl Jung's protégé, Dr Joseph Lang. I longed to know why they had chosen the mystical Jung's methods over his rival, Sigmund Freud. Miriam said that at the time of her death, her grandmother Emma was reading Freud's complete works.

Charles's illness coincided with the deaths, one by one, of the senior Rothschilds. Between 1905 and 1917 the generation that had dominated Rothschild finance since 1875 was picked off by illnesses and infirmity. Charles was expected to run the British branch, modernise the bank's practices and lead British Jewry. All he wanted, however, was to study natural history and spend time with his family.

In December 1919, Rozsika woke her children up early to give them the best possible news, an early Christmas present. Their father was coming home. The excitement in the nursery was palpable. Although the ground was covered in a thick layer of snow, Charles would surely help them catch bugs and play music. There would be jokes and games. Everything would be better again, as it had been before the war, before Daddy had to go away. The children organised an exhibition of all the bugs they had caught over the summer. There had been a spectacular heatwave in September when the hedgerows and garden had hummed with insects.

On the morning of their father's return, the children were dressed in their best clothes waiting in the hall. Just six, Nica was particularly thrilled; she hardly knew her father and wanted to show him all the things she had learned in his absence. Charles arrived by car; Rozsika and a nurse helped him out. He walked very slowly and with a bad limp. Later they were told that a nurse had accidentally spilled a boiling hot-water bottle on his foot. The children did not mind and rushed forward to embrace him. Rozsika raised her hand, a warning to stay back. The children stopped but could hardly contain their enthusiasm. Miriam, their leader, called out, 'Hello, Daddy.' But Charles did not even look at them. It was as if they were invisible. He hobbled straight past them, past the Christmas tree and into his study.

'And that is the end of the story, as far as I was concerned, because from there onwards my father was mad,' Miriam said, the memory still fresh. 'My poor mother. She adored my father. The man she married disappeared and she was left with this lunatic in the house.'

While Charles's illness followed no predictable pattern, the symptoms sound like a form of schizophrenia, moving without warning from high to low, from calm to manic. At times he was charming and sweet but moments later he could be aloof, irascible. He experienced bouts of extreme grandiosity and compulsive generosity in which he tried to give all his possessions away to the nearest person. For days on end he would not sleep, padding around the house, peering across rooms at no one or nothing in particular. Then he would crash, falling asleep in the middle of lunch. He became totally obsessed with a subject and, once fixated, would talk about it doggedly to anyone who would listen. The children and the staff alike lived in dread of being caught in the headlights of his mania.

Charles's brother Walter and his mother Emma tried to pretend that nothing was happening; Walter buried himself in research, Emma in running the estate. It was an almost intolerable situation for Rozsika, who had no real role at Tring, few friends and scant idea of how British life worked. Her parents had died during the First World War and her siblings were stuck on the other side of Europe. In one of his rare moments of tender lucidity Charles wrote to his wife: 'I wish you and I hadn't lived through this, I am sorry we lived to see this.' It was not clear if he was talking about his illness or the war.

In 1923 Rozsika decided to take her family to Ashton Wold, hoping that the onset of spring would bring out the wildlife and raise her husband's spirits. Charles particularly loved the abundance of insects and rare butterflies found in the garden. On good days he watched his children play and, for a brief period, his spirits rallied. The house was suddenly full of optimism, but it was short-lived. As summer gave way to autumn that year, Charles's mood darkened.

Seventy-five years later, Miriam and I were sitting near the fire in her drawing room at Ashton Wold. I had set up my camera opposite her wheelchair and perched on a chair next to it. What I heard next was so shocking and unexpected that I sat rooted, unable to move, for the next hour. 'One afternoon my father went into a bathroom and locked the door behind him. Then he took a knife and slit his throat,' Miriam said.

Although I had heard about Charles's suicide, I knew nothing of the details. My great-aunt's deadpan delivery of the facts was far more moving than if she'd cried or had betrayed a shred of self-pity.

We sat in silence while I tried to think what to say or whether, indeed, to say anything at all. Eventually I asked, 'Did you ever talk about it, afterwards, as a family?'

'No, never.'

Miriam had been speaking for so long that the light had faded and the fire had gone out. I changed the tape in my video recorder. Miriam reached for her cup of tea, which must have been stone cold. I asked if she'd like some more. On the side table, a nightlight still burned under a silver tea caddy. I half rose to fetch a warmer brew. She waved me back into my chair, not wanting to be interrupted.

'I will never forget the first time that my mother and grandmother met after it happened,' she continued. 'We came into the hall at Tring and my grandmother appeared at the top of the stairs and just looked at us. My mother couldn't bear it and ran away.'

The children were not told the cause of their father's death. The staff were forbidden from discussing it and there was an embargo on all newspapers being delivered to the house. Recently I found the following contemporary report in *The Times* of 16 October 1923. 'The heir presumptive of the present Lord Rothschild was found dead at his home at Ashton Wold on Friday. At an inquest on Saturday it was stated that he was found with his throat cut in his bathroom. The evidence was that he had been in indifferent health and had suffered from depression, though so far as was known, he had no cause for worry.' I read the last sentence several times: 'He had no cause for worry.' I realised that Charles had faced the added pressure of guilt – he had been unable to enjoy his perfect life.

For the Rothschild family his death was an unimaginable catastrophe. They had to cope with the loss of a beloved son, cousin, brother and father, but they also faced the terror of having lost the heir to the British family. Charles's death left both a vacuum and a terrible sense of shame.

In 1923 suicide was illegal, an affront to the law, to society and to the monarch. Miriam, Nica, Victor and Liberty had to endure an almost universal silence for some years regarding the nature of their father's illness followed by the added difficulty, years later, of finding out about the circumstances surrounding his death.

Suicide leaves in its wake a wash of confusion, anger, guilt, sorrow and loss. The suicide escapes, while the living are abandoned in a perpetual darkness, their questions unanswerable, their fears irresolvable. There is always the haunting, fleeting thought that it might not have happened if only something had been done differently. The survivors wrestle with the entirely futile desire to reach a hand back into the past, and seize the person, hold them tight and persuade them to do otherwise. Children feel all this without the knowledge or experience to temper their reactions. It is easy to imagine the devastating impact this has on a child, particularly when there is no one to confirm, deny or help interpret his or her fears. Nica and her siblings not only lacked that person but they also lived in the constant fear that the same thing might happen to their mother or to others they loved. There is also a lingering fear: could it happen to us? Is there a tiny mental ledge that we could step over at any time?

What becomes of that child in adulthood? Are there common anxiety disorders or behavioural traits? The medical and psychiatric reports on the subject are inconclusive and yet all-inclusive: the children of a suicide experience a gamut of symptoms, ranging from fear of intimacy to suicidal tendencies to a propensity for addiction. Every child suffers trauma of a kind at some stage but as the child psychiatrist Alice Miller succinctly puts it, 'It's not the trauma we suffer in childhood that makes us emotionally ill but the inability to express the trauma.' As Nica and her sisters had no one to share their unhappiness with, the process of intense grief was difficult for them to navigate alone and in silence.

Nica understood from a young age that suppressing one's own needs and natural vitality leads to terrible forms of self-destruction. It was one of the reasons she would, in the future, refuse to be trapped in an unhappy life. It also helps to explain why, many years later, she would risk her personal freedom to keep Thelonious Monk out of jail and then fight tooth and claw to let him live out his last years away from the demands of public life.

In accordance with the Jewish religion, Charles was buried within twenty-four hours. Only male family members and associates were allowed to attend the funeral. Women and children stayed at home.

Two years after Charles's suicide, Victor, then fifteen, called Miriam from Harrow School, asking her to visit him urgently. She drove straight there. 'He was terribly upset and said that some of the boys had been teasing him that his father had killed himself and only madmen or convicts did that.' Miriam, who was seventeen, had already adopted the role of protector in the family. She calmed her brother, saying it was a pack of lies, promising to sort out the confusion, while assuring Victor that their father was neither mad nor a criminal. Racing back to Tring Park, she confronted her mother, asking for the truth. Rozsika, Miriam told me, 'never looked up from her desk'. Hardly missing a beat, she told her daughter, 'It had been coming on a long time.' After that, the subject was closed. Her mother refused to discuss it ever again.

In accordance with family tradition, Charles left his entire estate (valued at £2,250,000) to his only son Victor. He left each daughter £5,000 – 2 per cent of their brother's inheritance. Despite having no formal training in finance, Rozsika took on the management of the estates belonging to her husband and her brother-in-law Walter, as well as her children's inheritance. Her business acumen was such that she doubled her son's assets by the end of her life. However, in the process the once gay and beautiful barrel jumper became an aloof and formidable chatelaine: she had to. Her mother-in-law Emma, formerly a powerhouse of activity, was crushed by the loss of her husband and then of her beloved son. Walter, heartbroken, became increasingly eccentric and hid himself in his museum.

Letters to friends show that Rozsika had another huge problem – the health of her second daughter, Liberty. From an early age, Liberty was physically delicate and seemed to contract every passing illness. She was so sensitive emotionally that the smallest event plunged her into a morass of despair. The sight of a bird with an injured wing, a lame horse or a change to routine affected her deeply. In a cache of letters written to a family friend, Rozsika's worries about her frail daughter haunt every page. 'She looks so fragile. I really am in constant intense worry about her.' In her brief periods of good health Liberty showed huge promise. Her paintings won a gold medal at the Royal Academy summer show and at twelve she was offered solo piano concerts in London. Attempting to keep Liberty on an even keel, Rozsika divided her time between caring for her second daughter and managing her children's finances. With Victor at Harrow and Miriam in London for the Season, Nica was frequently by herself.

Until she was sixteen, Nica, being the youngest, often ate alone in the nursery, while her nurse and governess went downstairs to the noisy, convivial servants' hall. When Nica was finally allowed to join her mother and siblings in the dining room, she had to get used to another set of rules. A footman in livery, with spotlessly white gloves, stood behind her chair. Her golden plate, stamped with the family's crest, was framed with rows of knives, forks and spoons, spelling out how many courses would follow. For the duration of the endless meal she would be expected to sit, back straight, eyes ahead, hands in lap, mouth kept dry with tiny pats of a heavy, monogrammed, white-linen napkin.

The most perfect remaining example of that way of life can be found today at Waddesdon Manor, now a National Trust property open to the public. The house has been preserved to perfectly capture the atmosphere of Nica's youth. There are now little red ropes to keep the visitor from stepping on a priceless carpet or touching a piece of porcelain. However, even during Nica's childhood, the curtains were kept drawn to protect the artworks from light and it was forbidden to run among the priceless Sèvres, the delicately placed Fabergé eggs and the eighteenth-century ormolu. Daylight was banished behind layers of embroidered damask and silk. Heavy French panelling and perfect examples of rare Savonnerie carpets muffled ambient noise.

Tring, like Waddesdon, was beautiful but also utterly suffocating, which partially explains why later in life Nica showed so little interest in possessions or formalities. Her kitchen cupboards contained little more than cat food and the odd dry biscuit. There were no dinner services or silver, no attempt to learn how to cook. Tring Park and even Ashton Wold, for all their beauty and comfort, represented places to escape from, rather than family homes.

The Great Hall at Tring.

8

Pure Pre-War Perfection

Even though Nica was a member of the first generation of emancipated British women, well-brought up young ladies were still expected to behave like the weaker, gentler sex. Submissiveness, modesty and humility were required female attributes. English society was so small and introspective that everyone knew everyone else's business. If events were not already listed in *The Times* or transmitted over the servants' network, gossip whistled round the hunting fields and drawing rooms. Nica's reputation as a wild child was broadcast before she even stepped on to the dance floor. My father's mother Barbara, who used to stay at Tring Park, wrote in her private diaries in 1929: 'Amazing red house with plate glass windows. Indoors yellow furniture in the bedrooms, blue bows on my bed and very few bathrooms. Wonderful Lady Rothschild with a lovely witchy face and Uncle Wally with spaghetti in his beard and the old housedog way of being treated. Little sister Nica full of fat and high spirits.'

In 1929, at sixteen, Nica exploded out of the nursery. Finally allowed to stay up after nine o'clock, Nica decided that sleep was a waste of time and switched her preferred waking hours from day to night-time. The Tring Park visitors' book shows that the house was now packed with people on most weekends. Selected guests were asked to attend secret late-night sessions in the attic. Between the hours of 2 and 5 a.m., after the stuffier adults had gone to bed and before the servants awoke, the young Rothschilds entertained their friends with bottles of family wine and jazz records. 'We used to call it corridor creeping,' my grandmother explained with a wicked giggle.

Rozsika had no idea how to manage her wayward daughter. Cut off from her native Hungary and its traditions, she could hardly rely on guidance from her ageing mother-in-law or the eccentric Walter. Adrift in a sea of arcane and fairly incomprehensible rules, Rozsika sought the counsel of society ladies. The first piece of advice both given and taken was to send Nica to a finishing school in Paris. While ostensibly a reputable establishment, it was in reality 'operated by wig-wearing lesbian sisters', she told the critic and writer Nat Hentoff in a profile for *Esquire* magazine in 1960. These redoubtable women, Nica said 'made passes at the girls. They taught us how to put on lipstick and gave us a little literature and philosophy to go with it and if you weren't a favourite, woe betide you. They used to charge the earth for corrupting all those girls. It was all quite revealing.'

Graduating from this lesbian seminary in the summer of 1930, Nica joined her sister Liberty on a grand tour of Europe. A governess, a chauffeur and a maid accompanied the young ladies. The network of maternal and paternal cousins meant that the sisters were in constant social demand. In France, they stayed at the magnificent Château Ferrière. In Austria, Nica waltzed at balls and rode Lipizzaner horses at the Spanish Riding School. In Vienna, she got involved in her first international scandal, although admittedly it was not, for once, of her making. An impoverished, opportunistic countess, hoping to restore her family's fortunes, announced that her son and Miss Pannonica Rothschild were engaged. There was little substance to the romance apart from a shared love of riding. It was the countess's bad luck that Rozsika, who took every foreign

Great-aunt Miriam at work.

newspaper, spotted the announcement and immediately published a robust disclaimer.

In Munich, the two sisters took a painting course. 'It was during Hitler's rise, but we weren't aware of what was going on until it finally occurred to us that the people who were behaving boorishly were those who knew we were Jewish,' Nica told *Esquire*. It was a rare moment of political awareness; the sisters were strangely oblivious to international events. Another major incident that appeared to pass them by was the Wall Street crash of 1929, although the collapse of the stock market and the ensuing depression bit deeply into the family's fortune.

With an unearned income at their disposal but no guiding Rothschild male role model, Nica and her siblings made up their own rules. The four children of Charles and Rozsika were driven by a sense of entitlement rather than duty. Miriam, Victor and Nica masked their insecurities with an air of utter imperiousness. None of them was popular or even well liked.

Despite her best efforts, the finishing schools and London party circuits, Rozsika was failing to marry off her daughters. Liberty, though greatly admired by her Rothschild cousin Alain, was too nervous to cope with affairs of the heart. Miriam was more interested in looking down a microscope than into the eyes of young men. In 1926, aged eighteen, she decided not to waste nights dancing and flirting, and enrolled secretly in evening classes at Chelsea Polytechnic. Having gained the most basic qualifications, she got a paid job, studying marine biology in Naples. Her family were baffled, while 1920s polite society was shocked. Why would anyone in her position choose a job over a comfortable life? Possessed by a determination to complete the research started by her father Charles, Miriam became one of Britain's leading naturalists, and a world expert in fleas, butterflies and chemical communications. Without the proper credentials to win a place as an undergraduate, she went on to be awarded eight honorary doctorates, from Oxford University in 1968 to Cambridge in 1999, as well as a Fellowship of the Royal Society in 1985 and she was later made a Dame of the British Empire.

Thus Miriam showed a generation of young women, including Nica, that there were alternative ways of living and that passions could transmute into careers. By the time Nica left the nursery, Miriam was well advanced in her studies. Following her apprenticeship in Naples, she spent the inter-war years developing a chicken feed made from seaweed rather than grain. However, the inspiration for her work still came from her father's unfinished research into butterflies and fleas. Miriam became the dutiful eldest daughter who stayed at home, worked assiduously and kept alight the flame of her parents' memory.

Without Miriam's involvement, encouragement and memories, this book could not have been written, yet her achievements and her forceful character also threatened to derail the project. Miriam was so strong and her recollections so vivid that her voice at times seemed to overpower Nica's. Sometimes when I asked Miriam about Nica, she would talk instead about herself or Liberty. I would question other people about Nica and they would only want to talk about Miriam. Why aren't you writing about her, they would say. She was the really distinguished, high-achieving one.

I wondered whether Nica resented living in the shadow of her

Victor and his first wife Barbara (née Hutchinson).

highly successful sister and brother. Was her later decision to live abroad an attempt to establish herself elsewhere, away from their spotlight? A by-product of coming from a highly successful family, as I know, is being treated as someone's daughter, sister, cousin, niece or mother rather than a person in one's own right. I stuck up for Nica and for this project. Perhaps Nica achieved something that cannot be measured in honorary degrees and paper qualifications,

I would remonstrate, something less public but nonetheless valid. Minor characters, I argued, are still important.

As the youngest child, Nica never felt obliged to continue any tradition, so she did what pleased her, when it pleased her. Liberty, however, could never make the most of her huge potential, and would remain incapacitated by psychological fragility for the rest of her life.

Victor had no intention of letting a career in banking get in the way of his real passions. From an early age, as the longed-for son and heir, he had been over-indulged and brought up to believe that his will was omnipotent. When as a tiny child he found fire amusing, his mother instructed a servant to walk backwards in front of his pram, lighting matches. At school when he was bored by lessons he was allowed to skip classes to concentrate on cricket. He went on to play at county level for Northamptonshire. Miriam became his manager and, in the absence of a father or an interested mother, she attended all his matches.

At Cambridge, Victor read Natural Sciences, hardly a surprising choice for a boy whose first memory was being asked by his father to catch a *gynandromorph* Orange-tip. There, a whole world opened up to him; Victor realised his intellectual potential and found his peer group. Though he was known at university for being a playboy who drove an open-top Bugatti and collected rare first editions, for the rest of his life Victor valued academic prowess over possessions. The people he really admired were scientists, dons, thinkers and intellectuals. His forebears had used assets and wealth to create a sense of identity; Victor relied on being clever and being surrounded by clever people. His other great passion was jazz music and he considered becoming a professional musician. Hearing that the great jazz pianist Teddy Wilson was giving lessons in London, Victor signed up and took his little sister Nica to watch. Years later Teddy Wilson was Nica's entrée to the New York club scene.

Victor's first group of university friends included two young men, Guy Burgess and Anthony Blunt, who persuaded him to join their discussion group, the Apostles. Victor saw them as allies who shared a love of literature and learning, and a hatred of fascism. In the period from 1927 to 1937, twenty out of twenty-six of the group's new members were socialists, Marxists, Marxist sympathisers or communists. For a young Jew watching the rise of Nazism in Germany, becoming a left-wing sympathiser was not unexpected.

Graduating from Cambridge, Victor was awarded a triple first and was elected a Fellow of Trinity. During the war he worked at MI6 and was awarded a George Medal for bomb disposal, claiming that years of copying Teddy Wilson and Art Tatum's chords was an ideal preparation for such a tricky task.

Yet for all this loyal service, when it emerged after the war that his two great friends Burgess and Blunt were Soviet spies and that two further members of the Apostles were also double agents, the finger of suspicion hovered over Victor for most of his life. One book claimed that he was the 'Fifth Man' and although this turned out to be John Cairncross, innuendoes continued to haunt Victor. On 3 December 1986, he took the unusual step of publishing a letter in the British press stating, 'I am not, and have never been, a Soviet agent.' Even when cleared by Mrs Thatcher, the whispers went on. Later he told his biographer Kenneth Rose that discovering Blunt was a double agent had been 'devastating and crushing beyond belief'.

Victor continued to work in the field of science and, in particular, on the reproductive system of sea urchins. Later he and Miriam became the only brother and sister to have both been made Fellows of the Royal Society. As Miriam put it, 'Of course my brother got into the Royal Society long before I did. Chiefly, I think, it was due to prejudice against women. Except for the fact that I hadn't been to a public school like my brother – I was educated, or uneducated, at home – I think I was always a rather better zoologist than he was.'

Despite their apparent differences, Victor always looked after his little sister Nica, and they shared a love for music and socialising. Nica was extremely pretty, not at all serious like her two sisters, and Victor liked to show her off. It was Victor who introduced her to the

Nica, the debutante, presented at court in 1932.

latest movements in modern jazz and encouraged her to learn to fly. A great lover of fast cars, Victor taught Nica to drive and bought her a racy sports car for her eighteenth birthday. Even when he became exasperated by her chosen lifestyle, Victor continued to take care of her, indulging her with random acts of kindness, although my father Jacob attests to the fact that Victor found it hard to show similar affection or generosity to any of his six children.

Nica was expected to marry a Jew but eligible suitors were in short supply. Having put her through finishing school and sent her on a grand European tour, Rozsika next decided to launch her daughter in society in 1932.

This annual British tradition, known as the Season, was open to well-connected young women and men. Following a custom that endured until 1958, Nica wore white and curtsied to a huge white cake at Queen Charlotte's Ball. For the next three months she took part in a merry race known to some as the marriage market. Given that only a handful of Jews attended, it was unlikely that Nica would meet any 'Mr Rights' among the hundreds of young debutantes and 'debs' delights' being presented to the King and Queen.

In June of that year, Nica was formally presented to King George V and Queen Mary and thrown into a swirl of debutante balls and coming-out parties. 'I burst forth on an astonished world and did my curtsies without falling down,' she told Nat Hentoff. Having already put two elder daughters through the Season, Rozsika could not face chaperoning Nica to a third. The task of seeing the young Miss Rothschild home to bed fell instead to Grandmother Emma's hapless chauffeur. Her cousin Rosemary remembers that Nica rarely came home at the appointed time.

The family lived in Kensington Palace Gardens, a gated road. While it was easy to give the chauffeur the slip, it was much harder to climb over high railings in the dark, wearing a floor-length ball gown. There were approximately four balls a week while the Houses of Parliament were in session between November and May. Wanting to get a flavour of what it was like, I interviewed Nica's near contemporary, Debo, the Dowager Duchess of Devonshire (née Mitford). Like the Rothschilds, the Mitford girls were rather eccentric. Unity used to take a pet rat to dances and Diana expounded her radical political views to her partners during the foxtrot. Debo explained that girls took the whole thing in their stride. 'It was rather like going to the office,' she said. 'It's just what one did but it was such fun.'

It is easy to trace Nica's progress through the London Season. Every dance was listed in *The Times*, often accompanied by a detailed description of what the debutante was wearing and which designer had made her dress. Daywear was prescriptive; there were many designers but few variations. In the year of Nica's coming out it was de rigueur to wear short fur cuffs that could be slipped off and turned into muffs. Dresses were often floral and trimmed with silk motifs. Skirts were to the knee and made from soft tweed or crêpe, occasionally adorned with velvet belts of two colours twisted and tied in sharp knots. Nica's clothes were made in Paris by leading couturiers Worth and Chanel. The Rothschild jewels, including emeralds the size of pigeons' eggs and strings of the finest white diamonds, belonged to Victor but were loaned out to his wife or sisters for special occasions.

Rozsika announced in *The Times* Court Circular that her daughter's coming-out ball would be held on 22 June 1931 at 148 Piccadilly, her mother-in-law Emma's house. My father's mother Barbara, who was being courted by Victor at the time, described the evening in her personal diary:

> At dinner there were three tables, the big middle one for all the old people – headed by the matriarch looking superb and matri-archal – the younger matriarch [Rozsika] next to Winston [Churchill] – the other table headed by the future matriarch Miriam and lastly Victor's table for Nica. The dance after was quite marvelous [sic], the great rooms with gilt and chandeliers, plush gold chairs and huge looking glasses, masses of champagne and people streaming up the stairs from the hall in all their jewels and grandest dresses. The park was open behind the house. Nica was pure prewar perfection. Some of us went to the Café de Madrid. Nica was chased in Piccadilly and rescued by Victor.*

My father's sister Miranda was one of the few Rothschilds who often visited her Aunt Nica in New York. She understood the nuances of English Rothschild life, as well as being sympathetic to what Nica was seeking in New York. 'The problem with putting all that "society stuff" in your book,' said Miranda during a recent con-versation, 'is that it makes Nica and Victor sound conventional. They were completely, totally eccentric. They were not like anyone else. My father [Victor] used to water-ski in a Schiaparelli silk dressing gown and he stripped naked whenever, wherever, he felt like it. Nica and her siblings only went to parties because it pleased their mother.'

The children were not, Miranda told me, remotely interested in being accepted in high society; had they been, the outcome for all of them, and the choices they made, would have been very different. Victor was a 'crashing intellectual snob', Nica something of a musical snob; but neither ever took the slightest notice of a person's social standing or background. What was really important to them, I asked. 'Music!' she replied. 'Victor and Nica were mad about music. Victor, who was a gifted pianist, toyed with a career as a jazz musician.' For Nica, the Season was nirvana, but not because of the young men: what she really loved was the music and musicians.

Nica's first love was the American bandleader Jack Harris. In film footage of Harris shot at the Café de Paris, London, in 1934, he shimmies across the dance floor, violin in hand. Swinging slightly from foot to foot, Harris sometimes draws a bow across his fiddle or sings a little, but more often than not he is caught returning the appreciative glances of fawning debutantes. Although fifty-five years had passed since their last meeting, Nica told me that she could remember every detail including his phone number, his favourite drink – brandy – and that he liked his eggs sunny side up. Whether or not he took her virginity is unclear, but Nica seized every opportunity to see her paramour. I asked Debo Devonshire whether she was shocked by Nica's infatuation. 'Shocked! Of course not. Everyone was in love with the bandleader. They were by far the most attractive men in the room. My particular favourite was a man called Snakehips Johnson. He was killed in the war. A tragedy.'

Big bands visited regularly from America. Some played at the debutantes' balls, others at London venues. Victor took his little sister to Streatham Town Hall to see Duke Ellington and Benny Goodman. Since the première of Stravinsky's *The Rite of Spring* in 1913, the year of Nica's birth, music had changed beyond all recognition. It was no longer something to be appreciated when perched on a gilt chair, or the accompaniment to executing perfectly co-ordinated steps: music had exploded out of the cradle of convention. It poured from radio sets and roared around the dance floors. The

*The Café de Paris, London's most fashionable party venue during the
1930s, where Nica met her first love, bandleader Jack Harris.*

emancipation of music freed the younger generation. Finally they
had something that their parents despised and couldn't understand
that was exclusively, gloriously theirs.

In Europe and America, musicians responded to social and political change by throwing out the long-established rule books of how
pieces should be constructed. On the dance floors none of the young
cared for an allegro or a scherzo; they wanted rhythm, something
they could dance and sing to, something that reflected new-found
opportunities and freedom. It was called swing. On opposite sides of
the Atlantic, separated by a vast ocean, Nica and a young African-
American high-school drop-out by the name of Thelonious Monk
were listening to the same music, at the same time. Their backgrounds were disparate, their circumstances could not have been
more different, but the soundtrack to their lives was exactly the same.

9

The Commander-in-Chief

Nica had come out three years earlier when, in the summer of 1935, her brother Victor took her to Le Touquet in France. This fashionable extension of British life, advertised itself as 'a new atmosphere in a familiar setting'. Since Noël Coward and his friends had begun to use it as a weekend destination in the 1920s, bright young things had flocked to the coastal resort to enjoy racing, gambling and parties.

At a lunch there given by a Rothschild cousin, Nica met her future husband. To a young fatherless girl brought up in a household dominated by women, Baron Jules de Koenigswarter seemed wonderfully assured and glamorous. A handsome Jewish widower, ten years Nica's senior, and father to a small boy, Jules was employed at the Banque de Paris as a mining expert. Originally from Austria, the de Koenigswarter family had lived in France for over a century and were part of the cosmopolitan group that moved effortlessly from country to country in their common pursuits of business, hunting and dancing. Rozsika knew them from her younger days. Although the family had some money, Jules had to work to support himself.

LE TOUQUET

THE WESTMINSTER

A new atmosphere in a familiar setting "

...there is dancing each night
at dinner. British and French
society meet daily in the new
bar with its sunny terrace...

*Open at Christmas and Easter,
then from Whitsun to September*

THREE GOLF COURSES (TWO 18 AND ONE 9 HOLES)
— POLO — RACING — 40 TENNIS COURTS — SWIMMING
POOL — TWO CASINOS — THE HOTEL IS 100 YARDS
FROM THE CASINO DE LA FÔRET AND UNDER A
MILE FROM THE NEW AÉRODROME

*Nica met her future husband, Baron Jules de Koenigswarter,
at the fashionable French resort of Le Touquet in 1935.*

Nica and Jules in Edinburgh.

Nica was literally swept off her feet. Before lunch ended, Jules took her straight from the restaurant to the airport and whisked her away in his Leopard Moth plane. There were clues in this first meeting that foreshadowed the pattern of their life together. For Jules, whom Nica later christened the Commander-in-Chief, accurate navigation, safety checks, maintenance procedures and the scheduling of flights were just as important as the sensation of being in the air. Nica later admitted that she was bored by his insistence on meticulous safety checks before their departure. Jules should also have spotted potential incompatibilities: Nica had been taught to fly by a saxophonist, Bob Wise, whom she met while dancing at the Savoy Hotel. Jules was appalled to discover that she didn't even have a licence or know how to map-read. Nica navigated using railway lines or main roads. 'It wasn't a problem unless it was foggy,' she told me.

For many years I struggled to find out more about Jules. The couple had separated long before I was born and after their break-up the Rothschild family lost touch with the baron. Nica described her former husband in disparaging terms: as an obsessive time-keeper, authoritarian and rather humourless. Clearly she had fallen in love with something, but what was it?

Hearing that Jules had published a memoir, I managed to track it down in a second-hand bookshop in Málaga. The title was *Savoir dire non* (or *Learning to Say No*). In it Jules presents him-self as a Jack the lad and tells tales of being arrested by his regiment for defying rules such as illegally entertaining a girl overnight in his room or cheating on his military homework. On three separate occasions, acting against the advice of friends, he recalls proudly how he flew and landed his plane in thick fog – exactly the kind of recklessness that he criticised his wife for. If Jules had been an Englishman, he would have been an upper-class toff who liked to portray himself as madly amusing and always at the heart of semi-daring exploits. In the early throes of romance, Nica chose to see a wild and dashing suitor. Unfortunately, the fug of early passion obfuscated Jules's more enduring character traits.

Over the next three months Jules was in determined pursuit of the young heiress around Europe, conducting their courtship like a military campaign. His first decision was to ask his mother to extend an invitation to Nica to stay with his family at their summer house in Deauville. Luckily for Jules, Rozsika approved of the de Koenigswarters and gave her daughter permission, so long as her chauffeur and a maid went as chaperones. It was Nica's first solo trip abroad and represented another exciting break from her restric-tive youth.

Nica drove the servants to Deauville in her low-slung sports car and for two days she and Jules kept their feet on the ground. Then on a whim they decided to fly to Salzburg in Jules's plane, and on to Vienna in a clear breach of etiquette. Their horrified mothers instructed the lady's maid and chauffeur to follow them. Each time the servants caught up with the courting couple, the lovebirds got back into the Leopard Moth and hopped on to the next capital. Having negotiated every pothole from Deauville to Salzburg, and from Vienna to Venice, the chauffeur and maid were finally reunited with Nica several weeks later in Monte Carlo.

Nica told her brother that Jules instructed, rather than asked, her to marry him. She had misgivings even at this early stage about their compatibility and asked him for time to reflect, being in no hurry to settle down into married life. But being young, naive and impressionable, with no father figure to advise her, Nica supposed that she must be madly in love.

In September 1935 Nica pretended that she needed to visit New York to seek the advice of her sister Liberty. What Nica really wanted was to go to America to hear, with her own ears, the extraordinary music being broadcast from her wireless. In Harlem's Savoy Ballroom she would hear Chick Webb, Teddy Hill and the King of

The New York Times

MISS ROTHSCHILD IS MARRIED HERE

Becomes Bride of Baron Jules de Koenigswarter in Chapel of Municipal Building.

ATTENDED BY HER SISTER

She Is Member of Famous Banking Family and Niece of Head of the London Branch.

Miss Kathleen Annie Pannonica Rothschild of London and Baron Jules de Koenigswarter of Paris, who revealed their intentions to marry when they obtained a license last Thursday at the Municipal Building, were married in the chapel there yesterday by Deputy City Clerk Philip A. Hines. The couple were attended by Miss Elizabeth Rothschild, a sister of the bride, and Lionel Harris.

The Baron and Baroness will sail in a few days for a world cruise, after which they will divide their time between Paris and London.

The Baroness de Koenigswarter, a member of the British branch of the international banking family, is the youngest daughter of the late Nathaniel Charles Rothschild and a granddaughter of the late Nathan Mayer Rothschild, the first

Swing, Benny Goodman. She could not wait to catch the two new recording stars, Ella Fitzgerald and Billie Holiday, who performed with Victor's tutor Teddy Wilson. Boundaries were being stretched across the whole spectrum of American arts. The same year, 1935, saw the première of Gershwin's opera *Porgy and Bess*, which scandalised polite society by focusing on the lives of poor African Americans. The Museum of Modern Art in New York caused controversy and some bewilderment among the chattering classes by mounting a show called 'African Negro Art'. In literature, William Faulkner, John Steinbeck and F. Scott Fitzgerald had secured literary acclaim, while a new wave of painters, Arshile Gorky, Willem de Kooning and Jackson Pollock, were establishing themselves on the East Coast. Europe, by contrast, felt anachronistic and tired. England was celebrating King George V's Silver Jubilee and the Royal Academy was mounting an exhibition of French paintings.

For Nica, this visit to New York was the first but not the last time she would seek refuge in the metropolis. The two-week voyage across the Atlantic was the young heiress's first experience of being alone. She soon discovered that she had underestimated Jules's determination. Even on the SS *Normandie*, bobbing between the two coasts, Jules bombarded her with flowers and telegrams. Only twenty-one, Nica was unable to withstand this romantic onslaught. Before arriving in New York, she was engaged. Jules took the next passage to America, determined that his fiancée should not escape.

Their marriage took place at the chapel of the Manhattan Municipal Building on 15 October 1935. Liberty acted as the sole family representative and chief bridesmaid. Nica was already newsworthy. The event was reported in the *New York Times* under the headline 'Mi$$ Rothschild marries'. Four paragraphs were devoted to the history of the Rothschild family with one short final one on Nica's new husband, who is described as a mining engineer, an aviation enthusiast and a member of several noted French clubs. Victor gave her an aeroplane as a wedding gift, but for the next few years Nica rarely had time to fly it.

Rozsika was pleased that at least one daughter was now married off but she faced another more serious problem. The family hoped that sending Liberty to New York would act as a tonic, giving her a chance to get away from familiar problems. As Liberty's passion was painting, Rozsika arranged for her be taught by a gifted artist, Maria de Kammerer, a Hungarian known to Rozsika's family. Both Liberty and Victor sat for de Kammerer and their portraits were shown at an exhibition in New York in 1936. For many years I have tried unsuccessfully to track down this portrait of Liberty; frustratingly, few images of her survive beyond childhood.

Unfortunately for Liberty, the move to New York was just a geographical relocation; her mental state became even worse. Liberty, the sickly child, had grown into a painfully nervous adult whose equilibrium could be shaken by every tiny event. Miriam was adamant that, like their father Charles, Liberty had inherited the family 'blues'. There is scarce information about Liberty's illness: a Hippocratic oath bound her doctors and Miriam burned all her medical records.

Shortly after Nica left on her honeymoon, Liberty suffered a major nervous breakdown. Attending a grand New York dinner party, she shocked fellow guests by eating the table decorations – some roses – rather than the food on offer. After that, Liberty was sent home to Tring and then placed in residential care at a private hospital under the guidance of a family friend, the psychiatrist Dr Freudenberger.

Nica had emerged from the chrysalis of nursery life at Tring, unfurled her damp, powdery wings and taken flight. But it was a limited form of independence. She was released from the close confines of her family to her husband's control. Physically, her tiny waist was nipped into shape by a fearsome corset. Society dictated the length of her skirts and the cut of her jacket. Her behaviour was kept in check by a myriad of do's and don'ts, shoulds and should nots, necessary for a young married woman in the 1930s.

The first clue that there were problems in the marriage comes in

Jules's memoir. Nica is never mentioned by name, even during their honeymoon, and is merely referred to twice as 'my wife'.

The couple went from New York to Los Angeles via Panama. From there they took the OSK line to the Far East. When Nica became sick on the long voyage, the ship's Japanese doctor was so overcome with nerves at being asked to treat a grand, titled woman that he spent most of the consultation bowing and forgot to prescribe any medicine.

In Peking they smoked opium, lying on hard pillows, while a beautiful geisha girl rolled out tiny balls of the narcotic to place in their pipes. They hired a plane and flew over the areas devastated by the Yellow River floods, where they could clearly see but were unable to help stranded families who waved desperately at them, hoping for rescue. Continuing their journey, Jules and Nica narrowly avoided death when their plane crash-landed in a remote area. They eventually got a lift in a cattle truck to a nearby village with a run-down hotel infested with giant cockroaches. They survived on a diet of chocolate and whisky. Making it back to civilisation, they moved on to Japan, where Jules won a sake-drinking contest against a newspaper magnate and bought a gun at a market. In Kobe they visited a sex shop and bought musical sex toys to send to friends and family back home. Outraged customs officials unfortunately confiscated these. When asked to account for his own package, Victor Rothschild denied knowing anyone called de Koenigswarter and could not, he said, imagine why he had been sent such shocking items.

Despite all the adventures on their honeymoon, Nica was ill at ease. Her husband was a compulsive planner and left nothing to chance. Their world tour, which had lasted for months, was a disappointment for Nica because, she told Nat Hentoff, 'My husband always did everything according to a schedule, and to do that with me is no easy feat. We had each hour planned from the time we arrived in the morning until we left for the next place, and, as a result, we never saw anything.' Nica began to realise that she had stepped out of one cage and into another.

10

You're the Top

Following their return from honeymoon, Jules and Nica settled in Paris while they looked for a house in the surrounding countryside. For any jazz lover, the city was a slice of heaven known as 'Harlem in Montmartre'. Following the First World War a platoon of African-American soldiers, known by some as the Harlem Hell Fighters, had been so enamoured of France's practice of liberty, equality and fraternity that they remained there. As a fighting unit, the so-called Hell Fighters was the most highly decorated American combat unit in the Great War. In peacetime they met the high demand for black musicians to fill the bandstands of the small nightclubs of Montmartre. An African-American community soon formed on the right bank of the Seine, made up mainly of itinerant musicians, all of them young unmarried males. An important milestone was the creation of the Hot Club of France, a quintet formed by a chance meeting of Django Reinhardt and Stéphane Grappelli. Although the founders of that group were white, similar Hot Clubs sprang up, made up of every nationality, colour and creed.

Paris became the 'must stop' place on every well-known musician's tour, giving Nica the chance to hear Coleman Hawkins,

Dizzy Gillespie, Charlie Parker and Duke Ellington among others. One of the few people whom she would not have seen was Thelonious Monk, who preferred to stick close to his neighbourhood in New York City and was, at the time, trying to find a band to play with.

Nica became close to her French cousins and caught up with them on the racecourses at Deauville or Longchamp where they loved to mix style and sport. There was terrific competition between both branches of the family; Edouard de Rothschild won the Prix de l'Arc de Triomphe in 1934 and 1938, and her cousin Hannah de Rothschild's inheritance helped her husband Lord Rosebery win the Derby no less than four times between 1894 and 1944.

Then, in late 1935, Nica became pregnant. She was twenty-three and fulfilling her family's wishes. Neither of her sisters was married and it looked to all as if the wayward Nica had been

FLYING BABY

© Daily Express

Both Baron Jules de Koenigswarter and his wife—the former Miss Nica Rothschild, niece of Lord Rothschild—are ardent fliers. Indications point to their month-old son Patrick developing an air-sense early. He left Croydon yesterday, with his mother, for the Continent.

Daily Express, *31 August 1936.*

tamed. Like many mothers, she wanted to give birth at home so the couple returned to London. Patrick was born in July and in August the *Express* newspaper photographed the couple at a private airstrip in south London. The caption reads: 'Indications point to their month-old son Patrick developing air sense early. He left yesterday, with his mother, for the Continent.'

While some of Nica's options were curtailed by marriage and impending motherhood, their earlier way of life was brought to an end by her brother Victor. Following the death of Uncle Walter in 1937, Victor decided to sell off the enormous family collection that he had inherited. This included Tring Park, its contents and his grandmother Emma's house at 147 Piccadilly. His wife Barbara was a Strachey and a leading light in the Bloomsbury set; her mother Mary was a friend of Matisse and T. S. Eliot. With no particular liking for French eighteenth-century treasures or hoards of silver and Sèvres, Barbara steered her husband instead towards book collecting and contemporary art.

Members of the family were puzzled and distraught by the brutal disposal of his inheritance. How could he cast off collections that had taken so many years to create, that had meant so much to earlier generations? One explanation is that Victor preferred cash to the responsibility of ownership. Another was Victor's ambivalence about being a Rothschild: he wanted to be recognised as a scientist and an intellectual but his surname and heritage got in the way. 'When people meet me,' he told Bernard Levin in a BBC interview, 'they assume I live in a house where gold runs out of the taps.' After Cambridge he became a socialist and he later sat on the Labour benches in the House of Lords. By disposing of his ostentatious possessions, Victor hoped to be regarded as normal. He and Barbara rented Merton Hall, in Cambridge, close to the university where he worked as a research Fellow. Barbara employed the English decorator Syrie Maugham to paint the interiors in the neutral white that was then fashionable. Merton Hall was a temple of modernism compared to the glitzy, gilded palaces of Victor's youth.

The Rothschild auction made headlines on both sides of the Atlantic and the BBC broadcast the event live. The main sale lasted four days while a further three were devoted to Nica's grandmother's extraordinary silver collection, inherited from the Frankfurt Rothschilds. On the first day, seventeen great paintings went for the knock-down price of £41,252. *The Courtyard* by Pieter de Hooch was brought for £17,500 by the legendary picture dealer Duveen. The contents of the house eventually fetched £125,000, the equivalent today of many tens of millions if one accounts for the rise in the value of the art market.

The international fascination with the auction was partly due to the fabulousness of the contents but also for what it represented: surely the mass dispersal of property marked the end of the hegemony of the Rothschild family over British financial life.

Following Rozsika's death, Victor gave the farm at Ashton to his sister Miriam. It was as if he were trying to expunge his family's past and start anew. Having denuded the family of notable Dutch masters, as well as paintings by Reynolds and Gainsborough, Victor chose to hang on his walls pictures of different animals' sperm, blown up beyond recognition. As a child and then as an adult visiting Victor's home, I saw hardly a trace of that former life; Nica was not the only family member seeking a massive break with the past.

The sales of the Rothschild houses deprived Nica of her childhood homes as well as a British base. She had to put aside any disquiet about her marriage since there was now no escape: her home and her life were now with her new husband in his native country, France. The couple set about house-hunting in earnest. To the outside world, it appeared as if the couple were having fun. They travelled widely and, in 1937, leaving their baby behind, they set off on an expedition in search of the treasure of Lima, supposedly sunk off the Cocos Islands, three hundred miles off the coast of Panama. They returned empty-handed but once again Nica was pregnant.

When she arrived in London to give birth to their second child Janka in 1938, Nica rented a house in Hyde Park Square. Their return to France was, once again, logged in the national press; on 26 November 1938, *The Times* Court Circular announced that 'the Baron and Baroness de Koenigswarter have left for the Continent'. This time it would be to their new home in Normandy.

The Château d'Abondant was every bit as palatial and vast as many Rothschild homes. It had belonged to an American family of bankers, the Harjes, who kept their own pack of hounds and had introduced polo to France. While her sister Miriam and brother Victor had chosen ascetic, academic lives, Nica looked as if she was reverting to type. The *New York Times* reported the purchase as 'one of the most interesting realty deals from abroad in the last months'. My hunch is that Nica spent a large proportion of her inherited capital on acquiring the place; in addition to the money her father

Château d'Abondant, south of Paris, was Nica and Jules's home from 1937 to 1940.

left her, she had also been given a small bequest in the wills of her grandmother Emma and her uncle Walter.

Nica became mistress of a vast red and yellow mansion set in two hundred acres of landscaped driveways and woodlands. As one of the finest examples of Louis XIII architecture in France, it was classified as a '*monument historique*'. The whole first floor comprised a series of highly decorated salons with windows twelve feet high. On the second and third floors there were seventeen grand bedrooms with dressing rooms and, unusually, fourteen modernised bathrooms. The entire top floor housed the servants' quarters, while the outbuildings included a garage for eight large cars and stabling for thirty horses. The property had its own dairy, and kennels for a private pack of staghounds.

It also had an intriguing earlier history: a previous occupant, the notorious widow 'Marie de la Noue', had owned the chateau in the seventeenth century. Described as 'fascinating and beautiful', the much married Marie – a talented musician and music lover – had built a theatre there that still stands, in which concerts and plays were performed nightly. Marie's daughter-in-law was employed by Marie Antoinette as governess to the royal household and was credited with disguising the Dauphin as a girl, thus saving his life, on the disastrous flight to Varennes.

Life at Château d'Abondant was similar to that at Tring but *haute* society in France was even more rule-bound and claustrophobic than in England. From the outset it must have been living torture for someone of Nica's disposition. Here was a young woman who loathed rules and timetables being put in charge of an establishment whose smooth running depended on order and hierarchy. She knew what to do, having been brought up to observe little else, but it was nevertheless exactly the life that she and her siblings most wanted to avoid. In the morning Nica would discuss menus with the chef and table placement with the head housekeeper. Large house parties would involve guests coming from every corner of Europe. Tables would be set for forty and conversation might flit from French to English, to Italian, to Spanish. Rooms had to be inspected and allocated. In the winter, guests would ride to hounds or shoot wild boar. In the summer there were walks and huge picnics in the park. But there was little time for children, who, according to the custom of the day, spent most of their time in the nursery being cared for by nannies, just as Nica had been.

Jules was in his element: his memoir reveals a highly social and hospitable man who loved huge gatherings. He invented gadgets to add to the efficiency of their new home, ensuring that everything happened on time and in the right order. One such invention was a train with two carriages, one for hot food, one for cold, that circulated continuously on a sixty-metre track between the kitchen and the dining room. All through dinner the train chuffed backwards and forwards, bringing different drinks and dishes. He also fitted telephones in every bedroom so that guests could phone their breakfast orders through to the kitchen.

Whatever her doubts, Nica seemed to make the best of being a chatelaine. Cousins who stayed at Château d'Abondant were amazed by the ease with which she had adapted: the wild child had morphed into a typical Rothschild matriarch.

11

Stormy Weather

In 1936, Victor wanted to take his new wife out to a restaurant in fashionable Mayfair. The maître d' recognised him and asked, 'You are Mr Rothschild?'

'Yes,' Victor replied.

The manager looked him up and down slowly. 'We don't serve Jews here.'

This kind of treatment was not unusual for Victor or his sisters but, as the decade progressed, it became harder to ignore.

The rise of anti-Semitism in Europe meant that no Jew could remain apolitical; in *Mein Kampf,* Hitler had set out his beliefs in black and white. In his opinion, the two great evils besetting the world were communism and Judaism. During the 1930s few Jews in mainland Europe felt safe as stories began to emerge from Germany of the persecution of innocent Jewish men, women and children. With Hitler's appointment as Chancellor in 1933, and his consolidation of power following the Night of the Long Knives the following year, many fears were being realised.

With the death of his uncle Walter, Victor inherited the title of Lord Rothschild and became the de facto head of British Jewry.

Although he longed for the life of an academic, he was forced into the political spotlight. The dilemma for the British family, and Victor in particular, was that, in deciding to pursue an independent career away from the powerbase of the bank, he lost both financial muscle and political leverage. In the past the Rothschilds, as bankers to royalty and governments, were consulted on foreign policy, often being asked to underwrite the cost of a war or a campaign. Yet all Victor's generation could do was protest publicly.

In 1934, Nica, Victor and other family members attended the screening of a new feature film, *The House of Rothschild*, for a charity event in aid of German refugees. This rather romanticised celluloid depiction of Rothschild history starred George Arliss and was nominated for an Academy Award.

From the outset, the Nazi regime used the Rothschild family as a model for the apotheosis of evil Judaism. In response to *The House of Rothschild*, Goebbels commissioned another feature film, *Die Rothschilds*, which blamed the family for the world's problems. In his diaries, Goebbels reveals that he discussed the production at length, often 'deep into the night', and his intention was to create a 'propaganda masterpiece'. However, the film was so garbled, and its message so obtuse, that audiences were left confused as to who exactly was supposed to be in the wrong. Goebbels recut the film, which survives as a 'curiosity', a piquant reminder of horrific prejudice.

An added problem was that family loyalties and policy had become fragmented and, as a result, the Rothschilds who had achieved so much by remaining close began to split apart. Since leaving Frankfurt over one hundred years earlier, the brothers and their descendants had made homes in new countries; now their allegiances were divided between kith and kin. Victor and his siblings did not see a conflict between being Jewish and being British, but there were many in public life who considered the claims of faith and nationality as an 'either-or' situation. British Rothschilds raised over £1 million to help German Jewry but one cousin warned against endangering their 'English citizenship if one becomes too strongly active in Jewish world actions'.

Few people anywhere could agree on a safe haven for Jewish refugees. The Nazis' preference, in the early days at least, was to send every last one to Madagascar. Jewish committees tried to raise funds to buy land in Brazil, Kenya and Rhodesia. Some Rothschilds campaigned noisily for international action to halt Hitler, while others argued for a more discreet approach. In France, Robert de Rothschild set up a fund to help the tide of refugees flowing over its borders from German-occupied Europe but advised that 'foreign elements learn how to assimilate as quickly as possible . . . If they are not happy here, they would do better to leave.'

An alternative lay with the settlements created in Palestine in 1882 by one of the French Rothschilds, Edmond. A leading proponent of the Zionist movement, Edmond spent over $50 million acquiring more than 125,000 acres, promoting industrialisation and encouraging economic development in Palestine. But there was not enough land to house the millions of Jews under threat from the Nazi regime, and Edmond foresaw other problems with his scheme. In a 1934 letter to the League of Nations, he stated with prescience that 'the struggle to put an end to the Wandering Jew, could not have as its result, the creation of the Wandering Arab'. At that time the British government viewed the Palestine question as 'appallingly complicated'.

Some Rothschilds feared that the promotion of a Jewish state would create another ghetto for Jews, another prison in which to keep them. Victor's own conflicted feelings were made clear in a speech made for Pathé News in 1938:

> We the British Jews will do what we can to protect this country; we will fight, as every good citizen should.
>
> In spite of our humanitarian feelings, we probably all agree that there is something unsatisfactory in refugees encroaching on the

privacy of our country even for relatively short periods of time. The refugees themselves share that feeling in a different way. To have to depart suddenly into a foreign country, with unknown customs, unknown language, with different food even, unwanted, and to feel that one is dependent both morally and materially on the charity of others, is one of the most humiliating experiences that I can imagine a human being can endure.

I have been the unhappy recipient of so many heart-rending letters from children; of commented reports and personal accounts from observers that it is difficult for me to believe that I shall ever become again the rather carefree and happy scientist that I was before all this began.

His speech is laced with double meanings. Victor was only a few generations away from being a refugee himself. His mother and grandmother had been immigrants but he considered himself British. He also knew that he had a responsibility to an international community of Jews who looked to the Rothschilds for financial and political support. The reports coming out of Germany were increasingly desperate but the answer was not obvious. Most members of the Commons supported the policy of appeasement while many in the Lords were actively pro-German. The Right Club, founded by Archibald Ramsey in 1939, was created 'to oppose and expose the activities of organized Jewry'. Its 'first objective' was 'to clear the Conservative Party of Jewish influence'. Members included Lord Redesdale, the Duke of Westminster, the 5th Duke of Wellington and others, many of whom had been guests of the Rothschilds and who saw no apparent conflict in accepting the family's hospitality while, at the same time, displaying hostility towards Jews. Nica's contemporary Unity Mitford moved to Germany to be near Adolf Hitler; Unity's brother-in-law Oswald Mosley founded the British Union of Fascists. While many practised subtler forms of anti-Semitism, the Black Shirts accused the Rothschilds of 'bleeding and sweating' profits from the public. The claustrophobic, insular nature of upper-class British life meant that Victor looked across the narrow benches in the House of Lords at, or attended parties with, members of the same families who had chased his father across the playing fields of Harrow, some of whom now wanted the young Lord Rothschild drummed out of public life. As a family, the Rothschilds remained passionately patriotic and grateful to England, and would risk their lives and fortunes during the war.

When the Conservative government signed the Munich Agreement in September 1938 there was little resistance in Parliament. One of the few resignations from Chamberlain's Cabinet was that of a Rothschild family friend, Duff Cooper. 'You say you expect I shall receive over a thousand [letters of support],' Duff wrote to Victor following his resignation. 'I have actually received over a thousand, and nearly as many telegrams – which shows that although I was alone in the Cabinet, I am not quite alone in the country.' The two men remained in constant correspondence during the 1930s, ardently discussing what could be done about the Nazi problem.

Victor is sometimes blamed for doing too little but he did push, against an apathetic Parliament, to publicise the plight of the Jews in Germany. He made speeches, wrote cheques and sold some of his remaining works of art, such as Joshua Reynolds's *The Braddyll Family*, to support Jewish refugees. In 1939 he flew to the USA to present the Jewish cause to President Roosevelt, the Secretary of State, Cordell Hull, and the Secretary of the Treasury, Henry Morgenthau Jnr. Another invitation came from J. Edgar Hoover, then head of the FBI, to discuss chemical warfare. During the same trip Victor managed to fit in some piano lessons with Teddy Wilson, travelling from Washington to the pianist's apartment in New York.

The Austrian branch of the Rothschild bank was forcibly closed in 1938 and its head, Baron Louis, was captured and imprisoned for a year. He was released following the payment of an enormous ransom by his brother Albert. Hitler and his officers had no qualms about freeing Jews for the right price or absorbing Jewish-owned art into their collections; priceless artworks belonging to

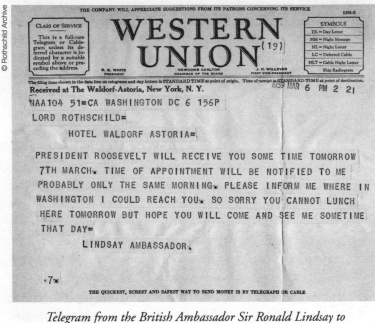

Telegram from the British Ambassador Sir Ronald Lindsay to Victor Rothschild on 6 March 1939 inviting him to meet President Roosevelt at the White House.

the German and Austrian Rothschilds were confiscated while Adolf Eichmann occupied the Rothschild Palace in Prinz Eugen-strasse, where he set up the infamous 'Zentralstelle für jüdische Auswanderung', the 'purpose' of which was to 'organise' the emigration of Jews from Austria. In theory, Jews could buy their way out of Austria; in practice, even after the Nazis' demands were met, many were given a one-way ticket to a concentration camp.

Having made France her home, despite the disturbing intelligence coming from her brother, Nica decided to stay at the Château d'Abondant during the late 1930s. In her letters and diaries Nica hardly mentions politics, nor does she take much interest in world events. For someone who thought little of jumping into a plane or a car, and was used to moving effortlessly around on a cushion of wealth and privilege, the threat of the advancing Nazi army must have seemed avoidable.

Even when the threats against the Jews and, in particular, against the Rothschilds infected the French leadership, Nica remained in denial. Like many wealthy people, she was able, for a time, to draw a financial curtain around herself; life continued as normal, bound up in dancing and fashion. The collections of 1939 were noted for their extravagant designs and gaiety. Schiaparelli presented an evening dress of ermine and introduced her famous high-heeled shoe. It was a glorious summer, too beautiful, most reasoned, to be an overture to war.

Between the summer of 1938 and the early months of 1939, some European members of the Rothschild family moved to New York. In January 1939, Hitler ordered the launch of Plan Z, a five-year naval expansion programme to build a fleet capable of crushing the Royal Navy. In a speech which he delivered at the Reichstag on 30 January 1939, calling for an 'export battle' to increase Germany's earnings abroad, Hitler was clearly thinking of his nemeses, the Rothschilds: 'I will once more be a prophet: if the international Jewish financiers in and outside Europe should succeed in plunging the nations once more into a world war, then the result will not be the Bolshevizing of the earth, and thus the victory of Jewry, but the annihilation of the Jewish race in Europe!'

In March, German troops annexed the last parts of Bohemia and Moravia; Czechoslovakia ceased to exist. In May, the Germans took back their former province of Memelland from Lithuania, and the two dictators Mussolini and Hitler signed the Pact of Steel. By the end of July, the last remaining Jewish enterprises operating in Germany were closed down. On 1 September the Nazis invaded Poland and war was declared.

Still Nica remained in France with her children at her chateau. One by one the men left, as the gardeners, chauffeurs and grooms went to join the army. Jules was not long in deciding to

go too. In his memoir I read incredulously that he buried a tin
of money in the garden and hid a car in a garage in case of an
emergency. He did not, however, tell Nica about this secret stash.
Perhaps his actions demonstrate his belief in her abilities: knowing Nica, he assumed she could make her own escape with their
children.

Leaving his wife with a hand-drawn map explaining how to get
to the coast, Jules joined up. At first he became a lieutenant in the
reserves in Rouen; then in January 1940 he was made commander
of an anti-aircraft battery, overseeing an advanced radar system to
warn of approaching enemy aircraft. On the night of the German
invasion of France, on 10 May 1940, he was at Bordeaux. Initially,
the battery did well, taking out a Heinkel bomber, but soon
enemy tanks surrounded them. Managing to cross the Somme,
Jules ordered his men to destroy whatever equipment or fuel
reserves they could not take with them, before escaping along the
riverbed.

When news reached Jules that the French government had sur-
rendered to Germany on 22 June 1940, he immediately resigned his
commission. Rounding up a group of 110 officers, NCOs and volunteers, he managed to get to England on the Polish boat *Sobieski*
to volunteer for the Free French Army.

Extraordinarily, Nica and her children remained in France,
where the only man left at the chateau was a fat chef. Ignoring the
advice of friends and family, she had opened her doors to passing
refugees and within weeks sixty evacuees were sleeping in the
beds once occupied by her guests. The wireless had been Nica's
conduit to her favourite music, bringing jazz over the airwaves
from America, but now the set was tuned to the World Service.
She heard her old friend Winston Churchill, who had attended
her coming-out ball and been a frequent guest at Tring, issue
his clarion call: 'I have nothing to offer but blood, toil, tears
and sweat . . . You ask, what is our policy? Victory – victory at
all costs.' I wonder whether Nica's decision to stay was based

on arrogance, bravery or foolishness. Is it too easy with hindsight to judge others' decisions, to assume that abandoning one's home with one's children and just a few possessions was a simple precautionary step?

News reached Nica of her cousin Marie de Rothschild's lucky escape from Château Lafite. Heavily pregnant with her second child Eric, and with her first, Beatrice, only two years old, Marie caught the last boat from Bordeaux just before the Nazis arrived and annexed their house.*

Jules got word to Nica that she must escape. The Germans were getting closer, and as a Jew, her fate was sealed. She made swift preparations for evacuation, but now there were no commercial ships, let alone commercial flights, while petrol was rarer than gold. Nica could not get hold of enough to fly her plane out of the country.

To leave France, she had to get exit visas for herself, her two children, her stepson Louis, her Swiss maid and her French nanny. Wishing to spare her mother anxiety, she telegrammed her sister Liberty in England. The family waited to see if and when she would arrive. They knew that the Germans were advancing towards the chateau; that the roads thronged with desperate refugees; that the chances of getting a place, let alone a berth, on a boat were slim. Rozsika described the wait as 'days of agony'. Writing to her sister in Hungary, she described her daughter's journey:

> Jules was unable to leave his post which was under continual bombardment but she [Nica] managed it most efficiently, leaving at dawn on Saturday, among streams of refugees from Belgium and Northern France. They were told they would reach the port in ten hours, instead of which it took them two days

---

*Charles's daughter, my great-aunt Miriam, used to send out a Christmas card with an image of swirling colours, and took great pleasure in correcting those who assumed that it was a lesser-known work of some famous Impressionist painter. 'You

and nights and no food after the first day when they shared their luncheon basket with other hungry travellers. On Tuesday they reached London and yesterday Wednesday, they were here. Nica was as fresh as a daisy and the three children none the worse for the journey. Nica's description is worth recording, but in spite of all the difficulties, her sense of humour never left her. Also she kept meeting English men who helped her gallantly and The Salvation Army whom she blesses for providing tea to thousands of poor refugees all alone. She really was wonderful arriving as if she came from a picnic.

Rozsika's account explains in part why Nica had dithered over leaving her French home. Brought up not to make a fuss, she had set out like an innocent, unworldly Jemima Puddle-duck with her luncheon basket, oblivious to the dangers posed by the nasty old Nazi fox. Contemporary footage clearly recorded the roads jammed with thousands heading for the coast, the chaotic state of the ports, the over-crammed ships, the rank fear on fleeing faces. However, arriving back at Ashton Wold, Nica knew what was expected of her: she had to keep up appearances, look 'as fresh as a daisy' and await Jules's instructions.

Three days after Nica left the chateau, the Germans arrived. Her mother-in-law, who refused to leave, was seized and her days were ended at Auschwitz. A similar fate befell Philippe de Rothschild's first wife Elisabeth, who was arrested in front of her daughter and taken to Ravensbrück, where she died.

Two young French Rothschilds, who had joined up in 1939, were captured in 1940. Alain was wounded and interned in a military hospital, while Elie, who had ridden off to war on a horse, was taken prisoner, along with most of his regiment, near the Belgian frontier. Both men tried to escape: Elie was sent to Colditz and then to Lübeck, a reprisal camp. However, they were lucky to be treated as officers rather than Jews. Their cousin Guy was on a boat that was torpedoed while making his way to London to fight for de Gaulle's Free French. Injured, he was sent to recuperate at Ashton Wold.

Some of the children who were evacuated to Waddesdon during the Second World War.

He found the house bursting at the seams and learned that some former employees had miraculously escaped from Dunkirk. 'The housemaid Ivy's two brothers had swum half way across the channel while Victor's chauffeur escaped with a family friend, now a Colonel, in a tiny dinghy,' Rozsika wrote to her sister. On the whole the news was very bleak. Many childhood friends would not be coming home.

Rothschild houses in Britain were requisitioned as billets by the army or used to board refugees. At Waddesdon, the staterooms were lined with beds for evacuated children. Alfred's former home

Halton became an officers' mess. Miriam joked that it was quite fun because she never knew who was going to turn up. One soldier billeted there turned out to be Clark Gable, whom she described as 'good-looking'; another was George Lane, whom she married.

In 1940 Victor became head of a tiny department at MI5 where he worked on enemy sabotage and bomb disposal. Years of dissecting frogs and playing jazz had given him a steady pair of hands. 'When one takes a fuse to pieces,' he wrote, 'there is no time to be frightened. One also becomes absorbed in its beautiful mechanism containing Swiss watches.' Later Victor admitted that at the final moment of dismantling, he would pull out the last wire from behind a chair, saying, 'I could face losing a hand or two but I really couldn't bear to lose my eyesight.' After the war he was awarded the George Medal 'for dangerous work in hazardous circumstances'.

Miriam joined Alan Turing's gang of decoders at Bletchley Park. She was briefly arrested as an enemy agent when carrier pigeons, a suitcase full of codes and a sack of corn were found at a cottage that she kept at Aberdovy on the Welsh coast. It turned out that keeping pigeons was just a family hobby and the so-called codes were mathematical puzzles that both she and Victor used to keep their minds razor sharp.

Since her return from America Liberty had grown terribly thin and more nervous, even given the care she was receiving from Dr Freudenberger. 'Dr F telephones that all is going well with Liberty. She does not worry over much and her spirits are not bad at all,' Rozsika wrote in a letter to her sister.

The postal service, surprisingly, worked well and letters from the cousins were safely delivered across the continent. Family correspondence reported that the spring and summer of 1940 were again beautiful, the gardens at Ashton bursting with lilac and laburnum, and the village hedgerows animated by dragonflies and butterflies. French cousins used the house as a staging post between Europe and America. Rozsika wrote to her sister, who was trapped in Hungary:

> If you could get a magic carpet here, you would find lovely summer days, millions of roses and most delicious huge strawberries, an abundance of vegetables even though several of our gardeners have been called up. There is no shortage of any food, we get all the meat and fish we want and have also got sugar for making jams of the soft fruits. I have bought a Frigidaire, which can make 18lbs of ice daily and besides plenty of room for keeping food.

Yet Nica was allowed to stay at Ashton for only a short time. While there, her children Patrick and Janka played with my father and aunt, who had been left in this safe haven with their grandmother. Rozsika wrote, 'The children [my father Jacob and his sister Sarah] have a pony cart. They are as brown as berries as they run about all day practically without any clothes.'

News reached Jules that the German Army had ransacked Château d'Abondant and only Nica's dogs were left. 'Alas last Tuesday,' Rozsika wrote, 'Nica and the children left for Canada. It was the wish of Jules who told her that for his sake and his peace of mind she must take the children overseas. She would have preferred to leave them with me and be near Jules but I think Jules has to be considered while he is fighting for his country since the first day of the war. Nica looked quite beautiful and saw all her friends in London and Miriam helped her to get off.'

I read and reread this letter, trying to decipher what was really going on. Again Jules's wishes were paramount: Nica had to leave behind her country of birth and her family against her will for 'his sake and his peace of mind'. She did her bit, which was to obey and look beautiful. The voyage across the Atlantic was perilous, with the boat narrowly escaping aerial bombardment. The American writer Virginia Cowles, who made the transatlantic crossing with

Nica's cousins, complained that their staple diet of caviar and foie gras was not very filling.

Nica was twenty-seven but still felt bound to follow her husband's instructions. Arriving in America, she received a cable, informing her that Rozsika had died on 30 June 1940 of a heart attack. Stuck on the far side of the Atlantic, she was unable to attend her mother's funeral. Settling her children with family friends in upstate New York, she returned to England. This was not an unusual decision at the time: my mother and her sister, aged four and two, were sent alone to America in 1940 to live with acquaintances to await the end of the war. What seems heartless now was normal then. For a time Nica worked as a volunteer but, without the presence of her husband or her mother, with Victor and Miriam away from home on war work, and her children thousands of miles away, she felt purposeless and lost.

Nica, who had married a Frenchman with a suspiciously Germanic-sounding name, had little chance of being accepted by the British Army. She could, like many of her relations, have stayed in New York or found some kind of work in England as part of the war effort. However, determined to play an active front-line role in the conflict, she decided to join the Free French Army in the hope that she would be able to fight alongside her husband.

12

Pistol-Packing Mama

Nica was not the only Rothschild woman to join the Free French Army. In response to a call from de Gaulle, her cousins Monique and Nadine also came to London to volunteer. 'The atmosphere of the capital fascinated me,' Monique wrote in her privately published memoir. 'It thronged constantly with soldiers of all ranks and all nationalities. At night, the underground was transformed into a huge dormitory; the English were endlessly patient, discreet and determined.'

The life of a new female conscript, as Monique de Rothschild said, was in complete contrast to that of a chatelaine:

o6h 30   Get up, wash, [do] hair, make beds, put on uniform.
o7h 30   Breakfast
o8h 30   Drill (Exercise)
o9h 30   Military training
12h 30   Lunch then free time
14h 30   Military Training
16h oo   Drill
17h oo   Driving instruction

18h 30   Dinner
21h 00   Lights out

The young Rothschild women presented themselves to General Koenig at Grosvenor Square. The commander was curt, informing them that, although their duties included acting as his chauffeur, he hated being driven by women. Hearing that Jules had joined the Allied offensive against the Germans in Africa, Nica begged to be sent out to join her husband and see some action, but was told there was absolutely no chance. All enlisted women had to remain in London. Nica decided to smuggle herself out there anyway. She did not let the general's orders to stay in England nor her own lack of military training get in the way of adventure. Her only preparation for life so far had been dancing lessons and being brave on the hunting field. With no means of self-defence and no idea how to survive in a hostile climate, she had little chance of reaching Jules alive.

Fellow conscripts in the Free French included Marcel Marceau, Antoine de Saint-Exupéry and a young soldier, Gaston Eve, who, between 1941 and 1943, kept an evocative diary of life in Africa with his unit. He described conditions in a typical French garrison: 'I have never again seen a camp so filthy. I had the bad luck of acquiring dysentery only 48 hours after my arrival, even though I had taken care to do as I was advised at night. We were told to wrap a long strip of fabric around our belly; [dysentery] was not a rare thing in Africa.'

Gaston Eve tells us all about the life of the new volunteers as they made their way across Africa. In Bangui, lions walked freely up the High Street. In Brazzaville, which had a significant European population, the food was rather good but for the rest of the time they lived off a diet of tinned corned beef. At Fort Archambault, they swam in the river, keeping an eye out for crocodiles. At night they were bitten by mosquitoes and attacked by ferocious black ants. In Kano, the Emir, whose teeth were filed into tiny sharp points, met the battalions with a display of his soldiers on dancing horses.

Nica ignored all the medical warnings. Within weeks of arriving in Africa she contracted malaria, got sunstroke and narrowly escaped death in a car crash for which she was solely responsible; she spent several weeks recovering in a field hospital. However, she did find Jules. Once her husband and his commanding officer got over the shock of her unexpected arrival and her audacity, Nica was given work as a decoder and a driver. Rumour has it that she flew Lancaster bombers in Africa.

There were few married couples in the army so Nica and Jules were often billeted apart at night, but were able, battles permitting, to meet in the daytime. As a woman, Nica was actively discouraged from taking part in direct fighting but, in the mayhem of war, rules rarely contained her.

Tracing Nica's movements during this period is difficult. According to an article in the *New York Times*, she narrowly escaped being torpedoed en route from Lagos to New York in January 1942. I can only assume that she made the journey to America to see her children, who were still living outside New York. Her visit coincided with the première of Duke Ellington's jazz symphony *Black, Brown and Beige* at Carnegie Hall on 23 January 1943. This piece of music would, she claimed, one day act as a calling.

Although New York was exciting, Nica missed Jules and was keen to follow him, even on to the battlefields. She smuggled herself back to Africa on a supply plane. In his memoir, which reads at times like a travelogue, Jules describes getting hold of a rickety old plane to travel between the Free French bases, enabling the couple to explore parts of Africa normally inaccessible to tourists, taking off and landing on scrubland or in clearings. En route between Brazzaville and Bangui, for example, they swooped down in the middle of a forest. There they met a pygmy tribe who explained that, to be considered a true hunter, a man had to kill an elephant by sliding under its belly, slitting it with a long knife and quickly getting out the way before the beast crushed its assailant to death. Another escapade placed them in Fort Lamy in Chad, where they got a lift from a man who was on his way to market to exchange his wife for some dogs.

In September 1943 the couple arrived in Cairo. Jules was immediately sent to Tunis; the Battle of Tunisia had lasted from 17 November 1942 to 13 May 1943. The Axis had been defeated, but the Allies needed to consolidate their position in Africa. Jules had played a key part in this, leading his men across the Mareth Line and joining the Allies in Triaga. The 90th Light Infantry German Division was holed up in the massif of Zaghouan. After a bitter battle on 13 May, victory fell to the Allies, but half of Jules's troops were killed. With only three hundred men remaining, Jules was put in charge of thousands of German and Italian prisoners.

Nica formed part of the back-up group who stayed in Cairo to help organise supplies and equipment. Cairo then was Africa's answer to New York: a cool multicultural scene and a stopping-off place for every decorated soldier or in-demand movie star – all the beautiful and the damned. In 1943, Vivien Leigh and Noël Coward were appearing there on stage; Gavin Astor was there too, accompanying Josephine Baker; Nica's old friend Winston Churchill was in town; the King of Egypt held nightly parties; there were two jazz clubs; and a new film, *Arsenic and Old Lace*, was showing at the picture house.

The author and critic Stanley Crouch was one of three interviewees to tell me the following story. An African-American soldier billeted in a Cairo hotel heard the most wonderful music coming from a gramophone in a room down the hall. The soldier, who also happened to be a musician, couldn't resist knocking on the door and was astonished when a beautiful woman with long dark hair opened it and invited him in. It was Nica and it appears that she seduced him. The only detail that changed in each of the three versions was the name of the musician. With all parties now dead, there is no way of proving or disproving the truth of it. War created

*Nica followed her husband Jules to Africa and
enlisted in the Free French Army.*

different rules, normal behaviour was skewed, and people stepped
out of character. Some will consider this typical of Nica, assuming
that she was promiscuous. My hunch is that she was motivated by
romantic rather than carnal love.

What of Nica's relationship with her husband at this time? The
very personality traits that had profoundly irritated Nica in peacetime became badges of honour during the war. Being decisive,
brave and dictatorial were essential qualifications for a military
leader. By following her husband to Africa, Nica saw Jules at his
best and possibly at his happiest and most fulfilled.

Reading Jules's memoirs gives another, more chilling insight into
his character and modus operandi. If one of his men committed
a serious fault, Jules had him dragged in front of the whole troop
and beaten up by a colleague, who happened to be a professional
boxer. Jules thought this a more effective and instantaneous way

of keeping control than referring the incident to a court martial. He described these methods as 'paternal but strict'.

No sooner had Nica got to Tunis than the soldiers were, once again, on the move, this time heading back to Tripoli and on to Algeria. Water was rationed to four and a half litres per person per day, just enough to prevent serious dehydration but not enough for comfort. For safety, it had to be boiled and served as tea, but most of the men had terrible dysentery and stomach pains. The dogs became so used to drinking shaving water that, following the war, they refused to touch anything without a soapy smell.

In April 1944, Jules's regiment, accompanied by Nica, began the journey from Bizerte to Naples and then on to Caserta, where Nica worked for the War Graves Commission, a post that involved identifying the bodies of dead soldiers left on the battlefields of Europe. It was a macabre and distressing job, following her husband's regiment as they battled across Europe, fighting their way to victory. In one bloody battle at Garigliano, the Germans, who occupied the hilltop position and the main road, should have won. Jules narrowly avoided death when a mortar exploded ten centimetres away from his head, knocking him unconscious and rendering him temporarily blind and deaf. Bit by bit, the Allies edged forwards, snatching tiny victories. Crossing the Gustav Line and then Pontecorvo on 23 May, the Germans were pushed north. Jules's battalion made its way to Brindisi to take a boat to the South of France, where it would join the offensive sweeping through France. After taking in the liberation of Lyons in September and Ronchamps in October, they marched north through the Alps in heavy snow towards Turin through the early months of 1945.

Following the liberation of Paris in August 1944, Nica had based herself in the capital, either at her husband's family home or the Rothschild mansion on Avenue Marigny, where her brother Victor was living while working for MI5. Malcolm Muggeridge painted a damning portrait of Victor in his memoirs *Chronicles of Wasted*

Time. This description contains clues that may explain why Nica decided eventually to opt out of Rothschild life:

> For Rothschild himself, of course, the Avenue Marigny house was a home from home, but at the same time, I felt, a prison. Installed there, he was de facto if not de jure head of the family. Other Rothschilds appeared from time to time, and offered obeisance. He both liked to feel they were looking to him, and abhorred their presence: his disposition was a curious, uneasy mixture of arrogance and diffidence. Somewhere between White's Club and the Ark of the Covenant, between Old and New Testament, between the Kremlin and the House of Lords, he had lost his way, and been floundering about ever since. Embedded deep down in him there was something touching and vulnerable and perceptive; at times loveable even. But so overlaid with the bogus certainties of science, and the equally bogus respect, accorded and expected, on account of his wealth and famous name, that it was only rarely apparent.

In an interview with the jazz critic and historian Nat Hentoff, Nica kept her recollections of the war short: 'I fought from Brazzaville to Cairo, from Tunis to Turkey and even got to Germany to see the last days of the Reich.' Another person I interviewed – Frank Richardson, an American boogie-woogie-playing jeep driver – shone more light on this period. During the war his company was stationed in Paris and he was one of four soldiers billeted at the de Koenigswarter house. There he met Nica and her sister-in-law Odile, who was much younger than her brother Jules.

'There were four men quartered in our room and an upright piano,' he told me. 'I was playing it one night and there was a knock on the door and Nica came in and introduced herself and asked if I'd like to come downstairs and play for her. She had a grand piano, of course.' Nica wasn't working at the time and Jules was away fighting. Although provisions were short, the de Koenigswarter house was warm and the two women, aided by the troops, were able to lay their hands on most supplies. Richardson clearly had a soft spot for Odile, who was nearer his own age than Nica. She was rather dashing; Django Reinhardt played at her birthday party and she wore white gloves up to her elbows.

On another occasion in late 1944, Richardson remembered the Baroness knocking on his door and asking if he would play for her and a friend. 'The other man was introduced as one of General de Gaulle's aides. So the three of us were there, I played the piano and they were sort of smooching, and then they went a little bit further and then further still. I thought I'd better go back upstairs.'

I asked Frank if he was shocked by their behaviour.

'Well, yes! My background being from a small town, and only twenty-one years old and not a man of the world, it shocked me.' But then he paused and added, 'It was wartime, I guess.'

Moments of relaxation were few and far between. Each battle brought news of the felling of friends. While the end of the war saw victory for the Allies, it also revealed the full horror of the Nazi regime. Having connections to privileged relations did not help everyone.

After the war, a tragic eyewitness account came to light of the fate of Nica's maternal aunt, Aranka von Wertheimstein. A Hungarian friend of the family had received a letter from an acquaintance, a Mr Racz, who happened to be on a death train with Aranka. The old lady was by then eighty, nearly blind and terrified. She had never married and worked on a farm near Rozsika's former family home.

On May 1st [1944], all Jews, including Miss Wertheimstein, were rounded up and put into a ghetto. They were kept there under awful conditions until May 28th, 1944, when they were forced into railway trucks (seventy-five in one wagon). The journey, a nightmare, lasted four days. No water, no food. Many women

Rozsika, Aranka and Charlotte von Wertheimstein in 1899.
Aranka was beaten to death by station guards on arrival
at Auschwitz in May 1944.

lost consciousness, some died, some became insane. On the fourth day I managed to obtain some water and gave some to Miss Wertheimstein who was in a bad state. After she [had] drunk and recovered she told me that she feared she would not live long and to try and have this letter conveyed somehow to the Rothschild family in London. When the train stopped at Auschwitz-Birkenau extermination camp, the SS guards were waiting there with sticks and truncheons. I saw Miss W pulled out of the wagon by an SS guard using a hooked stick. She fell forward onto the rails and was beaten to death on the spot.

On 8 May 1945, Nica's friend Winston Churchill announced the end of the war; although hostilities ceased, the repercussions had only just started. Countries, families, lives, dreams and futures lay in tatters. Survivors had to reconstruct a life out of debris and desolation. The way of life that had been shaken by the First World War was shattered by the Second.

Nica and Jules were decorated for their efforts. Jules was awarded the rare distinction of the Ordre de la Libération: the second highest honour existing in France, bestowed on heroes of the liberation of France during the Second World War. The few foreigners who received it included Winston Churchill and General Dwight Eisenhower. Nica was also decorated for her war services and made a lieutenant.

The couple faced an uncertain future. Their children were still in America. The Germans had smashed their home to pieces. Jules was unemployed. Nica's mother had died. Victor's marriage was floundering. Liberty's health was deteriorating. Only Miriam, newly married and settled at Ashton Wold, seemed purposeful and happy.

For Nica, the war was a personal turning point. Finally, aged thirty-two, she had been set free and shown another way to live.

13

Take the A-Train

Two photographs of Nica taken after the war reveal a sad and remote-looking woman. The first, shot in Norway, shows her behind the wheel of a large Rolls-Royce, staring blankly at the photographer. She looks beautiful in crisp white linen, her hair and make-up perfect, but while the child and servant are beaming at the camera, my great-aunt's expression is fixed, blank, resigned. Another picture taken on a pebbly beach a few years later should, like many of its kind, radiate with the joy of a holiday or a day out at the seaside. In the background there are beach huts and, in the foreground, Nica sits in an exquisite trouser suit, with two of her children, looking elegant and soignée. Again the crackling energy and intensity, the *joie de vivre* so evident in portraits of the young Nica, have gone.

For Nica, as for many of her contemporaries, the war offered women personal liberation as well as a chance to prove their worth outside the home. Some went out to work for the first time and, with their husbands away, had the opportunity to run their households, budgets and businesses alone. Nica had distinguished herself without the aid of servants, helpers and family. Brought up to believe that the simplest domestic duties should be done by others had been both spoiling and strangely disabling. Nica and her siblings had been pampered to the point of infantilism. As Miriam said, 'We had no idea how to do anything for ourselves.'

In peacetime, Nica's marriage was, in effect, a carbon copy of her childhood. As a married woman she was there to entertain, to inform and to breed. There was a temporary suspension of duties during the conflict but now she was expected to snap back into an uxorial role. Years earlier, a Rothschild cousin had warned her, 'I should imagine you will soon get married – so you should learn as soon as possible that you are a <u>worm</u>. A woman to be a successful wife must be <u>a worm</u>.'*

Nica was not worm material. Furthermore, the war had given her confidence, plus the opportunity to think, to act and to be herself. She had managed, alone, to get her children to safety from France to America; she had survived torpedoes and malaria, and had smuggled herself across continents. At various times, the Free French had employed her as a decoder, a driver and a broadcaster, and at the end of the war she had been decorated by a foreign army. Slipping back into domestic life, even a uniquely privileged and comfortable one, was never going to be easy.

Peace also created a vacuum of purpose for Jules. Life in the army suited him; peacetime meant sudden unemployment. Their home at Château d'Abondant had been wrecked by Nazi troops and was uninhabitable, while they themselves no longer had the money to live in pre-war style. Since no one wanted a house on such a vast scale, it sat empty in the French countryside like a great white elephant. The family relocated to Paris, where Jules found employment as the general secretary of the Free French Association and was placed in charge of stage-managing morale-boosting events. On one occasion he persuaded the French soprano Lily Pons to give a recital. Another time, surrounding the Opéra with tanks, he organised a march-past by Resistance fighters. When she heard that her husband

are looking at the greatly magnified reproductive organ of a butterfly,' she would tell princes and statesmen with glee.

was in charge of a huge festival of music in the capital, Nica's spirits rose, to fall swiftly on learning that only military bands qualified for inclusion. She hated marching bands, finding their style of playing too regimented and controlled. 'The reason my marriage broke up,' Nica told *Esquire* magazine, was 'that my husband liked drum music and used to break my records if I was late for dinner. I was frequently late for dinner.' In an interview with a Philippine newspaper, her son Patrick confirmed her story: 'My father had no particular interest in the subjects that fascinated her: art and music. He would quip that these were not serious matters.'

Nica was the beneficiary of a trust fund based in Britain. The capital, in a stable economic climate, could generate a healthy income but following the war, with taxation levelled up to 83 per cent, Nica faced relative economic hardship for the first time in her life. Even the Rothschild family could not afford to recreate their pre-war standard of living. They did not look for sympathy or feel self-pity, knowing they were still fortunate compared to most. Nevertheless it was a shock, particularly for a woman who had not been prepared, either by family culture or education, to find employment outside the home or to attempt to create a fulfilling role within it.

The French Rothschilds' assets had been seized first by the Nazis and then by the Vichy French, claiming that any Frenchman who removed himself from his native country had forfeited his right to his own property. An inventory* of the artworks taken from prominent Jewish families at 203 locations up to 13 July 1944 reads as follows:

1. Rothschild, 3,978 inventory entries
2. Kahn, 1,202 inventory entries
3. David Weill, 1,121 inventory entries
4. Levy de Venzionn, 989 inventory entries
5. Seligmann Brothers, 556 inventory entries

*Unfortunately no further details exist.

American troops holding paintings confiscated from Jews during the war.
3,978 works of art were stolen from the Rothschild family alone.

It took the family many years to get even a fraction of their belongings returned. By then the bottom had fallen out of the art market and the once-priceless treasures were greatly reduced in value. Not all their artworks survived. Many are still missing, while some were destroyed.

One picture that survived did so thanks to an extraordinary, reckless act of bravery. When the Nazis took over Château Mouton Rothschild in Bordeaux, they secured the cellars but used the family portraits for target practice. In the middle of a 'shoot', the family cook, a woman who had worked for Philippe de Rothschild for many years, marched out in front of the officers while they were firing, took her employer's picture off the wall, tucked it under her arm and left the chateau. She came back (with the painting) only when Philippe returned to his home in 1946.

In England, the great Rothschild fortune had crumbled, a

casualty of war and the breakdown of family ties. Halton House was sold to the RAF; Aston Clinton was turned into a hotel; and Gunnersbury became a public park. Tring Park became a school for the performing arts. Waddesdon was taken back by the family for thirteen years before being given, like Ascott House, to the National Trust. Only the house belonging to my name-sake Hannah Rothschild, Mentmore Towers, was lived in by her descendants the Roseberys until the 1970s. At the time of Nica's birth the Rothschilds had owned over forty stately homes across England and Europe. Today only Waddesdon, owned by the National Trust, has its original collection intact.

The war had also destroyed the Rothschilds' way of living. Their stronghold in the Vale of Aylesbury was at an end, as were the weekends spent at one another's houses; the system of inter-dependence was gone. Victor was a new kind of family leader who had eschewed his inheritance, disposing of the goods and chattels that his forebears had so carefully accrued. For Victor, if some-thing did not interest him or fit into his way of life, it had no value.

Victor used to say that for every Rothschild who made money, there were a dozen who spent it; that certainly included himself. He inherited a family fortune of £2.5 million as well as houses in Piccadilly and Tring, plus an enormous art collection. He left a net estate of £270,410, having dissipated most of his inheri-tance. Showing no interest in, or aptitude for, trying to rebuild the British bank's fortunes, in 1949 Victor accepted a post from the Labour government that he held for ten years as chairman of the Agricultural Research Council. He continued his research at the department of zoology in Cambridge, where he devoted himself to the subject of gametology: the study of sperm, eggs and fertili-sation. Having scant regard for the past, he knocked down the existing cottages at Rushbrooke in Suffolk to build a model eco-village with identical housing for all the workers on the estate.

*

Tired of organising victory parades, Jules applied for a post in the French Foreign Office. He was accepted and, on their way to his first posting in Norway in 1947, he and Nica were reunited with their two elder children and his son Louis. Jules had not seen them for five years, Nica for more than three.

Despite their reduced economic circumstances, the couple still entertained notions of grandeur and looked for a suitably magnificent abode. Nevertheless, their decision to set up home in Gimle Castle in Oslo was extraordinary; it had belonged to the convicted Nazi Vidkun Quisling, who was often referred to as Norway's Hitler. Executed in October 1945 by firing squad following his conviction for high treason for having mounted a *coup d'état* in April 1940, Quisling was guilty of other crimes including encouraging Norwegians to serve in the Nordic SS division and assisting in the deportation of Jews to concentration camps. Why the de Koenigswarters would want to live in a place redolent of so many appalling memories is not clear.* Jules, who boasted that its grand façade dominated the entire fjord, took pleasure in the fact that its sitting room could accommodate a hundred guests and its dining table could seat sixty.

For Jules, the post of Ambassador to Norway was a way of supporting his family while continuing to represent his country. Nica hated it.

A childhood friend of the couple's eldest son, Patrick de Koenigswarter, remembers the boy singing 'Don't Fence Me In' and running in and out of Nica's bedroom while his mother lay in bed most of the time, looking glamorous, framed by long dark hair.†

Diplomatic life offered Jules a wonderfully ordered existence with clear-cut rules and established protocol. As an ambassador he

---

*To this day Eric de Rothschild refuses to rip out the line of showers the German officers installed in his chateau to serve as a reminder of what could have happened.

*Gimle Castle in Oslo was Nica and Jules' home during his posting
as French Ambassador to Norway in 1947.*

wielded power and influence over his embassy and could affect foreign policy in the region. For the 'Commander-in-Chief', it was
perfect. Norway represented something of a diplomatic wilderness
in comparison to the major prizes such as Washington, London or
Berlin, but in the aftermath of the war every embassy had a role to
play and any posting could lead, potentially, to a more significant
one after a few years.

The role of an ambassador's wife was entirely separate, as
Marilyn Pifer, wife of Steven Pifer, US Ambassador to the Ukraine,
explained in an interview some years later. 'I expected that the "wife
of" role would involve finding a balance between two opposing
perceptions: Embassy Morale Officer, helping set the tone for the
community, and Most Despised Person in the Embassy, an authority figure who must be obeyed, but who has no real authority at all,
and whose requests are therefore all unreasonable.' An ambassador's
wife's main concern was with protocol, making sure people sat in

the right places or that their name cards had the right title. They had to make sure that visiting dignitaries were fed the right food and were addressed in the right way. Above all, they had to be a blank but magnificent canvas, reflecting the good works of their spouse and the ideals of their country. This isn't to negate the extraordinary good work done by many diplomatic wives but merely to point out that Nica was not an obvious candidate for acquiescent consort.

Some elements of the marriage worked: the couple had another three children after the war – Berit in 1946, Shaun in 1948 and Kari in 1950. They continued to travel and explore foreign cities. Both were party-loving social animals. Marriages rarely collapse over one incident, rather it is a steady accumulation, a layering of individual instances and incompatibilities, that create a fault line, an accident waiting to happen.

One incident from Jules's memoir seems to epitomise his character and their incompatibility. The couple entertained frequently, giving dinners for up to sixty guests at the long dining-room table in the banqueting hall. According to the social protocol of the time, once the pudding course was finished, ladies were expected to leave the dining room immediately so that their husbands and partners could talk and smoke freely. It was the role of the hostess to lead her female guests out of the room. Nica, according to Jules, often forgot to leave the table so, to remind her, he installed a light bulb in front of her seat, which he could operate from his chair. Once the last plate was cleared, Jules would flick the switch on and off. The naked bulb in full view of Nica flashed insistently until she rose and left the room.

Their son Patrick admitted, 'My father was a very controlling person. He reminded my mother of her own domineering mother. He was adamant about punctuality, while Nica was notorious for being late. She missed appointments, sometimes by days, and was constantly missing planes.'

Nica was headstrong and wilful. To hear the word 'no' was a rarity rather than the norm during her childhood. She had disobeyed her mother to flit off with Jules before they were married and she had completely ignored General Koenig's orders to stay in England. Now she was being asked to live a life that had become anathema to her. Cut off from her friends, her extended family and the music scene, Nica was stranded in a sea of rules and regulations. She had borne five children but never seemed to find comfort in mother-hood. Perhaps she never tried; perhaps she just accepted that child-rearing was best left to the professionals, heeding the maxim 'Nanny knows best'. Perhaps, if war had not broken out, if she had not had that heady glimpse of freedom, she might have stayed with her husband, albeit resentfully.

There was another factor that contributed to the breakdown of her marriage. Nica knew that to ossify in a particular situation, to carry on because that was what others expected, led to dire personal consequences. She had watched her father try to become someone else and live at odds with his personality, against the grain of his passions; she had also witnessed the tragic outcome.

Nica had moved with Jules from London to Paris to Africa and then to Norway. Two years after his posting to Oslo, Jules's job took the family to Mexico. Nica hoped that being in South America would bring her closer to her kind of civilisation; she found more excuses to visit New York. Increasingly unhappy and desperate, she was looking for a way out.

14

Black, Brown and Beige

In 2004, I contacted the producer Bruce Ricker to see if, by any chance, he had kept the out-takes of Nica's interviews for the Thelonius Monk documentary *Straight, No Chaser*. Nearly forty years had passed since the Blackwood brothers shot the original footage of Nica and Monk, and twenty years had elapsed since Ricker, Clint Eastwood and Charlotte Zwerin had updated the story. It was highly unlikely that any material had survived. Returning to my hotel from a concert late one night in New York, I found a package at reception containing a CD with 'Nica' scrawled on it. I put it into a player and suddenly heard Nica. The sound of her booming voice was so unexpected, so immediate, that I expected her ghost to tap my shoulder at any moment. She sounded exactly as I remembered: gravelly and hoarse from cigarettes, her words punctuated by her inimitable throaty giggle.

The interview was recorded in 1988. Ricker had gone round to Nica's house in Weehawken to capture her memories of Monk. Hoping to loosen her tongue, he had opened one and then two bottles of wine. Nica drank only tea; Ricker got so drunk that, by the end of the interview, he was hardly coherent, a story he loved to tell against himself. Throughout the interview, Nica is precise about her recollections. She sounds frail and sad as she summons up the past but always uses words succinctly and is quick to reprimand the interviewer for any inaccuracies.

'No, Bruce, that's not what happened,' she corrects him. 'What are you talking about now?' she chides. 'Not true,' she reprimands.

Unable to sleep, I whizzed backwards and forwards through the disc, writing notes, trying to fix timelines and readjusting old presumptions. Sitting there until dawn broke, I became ever more excited by this quest. Finally I had answers to some key questions and, bit by bit, a blurry picture was coming into focus.

'Should I tell you that at a certain point in my life I got a call?' Nica's voice echoed around my room. Then she let out a guffaw of laughter to underline rather than undermine the importance of what she was about to say. Laughter was often used by her generation as an indication that what they were about to tell you was slightly embarrassing but very important. 'A call.' She repeats the word carefully. 'I did. I did. Can you imagine such a thing?'

Normally it is holy people who get a calling, a sign or an overwhelming desire to devote the rest of their lives to God. It was hard to imagine Nica, brought up without religion, suddenly getting this message.

'I was in Mexico, when I was in the throes of diplomatic life and all the bullshit, and I had a friend who was from the musical circle. He used to get hold of records for me and I would go to his pad to hear them. I couldn't have listened to them in my own house with that atmosphere.'

Then I heard Nica describe how this friend had got hold of a 78-rpm recording of Duke Ellington's symphony *Black, Brown and Beige*, first played in New York in 1943. Ellington introduced the piece as a 'parallel to the history of the Negro in America'.

To some, this music became a political statement, to others it was simply a wonderful jazz symphony, but for Nica it meant something completely different.

'I got the message that I belonged where that music was. There was something I was supposed to do. I was supposed to be involved in it in some way. I got a really clear message. It wasn't long afterwards that it happened, that I cut out from there. It was a real calling. Very strange.'

Nica with her brother Victor in Mexico, 1947.

I wondered about her statement in the light of what I knew about the family. Earlier Rothschild generations had had a calling to finance: they had united to create a behemoth of a bank. Some claimed they helped create the 'worship of materialism'. Nica's brother Victor and sister Miriam had also had a calling, although theirs was to science. Would Liberty's life have turned out differently, I wondered, if she had found a great passion? Would Charles's life have ended more happily if he'd been allowed to follow his? Perhaps Nica's calling was another way of describing an inherited obsessive-compulsive trait: I have noticed that the Rothschilds – down to the present generation – often fix on a subject with absolute, single-minded determination.

Nica did not immediately know how to act on her calling. She stayed on in Mexico, where Jules worked in that 'bullshit' diplomatic life. As the 'atmosphere' grew worse, Nica found more excuses to stay away from home and more reasons to visit New York. On one particular trip, the chance hearing of a piece of music would change her life for ever.

'I was on my way back to Mexico where we were living at the time – I think it was 1948 or 1949,' Nica said, 'and I stopped off to see Teddy Wilson on my way to the airport to say goodbye.

'Teddy was one of the people who sent her records, and on this occasion he asked if she had heard of a young artist, Thelonious Monk, who had just cut his first record. 'I'd never even heard of Thelonious. So Teddy galloped off to find it somewhere and when he came back he played it. Well, I couldn't believe my ears. I'd never heard anything remotely like it. I must have played it twenty times in a row. Missed my plane. In fact I never went home.'

Over the years, this story has become a well-honed piece of jazz folklore: 'Did you hear the one about the crazy baroness who was bewitched by a song?' It was, for example, one of the first things that the writer Stanley Crouch told me as we sat in New York on a hot May afternoon in a one-sided 'conversation' that lasted for four and a half hours. Crouch occasionally stopped to mop his brow with a large white handkerchief, taking a momentary pause from his seemingly inexhaustible reserves of knowledge.

'She told me that the musician Teddy Wilson had this recording and he wanted to play it for her.' Crouch shook his head in amazement as he recalled the details. 'He said he wanted her to hear something unique. It was "'Round Midnight" and she said she'd never heard anything like the sound of it, just the sound and the feeling of it, and she just kept asking him to play it over and over, and she led one to imagine that this was like the vinyl version of a spell being cast on someone, except that it is not a spell that arrives by itself, it is spell that is assisted by you. You. Just you. She kept getting deeper and deeper into it as she heard it. You can't explain music, we do not know where she went or where that song took her, but from that point on, she had concluded that she was going to have to meet the guy who played this music.'

Suddenly it was light outside my hotel room. The garbage trucks were grinding up the street, clanking and banging the waste bins. A lone police car made its way downtown, its siren as nagging and persistent as a mosquito's whine. Ignoring the outside world, I replayed this section of the CD over and over again, trying to decide what was more surprising: the simplicity of Nica's account, as if it were perfectly normal to miss planes, let alone leave a marriage and a life as a result of merely hearing a tune, or the entirely insouciant way in which she delivered the story, like a person giving directions to a local landmark.

I put "'Round Midnight' on my iPod and listened to it, really listened to it, as if for the first time. It cannot be described as a typical Monk composition, but then nothing is typical about the man or his music. It is a mournful, lazy, sexy-sounding ballad shot through with a little blues and even a dash of stride. A grand trumpet solo introduces the melody, then the piano nudges in and plays with the horn for a while, batting the tune around between wind and percussion, before dismissing the trumpet into the background where it stays on the touchline for the rest of the session, along with the strings and the drums. While the rest of the quartet languishes, repeating a background harmony, the pianist takes off, letting his fingers dance around the notes, sometimes hitting two or three at a time, sometimes shooting to the top of a scale, playing around with a high arpeggio and then landing at random elsewhere on the keys, at another point in the tune, breaking and confounding and thrilling. The lyrics were added later to some versions but when Nica heard it she grafted her own feelings on to the tune.

Monk never said what event or person inspired it. He was only nineteen when he composed it but did not have the chance to record it until 1947. Since then ''Round Midnight' has become one of the most recorded jazz standards of all time, appearing on no fewer than 1,165 albums. One critic has called it the 'National Anthem of Jazz' and others see it as a lucky song. When Nica heard it, ''Round Midnight' had not even made it into the jazz charts. The song was like her: a beauty on the threshold of being discovered.

Nica heard the melody but she also heard something intangible. Her friend, the photographer and writer Val Wilmer, explained: 'For the fan the music becomes deeply personal, as if the player is talking to you alone. The musicians are reaching out and telling you their own life history, their experiences. They are testifying on their instruments.'

Jazz and Nica grew up together. It was the soundtrack to her life. Her father had played the great early recordings of Scott Joplin, George Gershwin and Louis Armstrong. She swung herself into society on a wave of Tommy Dorsey, Benny Goodman and Duke Ellington. Those who didn't actually perform in London's grandest ballrooms called to her over the wireless.

Even in deepest Africa, on daring Free French missions, the radio was Nica's constant companion, the Circe drawing her, beckoning her towards another world, another life. While she was enduring an unfulfilling marriage, living in a disoriented society that, after the war, was trying to rebuild itself, bebop burst across the airwaves. Its discordant, anarchic and explosive phrases seemed to match her mood exactly. Those musicians were throwing out the rule book, playing the notes out of sequence, ignoring structure with great speed and dexterity. Bebop was music you couldn't dance or sing to. For many, it was as tuneful as a hundred cats scratching on a blackboard, as comprehensible as a buckling freight train. It was music that said, 'I really don't give a shit about convention or what anyone thinks, I am going to be uncompromisingly myself and there's nothing anyone can do about it.' It was the exact antidote Nica had been looking for. For those, like Nica, who succumb, jazz is something that reaches out and saves you.

'It was the music that drew me first,' she said. 'I didn't know any musicians then. In time, I grew to feel that if the music is beautiful, the musicians must be beautiful too in some way. Now I know that it's not possible to play with Bird [Charlie Parker], Monk, Sir Charles Thompson and Teddy Wilson and not be very much worth digging yourself. They're all rather like their music.'

Nica's friend, the musician and producer Quincy Jones, told me: 'Jazz has a way of transforming darkness into light through comedy or taking the pain away from a bad love relationship or whatever and then make it either funny or express it in order to release it . . . That is why it was so strong and that is why it has permeated the planet and almost every country in the world.' For all the awards Jones has won, the multimillion-selling albums, he can still remember the thrill of arriving in New York in the late 1940s with nothing but his trumpet. 'It was like walking into Wonderland.' Through his eyes, I could imagine the city.

At that time, Monk, Quincy Jones and other jazz musicians

were just a bunch of unknowns: a collection of diverse individuals drawn to the same place. 'She had no idea they would some day become famous. No one could have imagined it. They were virtually social pariahs,' her son Patrick observed in a newspaper interview. Nica's friend and contemporary Phoebe Jacobs pointed out, 'Nice girls like the Baroness didn't associate with jazz musicians because everyone knows that jazz had just come out of the whorehouses and crack dens and, anyway, jazz musicians were junkies. Heroin addicts.' Nica, however, never cared much what people thought.

The more I researched, the more I realised that jazz has a symbolic value and a cultural significance beyond its arrangements, and an emotional impact beyond the tunes. It became linked with the struggle of African Americans to achieve freedom and equality. It gave a voice to a generation and hope to thousands. For slaves who had been stripped of their culture, belongings, heritage – even their language – music was one of the few imports they could bring to their new homeland. Traders could take away their possessions but not their voice.* Blues and jazz evolved in the cotton fields where workers' songs soared above the crops: optimism and despair set to music, uniting disparate people in desolate places.

First jazz gave black immigrants hope; later it gave them a livelihood. Following the abolition of slavery, opportunities for many African Americans were limited and 'low-class' entertainment was a popular employment option. At the end of the civil war, when the armies dumped their instruments, their pipes and bugles were rescued and adapted by these entertainers. Many of these instruments bear a striking resemblance to models found in West Coast Africa. In 1895 the first ragtime sheet music appeared, followed in

*This came from the distinguished chatelaine of Waddesdon Manor, the author, benefactress and indefatigable charity worker Mrs James de Rothschild.

1899 by the international hit 'Maple Leaf Rag', written by a young, classically trained African-American pianist by the name of Scott Joplin. Since then jazz has been celebrated and dismissed, loved and hated, studied and overlooked by generation after generation. Defying simple definition, jazz encompasses diverse rhythms, scales, syncopations and styles ranging from early New Orleans Dixie and ragtime waltzes to fusion.

While it's far-fetched to correlate Nica's experiences with those of African Americans, there were common elements. She and her family had long since left the ghetto behind but their forebears' experience of being Jewish refugees, of being born into another race, inspired them during the war to risk their own lives.

Nica detected the passion and heartbreak underlying the music. It resonated too with her that many women and black musicians had fought in a bitter and bloody war on the principle of freedom, yet both groups returned to a society that refused, by and large, to entertain change. Robert Kraft, a musician and record producer who knew Nica, put it very succinctly: 'America had just fought a war of freedom and soldiers, black and white, had gone to liberate whole populations in fascistic, Neolithic, incredibly difficult times in Europe and Asia. Yet black soldiers were returning to America and could not enter the front door of the restaurants they were performing in. They couldn't sleep in white hotels when they performed on the bandstands of those hotels. They had to sleep in other hotels. There had to have been a phenomenal amount of conflict, rage, dissonance and of course it's the artist's role to call attention to that.'

Artists took their role seriously, as the great jazz legend, Nica's friend Sonny Rollins, explained to me. 'People who played bebop wanted to be accepted as fully fledged human beings, not just as talented artists. Charlie Parker was a very dignified person and he wanted to present the music in a very dignified manner. When Charlie Parker used to play he wouldn't move. He would just stand up straight and he would play. There would be no clowning around and no entertaining.' These thoughts are echoed by Quincy Jones: 'Musicians were saying, I don't want to have to entertain an audience, I want to be an artist like Stravinsky or whoever, that pure art without dancing and rolling eyes and dancing to minstrel stuff.'

'Music, as you and I know, transcends social policy and patriotism,' Rollins continued. 'It draws together a lot of people from all ethnic backgrounds.' For Nica, who had grown up in a rule-bound, class-obsessed society, this defiance was intoxicating and inspirational. 'It was rebellious, it was sexy and it was exciting. The Baroness liked that,' Monk's former manager Harry Colomby explained.

Most importantly, perhaps, jazz helped Nica feel less alone, more connected. As Proust discovered, music 'helped me to descend into myself, to discover new things: the variety that I had sought in vain in life, in travel, but a longing for which was none the less renewed in me by this sonorous tide whose sunlit waves now came to expire at my feet'. For Proust, and for Nica perhaps, music provides the 'means of communication between souls'. Music was her balm. It soothed and harmonised. It was wildly mood-altering: uplifting one moment, heartrending the next. Music linked and transported her away from the 'atmosphere' and the 'bullshit'.

I took the subway up to Roosevelt Avenue in Queens where Teddy Wilson lived and found a corner table in a coffee shop. Daft as it sounds, I ordered a Coke, played ''Round Midnight' on my iPod and imagined I was Nica some sixty years earlier. In a few hours she had to leave New York, a city that represented freedom and escape. Suddenly she could not return to a marriage that for fifteen years had felt increasingly like a prison. Perhaps in that room overlooking Roosevelt Avenue she heard in ''Round Midnight' something that made sense of her life. Nica had never met or even heard of Monk at that moment. He could have been a hundred years old or a teenager: she had no idea then how much they would come to

52nd Street, the oasis of jazz in the 1940s and 1950s.

share and how extraordinarily important he would be in her life. Perhaps I have to suspend my disbelief and accept that in that one tune, which lasts only three minutes and eleven seconds, Nica's life changed.

Once the decision not to go back to Mexico was made, Nica was determined to meet the man who played this music.

15

A Blast

Nica left home in style. She did not take a discreet apartment in London, or a cottage on one of the family's estates. Instead she moved into a suite at the Stanhope Hotel, a grand establishment overlooking the Metropolitan Museum of Art on the edge of New York's Central Park. Built in 1927, it was, like many Rothschild houses, a faux version of a European chateau. Guests passed through a neo-Italianate entrance into an opulent, eighteenth-century, French-style lobby with antiques, marble floors and hand-carved wall mouldings burnished with 24-carat gold leaf. Male guests were expected to wear suits and ties, and women rarely left the premises without hats and gloves. Like many hotels, the Stanhope rigorously maintained a policy of segregation: blacks were allowed in only through the service entrance, and would certainly not have been permitted to rent a room or to frequent public areas or guests' bedrooms.

The hotel wasn't a stranger to controversy. In 1946, the American socialite Kiki Preston jumped to her death out of a high window. The alleged mother of one of HRH Prince George's illegitimate children, a member of the Happy Valley set and a niece of Gloria

Nica's first home in New York, a suite at the
Stanhope Hotel, overlooking Central Park.

Vanderbilt, she had been given the nickname 'the girl with the silver syringe' on account of her penchant for narcotics. Ms Preston's unfortunate leap raised many questions about life behind the heavy, ruched curtains at the Stanhope Hotel. The last thing the management needed was another scandal, yet the ink was hardly dry on Nica's registration form when she began to cause trouble.

'One of the stories that I used to hear about her,' my father Jacob told me, 'was that she liked to practise her pistol shooting on the light bulbs. She had to keep her "eye in" following the war. From time to time my grandfather [Nica's brother Victor] had to go over to New York to persuade the management to allow her to stay.' Nica confirmed the story to me but added, 'The manager said, "We don't mind if you shoot our staff but please leave our chandeliers alone."'

Nica's first New York car, a 1953 Rolls-Royce Silver Dawn.

Nica's first major purchase was a new Rolls-Royce that she would park in front of the Stanhope, leaving the engine running in case she needed to depart in a hurry. Later she would switch her allegiance to Bentleys, although all her cars were treated with gay abandon. 'She always drove as if she were competing at Le Mans, and she paid very little attention to traffic rules,' her son Patrick told a journalist. 'In my parents' divorce settlement there's a clause my father insisted upon: under no conditions were any of us children to ride in a car driven by Nica. A condition that was largely ignored.'

One late night in Manhattan, at a red light, a shiny sports car pulled up next to her Bentley Continental Convertible. The elegant gentleman driving the sports car signalled her to roll down her window.

'Madam, you should be ashamed of yourself. You have a rare and beautiful car, but you treat it in a disgraceful manner.'

She looked at the gentleman concerned and replied, 'Fuck you!' Then she sped off.

He caught up with her at the next red light and, once again, asked her to roll down her window. Despite their previous encounter, she did so. The gentleman said, 'Madam, with all due respect, the same to you!'

He was, she declared, 'a lovely man'.

Although these stories made me laugh, they also made me uncomfortable. Nica's newly chosen lifestyle of grand hotels and fast cars seemed like pure hedonism rather than a spiritual 'calling'. I saw an analogy between the way Nica drove the Bentley and the manner in which she discarded her former life; both were, in many respects, rare and beautiful and she treated both with a careless disdain. I wondered, too, whether there were parallels between Victor disposing so readily of his inheritance to pursue his own passions and Nica walking away from her responsibilities.

Jules's behaviour might have been controlling and authoritarian, but I felt nothing but sympathy with his desire to protect his children. Of course he did not want them to be driven by a woman who drank and crashed cars. Wanting to believe that Nica had put up a great fight to keep custody of all her children, I tried to find out details of the couple's divorce settlement. I combed contemporary newspapers, looking for any mention of custody battles, and searched family letters for references. I found nothing. My respect for Nica wavered. Perhaps she was nothing more than a wealthy, irresponsible gadfly after all.

A civil war of opinion raged in my head. Was she good or bad? Naive or callous? I wasted hours in pointless speculation and then called a mental truce. It was time to stop judging Nica and attempt instead to understand her actions through the prism of her own experiences and the conventions of that time. What of her own childhood? She had never been parented; her father had died abruptly and violently. Rozsika was a ghostly figure who left the business of mothering to the servants. The children learned to avoid intimacy. Victor used cruelty to keep others at arm's length; he tormented and bullied many of his six children as well as his two wives.

Liberty could not cope with relationships of any kind. Miriam worked obsessively. Nica dodged getting close to anyone by scattering her love widely. Her photograph albums show a woman permanently surrounded – either by cats, children or adults.

Nica's marriage and her subsequent peripatetic lifestyle meant that she could, when she chose, easily lose contact with people. One Rothschild cousin described her feelings about Nica with both sadness and mystification. The two women were contemporaries and lived in neighbouring houses. As children, they played, hunted hounds and husbands together. Their close friendship endured even when Nica and Jules went to live in France. However, once Nica left Jules she never contacted her cousin nor returned her calls or letters, as if 'she simply didn't want to know me any more'.

One of Nica's favourite expressions came from the hunting field. 'If you throw your heart over the fence, your head will follow,' she told me. Perhaps she should have added, 'And do not look back.' She moved to America confident that everything would work out; others would provide and her children would be well cared for by Jules. Her eldest son Patrick said of her financial affairs, 'My mother was comfortable, she had a trust fund, but she always had money worries.' Nica spent money she did not have, assuming correctly that her family would bail her out of difficulties. Our cousin Evelyn de Rothschild remembers that a senior bank manager, Mr Hobbs, was regularly sent to New York to keep tabs on Nica's spending and encourage a more cautious existence. I imagined Mr Hobbs as a suburban chap with a bowler hat, being unprepared for travel to America in pursuit of a wayward Rothschild. 'No! You've

R. W. C. Hobbs Esq.

got it all wrong,' another cousin corrected me. 'Hobbs was a ladies' man. He looked after all the Rothschild women and he *loved* it.'

There was another practical explanation for the terms of Nica's separation. Prior to an Act of Parliament passed in 1969, many years after Nica's marriage ended, wives were rarely granted alimony or gained custody of their children. When Frances Shand Kydd, the mother of Diana, the Princess of Wales, left her husband for another man in 1967, she lost custody of her children and received no financial support. Until Princess Margaret got divorced in 1969, only two groups of people were banned from the royal enclosure at racecourses: convicted felons and divorcees. Perhaps Nica did not fight harder for custody of her younger children because she knew she could not win. Perhaps she was honest enough to admit that her younger children would have a more stable life with their father.

Nica's eldest daughter Janka joined her mother in New York when she was sixteen. In her letters, Nica treats her like a younger sister rather than a child, taking pride in Janka's knowledge of jazz and their shared love of music and musicians. Later Patrick tried living with Nica but complained that the all-night jam sessions made studying impossible. The three younger children, Shaun, Berit and Kari, lived with their father in New York from 1953 until 1957 while Jules held the position of French Minister Plenipotentiary to the United States and Canada. Later they moved with him to Peru where Jules was made Ambassador.

For those in search of a new life, post-war New York was the crucible of creative innovation and a locus of tremendous energy. The economy was booming. It was also a place where being a foreigner was normal. A cacophony of different languages could be heard on any block. Within a few miles of each other, Chinese neighbourhoods bordered Italians, Koreans, Africans, West Indians, Russians, Poles, Jews, Muslims and Hispanics. Most of them lived happily cheek by jowl. What better destination, then, for Nica, a woman of Hungarian-British-German-Jewish extraction, married to a

Frenchman of Austrian lineage, who had lived in Europe, Africa and South America?

As the cost of living was relatively cheap, New York became a magnet for leading protagonists in the worlds of art, literature, dance, poetry, music, philosophy and psychoanalysis. Ideas, images and thoughts were incubated in cafés, bars and jazz clubs. Nica's friend Phoebe Jacobs sums up the city's attraction: 'She came here because we had a freedom that didn't exist elsewhere. We said to hell with manners or good taste. It was so exciting and she wanted to be one of the crowd, one of the boys.'

Like Nica, Sal Paradise, the hero of Jack Kerouac's novel *On the Road*, ends up in New York in the 1950s.

> Suddenly I found myself on Times Square; and right in the middle of a rush hour, too, seeing with my innocent road-eyes the absolute madness and fantastic furore of New York with its millions and millions hustling forever for a buck among themselves, the mad dream – grabbing, taking, giving, sighing, dying, just so they could be buried in those awful cemetery cities beyond Long Island City. The high towers of the land – the other end of the land, the place where Paper America is born.

The jazz clubs on 52nd Street were tiny and the same clientele went night after night. Nica sat with Kerouac, William Burroughs, Allen Ginsberg and Abstract Expressionist painters like Jackson Pollock, Willem de Kooning, Franz Kline and Frank Stella, listening to Charlie Parker, Dizzy Gillespie, John Coltrane and Miles Davis. They were joined by an emerging generation of American novelists including Saul Bellow and Norman Mailer, who were also transfixed by the jazz scene. The music bled into other art forms, inspiring the Black Mountain poets to reject control and structure. Painters like Robert Rauschenberg used the cut-up technique on canvas, while William Burroughs clipped phrases from newspapers to create a collage of words and meaning.

John Dankworth, Nica's British saxophone-playing friend, was in New York at that time, listening to the same music. 'It was a fantasy world especially if you had just come from war-torn Europe where everything was still rationed and we were suffering the worst weather we had had for half a century. New York was the nearest thing to heaven I could ever remember. I can well understand Nica wanting to be part of it.'

Since the Cotton Club had opened its doors in the 1920s, many white people frequented jazz clubs. What set Nica apart, though, was that she didn't want to go home when the joints closed. Clint Eastwood, the film director, who got to know Nica when he was making the film *Bird* about Charlie Parker, told me, 'Society people would slum it and go down to hear swing or jazz bands. Nica embraced the whole culture of jazz and bebop and loved the rebelliousness of it.'

Robin Kelley, Monk's biographer, added another dimension to Nica's behaviour. 'From everything I have heard, she lived a very protected life as a child. She almost died when she caught measles as an adult. I think that kind of seclusion, that kind of protection, is enough to make you go wild when you become an adult.'

For the next thirty years Nica's lifestyle barely changed. She did not just listen to jazz; she lived it. She got up as darkness fell. She wasted daylight, treating it with utter disdain.

Within months of settling in America, Nica replaced the internecine web of cousins with an equally complicated maze of musicians. The aristocracy that she knew so well in England was now replaced by a 'jazzocracy'. She learned who had influenced, betrayed, loved, nurtured and copied whom. Adopting the patois, the hours and habits, Nica became a jazz native.

When Nica arrived on the scene with her gleaming white Rolls-Royce, her chequebook and her unbounded enthusiasm for their music, the musicians could not believe their luck. She took them seriously and was happy to pay for a night out, offering both cash and cachet. 'I remember one night we had dinner at her place,'

Horace Silver wrote in his autobiography. 'We decided to go to Birdland.* We got in her Rolls-Royce, with her driving, and proceeded down Broadway. I remember all the white people staring at us as if to say, "What are those niggers doing in a Rolls-Royce with a white lady?"'

Nica was not worried about spending money: that was what it was there for. What she wanted was an entrée to a different life and the musicians gave it to her. Her grandson Steven told me: 'To her that music was the ultimate expression of freedom and that was something that she had never experienced until she went to New York: that was what it was all about. Her passion for liberty was expressed by African-American musicians. It could have been expressed by Chinamen; it wouldn't have made any difference. She saw in them [the musicians] the embodiment of life and freedom.'

Nica's words, told to Nat Hentoff in *Esquire*, confirm her grandson's hunch. 'The music is what moves me. It has something I also hear in the playing of the Hungarian gypsies, something very sad and beautiful. It's everything that really matters, everything worth digging. It's a desire for freedom. And in all my life, I've never known any people who warmed me as much by their friendship as the Jazz musicians I've come to know.'

Nica had found her calling, her version of paradise. No one told her when to get up or go to bed, how to dress, what to eat, who to talk to, what not to drink. There were no cooks, maids or nannies or disapproving husbands. If she wanted to eat, she called room service; if she wanted to go out, she hopped into her car. She could have reverted to her maiden name or used her husband's but she preferred to be known as the Baroness.

Many assumed that Nica's relationship with the musicians was physical. 'Black man, white woman, it had to be all about sex didn't it? That's the normal, offensive, old prejudice coming out,' her

*Papers left by Field Marshal Keitel, Commander of the German Armed Forces, and Alfred Rosenberg, Custodian of the Arts.

Nica with Teddy Wilson at London's Stork Club in 1954.

friend, the trombonist Curtis Fuller, said sadly. Curtis spent a lot of time with Nica from the late 1940s. 'I never saw any touchy-feely stuff. Besides, if you had had five kids, wouldn't you just want a bit of a rest from all that?'

The drummer and ladies' man Art Blakey was the first musician with whom Nica was romantically linked. She bought him a Cadillac and fitted out his band with suits. Many thought Blakey used Nica but to her he was an amusing, talented guide to the jazz world, introducing her to musicians and clubs, and teaching her about music. Another musician with whom she was supposed to have had an affair was Al Timothy, a Trinidadian saxophonist who had arrived in Britain in 1948 and met Nica through their mutual friend Teddy Wilson. Apparently, Nica loved Timothy or his music or both, and when she returned briefly to live in London in 1954, she reopened the club Studio 51 and made him resident bandleader. Later Timothy came to visit Nica in New York, where she photographed him with Monk and Sonny Rollins.

Gossip and speculation stalked Nica but there is no evidence that any of these relationships were consummated. One of her closest friends was her brother's old piano teacher Teddy Wilson. When he went on tour in Scotland in 1953, Nica drove him from London to Edinburgh. Again the newspapers had a field day. 'Blues Man Gets Rolls Royce' was one headline. For Wilson, seeing the United Kingdom 'in a four-door sedan, with the sun roof open, at highway speeds', was seeing the country at its best. For Nica, with time on her hands and a car at her disposal, it was 'a blast'.

The irony was that she still could not find the man who wrote ''Round Midnight'. Nica combed the clubs, looking for the High Priest of Jazz, but Thelonious Monk had lost his performer's licence following a drugs bust. Let out of prison, he was unemployable and broke, living as a virtual prisoner in his own apartment.

16

Loneliest Monk

A mere twenty blocks south-west of the Stanhope Hotel, in a tiny two-bed walk-up in the San Juan district, on the opposite side of Central Park, Thelonious Sphere Monk was struggling. Busted for possession of heroin in 1951, he had lost his cabaret card for seven years and with it the right to play in most Manhattan clubs. While his contemporaries were graduating from slipstream to mainstream, Monk was becalmed. Occasionally he was booked to play in Brooklyn or some other place out of town, but mostly Monk played alone on an upright piano in his kitchen. His only audience was his wife Nellie and their two children, Toot and Barbara. At night, if he could bear it, Monk listened to his contemporaries on the radio. More often than not, during what he called the 'unyears' (his nickname for these unproductive times), Monk lay on his back in silence looking at a picture of Billie Holiday tacked to the ceiling above his bed.

The family lived on Nellie's meagre wages. Over the years she found work as a lift operator, in an ice-cream bar and as a seamstress, but ill health often kept her at home, forcing the couple to rely on their families for handouts. Fear of penury constantly dogged the couple. Even in better times, on their world tours Nellie collected empty Coca-Cola bottles in order to get the refund on the glass back home. The fear of arrest never left Monk either; he always carried $1,000 in cash in case he needed bail money. While many would have tried to get a normal job, Monk could not stick regular employment, and employers couldn't hack his scant regard for authority or timekeeping. A person with less self-belief might have buckled.

At first glance, the differences between Monk and Nica – their backgrounds, their experiences and their characters – seemed irreconcilable; the only thing they appeared to share was a love of his music. Even if Nica did find him, it was unlikely that the two would have anything in common. Their friend, the writer Stanley Crouch, was equally sceptical. 'Monk was a country Negro, he wasn't even brought up in New York, he was from North Carolina. Monk and the Baroness came from very, very different places socially and economically.'

I realised that one of the questions at the heart of my quest was: what attracts two people to each other? Why does one fall in love with one person rather than another? Monk was black, she was white; he was poor, she was rich; he was a Christian, she was a Jew: the list is endless and rather fatuous. Were there deeper shared connections, not visible immediately to the casual observer? Was it possible, I wondered, to strip away the surface and find other connections between them? Were people wrong to claim that their friendship was built on the attraction of opposites?

Thelonious was born in Rocky Mount, North Carolina, in 1917, four years after Nica. His great-grandfather came from West Africa on a slave ship in the mid-nineteenth century and was given the name of his plantation owner, Archibald Monk. Thelonious and his father, Thelonious Snr, were named after a Benedictine missionary saint of the seventh century. The pianist later added a middle name, 'Sphere', as a variation, a riff on his mother's family name Speer.

Like Charles Rothschild, Monk's father was in poor health, physically and mentally. Both men suffered from bouts of erratic behaviour and depression. Monk's mother Barbara had to cope with her husband's terrible temper, wild drinking, mood swings and, eventually, his withdrawal from family life and society. Perhaps to escape her marriage or to search for a better life, in 1921 Barbara took four-year-old Thelonious, his brother Thomas and his sister Marion to New York to live. It was a brave and highly unusual act then for a woman to leave her husband and her extended family. Barbara was determined; there were few opportunities for black people in the South. Jim Crow's system was still operating, practically if not legally.

By the time Monk Snr caught up with his family some three or four years later, Barbara had settled their children in the San Juan Hill district, a neighbourhood that had become home to thousands of émigrés from the Southern states and the Caribbean. For a brief period the Monks lived together as a family but their small tenement flat was a damp and sunless place that set off Monk Snr's asthma attacks as well as his mental problems.

I wondered if their respective fathers' afflictions offered a potential bond between Nica and Thelonious. Both had grown up with a parent who was stricken with mental illness exacerbated by random conditions. Charles's depression became worse after he contracted Spanish flu, Monk Snr's worsened when he had bronchial problems. Despite their vastly different financial circumstances, there was an atmosphere in Monk's and Nica's homes that shaped the childhoods of both and altered their way of looking at the world. When they were children, neither could predict which mood or persona their parents would adopt at any given time. Monk Snr would disappear to bars; Charles Rothschild would shut himself in his room.

After a few years, Monk Snr returned south to live with his brother. Overwhelmed by his illness, the family committed him to a mental asylum where he spent the remainder of his life. There

The young Thelonious Monk.

was a huge difference between Charles Rothschild's comfortable Swiss sanatorium, where he was allowed to take a companion and his work, and the State Hospital for the Colored Insane in Goldsboro, North Carolina, where Thelonious Snr was incarcerated. The latter was a miserable place with few facilities and little hope of discharge.

Young Nica and Thelonious had extremely strong mothers who kept their families together. While Rozsika Rothschild enjoyed the ministrations of over forty members of staff, Barbara Monk worked as a cleaner at Children's Court on 137 East 22nd Street. Young Thelonious was enrolled at the prestigious Peter Stuyvesant School where he had access to a broader education than Nica. After an initial flurry of academic promise, he turned into an undistinguished middle-grade student. Although he did not join the school orchestra, music played a key part in the young man's life. Like Nica, he was brought up listening to a mixture of classical music and jazz. Nica could hear the best classical orchestras in her family's ballrooms and then dance to the leading big bands at society parties. Barbara took her children to Central Park to listen to the Goldman series of classical concerts where top orchestras played works by Schubert, Tchaikovsky, Wagner, Chopin and Strauss. Monk's son Toot told me, 'If you had come to my father's home you would have seen stacks of Chopin, Liszt, Haydn, Handel, Beethoven, Wagner. His music didn't come out of a vacuum.'

Nica was not expected to get a job, but Monk's outlook was as bleak. Employment opportunities for young blacks were extremely limited. I asked Monk's contemporary, the legendary drummer Chico Hamilton, about his career prospects in the 1930s.

'I had a choice of being a musician or a pimp,' Hamilton replied.

Assuming he'd made a joke, I smiled and was promptly excoriated.

'You might smile,' he said, leaning towards me, his eyes blazing with fury, jabbing a drumstick in my direction, 'but when I was eight, nine, ten and eleven years old, I shined shoes: that was how

I bought my first set of drums, shining shoes for a nickel. You remember what a nickel was. I would go out on a Wednesday and a Saturday from school, I would stay out all day Saturday until I made a dollar and then come home. I made enough money shining shoes, like I said, to buy my first set of drums. I have been making my living ever since. I was a lucky one.'

In 1932, while Nica went husband hunting, curtsying to Queen Charlotte's cake and marking her dance card with the names of suitable swains, Monk set up his first informal band, left school and got a girlfriend. He also met but hardly noticed Nellie, the younger sister of his friend Sonny Smith, a tiny, skinny ten-year-old who was to become his wife and the mother of his children.

In the year that Nica married, 1935, Monk went on tour supporting a woman preacher. He told Nat Hentoff, 'While still in my teens, I went on the road with a group that played church music for an evangelist. Rock and roll or rhythm and blues. That's what we were doing. Only now they put different words to it. She preached and healed and we played. We travelled for about two years.' It was one of the pianist's longest periods of steady employment.

On his return to New York, Monk briefly joined some of the big bands, working with Lucky Millinder, Skippy Williams and Dizzy Gillespie. 'The bands never did knock me out. I wanted to play my own chords,' he told George Simon. His son Toot was keen to stress that, while Monk might not have been a star on the bandstand, 'He was the star of the neighbourhood long before he ever got any international recognition. In those days everybody didn't have a record player so the party would be where you had the live music.'

The club that launched a thousand dreams and changed the history of jazz was Minton's Playhouse in Harlem. Small and nondescript, it became known for its innovative Monday-night jam sessions where musicians could leave tightly arranged sessions behind on the bandstand and play unregulated, abandoned jazz. It was here that Monk met jazz greats such as Coleman Hawkins, Ben Webster and Lester Young.

Thelonious Monk, Howard McGhee, Roy Eldridge and Teddy Hill
outside Minton's Playhouse in September 1947.

At Minton's, four young men – Thelonious Monk, Charlie Parker, Max Roach and Dizzy Gillespie – were at the forefront of a new form of jazz called bebop. 'Everyone called bebop a revolution but it was an evolution,' the critic and writer Ira Gitler told me. 'Bebop echoed the faster means of transportation, the uncertainty of wartime, the hope for the future. It captured all the young musicians in a very, very powerful way.'

I visited Gitler in the Upper East Side basement apartment that he shares with his wife Mary Joy and which Nica also visited. Like her, Ira Gitler was an habitué of the New York scene and has devoted his life to writing about jazz. Every nook and cranny, corner and surface of the apartment was piled high with jazz memorabilia: musical instruments, photographs and records collected over the previous seventy years. Gitler was one of the small group of people who really helped me understand Nica and the jazz scene.

'I knew of Nica from the time she arrived here because people in jazz started talking about this baroness who was driving around in a Rolls-Royce. I first saw her at the Open Door in Greenwich Village where jam sessions were held at this club late Sunday afternoon to Sunday night. Charlie Parker started to play there and naturally that attracted a lot of attention.'

Surely, I said, it must have been hard for Monk being stuck at home while all that was going on? Gitler nodded but explained that Monk's career was never easy.

Nica was in Africa and then in France when bebop was born. If the music reached her at all, it was over the wireless rather than on a record. There was a recording ban during the early 1940s while the record companies negotiated a new form of contract, so much early bebop was not recorded. It was not until 1945, when small record companies sprang up, that this new music was captured on shellac and its influence spread.* The writer Gary Giddins explained: 'Jazz was a music that brought people together and that was kind of, you know, somewhat of an oasis in all this quagmire.'

Monk's compositions aren't classic forms of any style. They are suffused with strains of gospel, stride and blues, a hotchpotch of his early influences from the Church, gospel tours and the radio. His sound is completely individual. Three chords in, like it or loathe it, anyone can spot Monk's signature playing. So what, I wanted to understand, did Monk do for music and musicians?

*Gimle Castle has since been renamed the Grand Villa and is Norway's Holocaust Museum.
†Mrs Mary Jean Onslow, the daughter of a military attaché to the British Embassy in Norway.

'Thelonious was the father of modern jazz because it is the harmonic possibilities that he brought to the table that freed the Charlie Parkers and the John Coltranes and Dizzy Gillespies from the chains of popular American music,' Toot explained. Until then, most music was played according to simple chord structures. The beboppers threw that rule book out of the window. To many, though, it sounded as if someone had thrown a big hammer against a beautiful pane of glass: bebop was sound fractured into a thousand pieces.

Monk took the musical anarchy even further than his contemporaries. They were playing notes in strange sequences, ignoring melodies and subverting the chord structures. Monk added to this his own variation. My favourite explanation of why Monk's playing was ground-breaking came from Chico Hamilton: 'Man, I have played with piano players who play with all the white keys, I have played with piano players who have played with all the black keys, but I have never played with no motherfucker who played in between the cracks.'

Monk might have been a hero to other musicians but at the time Nica first heard him, the critics hated his music and his compositions. The influential promoter George Wein admitted to me, 'The first time I heard him play was back in the late forties and I just thought he was a bad piano player.' The most important music magazine at the time, Downbeat, described him as 'The pianist who did NOT invent bop, and generally plays bad, though interesting piano.'

Were it not for a young female promoter, Nica might never have heard Monk. Lorraine Lion Gordon* fell in love with his sound and was determined to bring the pianist to a wider audience. She went to see Monk at home. 'Monk had an upright piano in his narrow room, which looked to me like Van Gogh's room in Arles,

*There are many irrefutable factors linking jazz to Africa. Fundamental to the nature of the music is the call-and-response pattern common in the African tradition, reflecting African speech patterns and the African use of pentatonic scales.

with the bed and the dresser.' She had to sit on the bed while Monk played. 'Thelonious played with his back to us various numbers we had never heard before. I thought: is he a great blues pianist! That's why I liked him so much.'

Lorraine drove her suitcase of Monk records all over the country. 'I went to Philly, Baltimore, a whole line-up, Cleveland, Chicago. I was a kid, doing all this for him and for other Blue Notes. I went to Harlem to try to sell Monk there. The guys in the record stores would say, "He can't play. He has two left hands." I had to battle all the way to get them to buy a Monk record and listen to him.' Lorraine admitted to being Monk's gofer. 'He used to call me up. "Will you take me here? Will you take me there?" So I kind of pampered him in that way because I did feel he was very special even then. I was the errand lady.'

Monk had a certain talent for finding women to care for him: his mother, his wife Nellie, Lorraine and later Nica. Although he had one brief job in the 1930s, he was happier composing, hanging out and playing music, and decided that regular work wasn't really for him. He lived at a time when geniuses were expected to be eccentrics and had a licence to misbehave, as if their refusal to take responsibility for anything and their self-indulgent lifestyles were justified in the name of artistry. Lorraine Lion Gordon had started the ball rolling by comparing Monk's apartment to Van Gogh's. Subsequent authors and managers promoted the myth by alluding to his dancing, his hats and his erratic behaviour.

In late March 1943, when Nica was in Africa fighting for the Free French, Monk was called up and told to 'report for induction'. According to family lore, Monk told the recruiting officer that he refused to fight for an America that had kept his family in slavery and done so little to stamp out racism. He was duly classified as a 4F, a 'psychiatric reject'. It was rare for Monk to take a political stand. He did not, like many of his contemporaries, join the Nation of Islam or march for equality: his duty was to play music.

'What do you think I am, a social worker?' he told an interviewer. 'I don't care about what happens to this person, that person. I'm just busy making music and thinking about my family.'

Monk was never under any illusions about his own genius. 'I feel like I have contributed more to modern jazz than all of the other musicians combined,' he told a French jazz magazine. 'That's why I don't like to hear: "Gillespie and Parker brought the revolution to Jazz," when I know most of the ideas came from me. Dizzy and Bird did nothing for me musically, they didn't teach me anything. In fact they were the ones who came to me with questions, but they got all the credit.'

His reputation endured and among the cognoscenti he became known as the High Priest of Jazz. He taught young musicians such as the saxophonist Theodore 'Sonny' Rollins and the trumpeter Miles Davis. 'Monk taught me more than anyone on the street when I was down there. [He's] the one who really showed me everything,' Davis said.

Admiration did not equal fame or fortune. Monk became increasingly resentful as he watched Dizzy Gillespie and Charlie Parker get more work and greater accolades. In the mid-forties, Dizzy was earning thousands of dollars a week; Monk still did not have a regular gig or income. By late 1946, Monk had so little work that he let his union membership lapse. 'It's my feeling that by playing with me, by copying my harmonies, by asking me for advice, by asking me how to get the best sound, how to write good arrangements, and relying on me to correct their music, they composed themes that came directly from me . . . meanwhile I wasn't even able to find a gig. Sometimes I couldn't even enter Birdland. Do you realise what it's like for a musician to hear his own compositions and not even be able to get inside [a club]?'

Monk cut his first disc in 1948. 'Thelonious' was on the A side and 'Suburban Eyes' on the B side. Shortly afterwards he was busted for possessing marijuana and sentenced to thirty days in jail. Locked up in a tiny cell in high summer, Monk knew that following his release his cabaret card would be revoked for at least a year. His prospects were then knocked further with the publication of Leonard Feather's *Inside Bebop*, which dismissed Monk in one paragraph: 'He's written a few attractive tunes, but his lack of technique and continuity prevented him from accomplishing much as a pianist.' Running into the author early in the winter of 1949, Monk grabbed Feather and screamed at him, 'You're taking bread out of my mouth.'

Monk and Nellie married in 1948. Unable to afford a place of their own, the newly-weds lived with her sister and their children, or with his mother Barbara. Although Nellie was in severe pain for much of her life with recurring stomach problems, Monk would not seek regular employment to lighten her load or take responsibility for supporting his family: he was a musician with a mission.

Nellie and Thelonius Monk in New York.

Drug taking was an endemic part of the jazz lifestyle. Monk regularly took a cocktail of booze and Benzedrine, marijuana, heroin, acid and prescription drugs. He had a strong physical constitution but few people could cope with this onslaught of mood-altering substances. Some have tried to excuse his drug use, calling it recreational. On the night of his son's birth, Monk was holed up in a shooting alley. Nellie made her way alone to the City Hospital on 'Welfare Island', sometimes described as 'hell in mid-channel' because of its close proximity to asylums and prisons. The new baby's clothes came from the local welfare shop. As soon as she had recovered from the birth, Nellie was back at work, this time tailoring at Marvel Cleaners for $45 a week.

While music always came first, Monk placed friendship before personal freedom. On 9 August 1951, he was driving his protégé Bud Powell in New York when the police pulled them over. Powell,

Bud Powell.

a well-known addict, had a wrap of heroin in his pocket and, pan-
icking, threw the drugs out of the car window where the packet
landed at the policeman's feet. The two musicians were hauled out
of the car, slammed face down on the bonnet, kicked and then
handcuffed. Monk knew, even if the cop or Powell did not, that his
friend Bud would never survive another term in jail. Many attrib-
ute the young pianist's mental problems, suicidal tendencies and
frequent breakdowns to the severe police beatings administered
while he was in custody in 1945. At the time Powell had been sec-
tioned at Creedmoor Psychiatric Center for over a year where,
according to friends, the intensive course of electroconvulsive therapy succeeded only in impairing his memory and exacerbating his
mood swings.

Monk claimed the drugs were his. Perhaps they were but he
insisted that Bud went free. Monk was sent to the notorious Rikers
Island prison for ninety days. He was not the first, nor would he
be the last, person to be profoundly damaged by that experience.
In 1998, over forty years later, despite advances in prisoners' and,
indeed, human rights, the *New York Times* reported that 'Inmates
at the Rikers Island jail complex for years have been subjected to
impromptu beatings and planned assaults by guards, according to
court papers. In the last decade, Rikers inmates have been brutally
beaten, some suffering broken bones, ruptured eardrums or severe
head injuries.' Toot was sanguine about that period: 'Life was going
to be tough for Thelonious anyway. Thelonious was not one of
those guys who was going to toe the line or play the game.' There
was one great by-product to Monk's enforced home rest: he wrote
some of the great standards of jazz.

I saw parallels between Monk and Nica. Both were capable of
being irresponsible and leaving others to take care of basic domestic
duties. Timekeeping, a structured routine, financial responsibility
and other bourgeois attributes were anathema to both. However, on
points of principle, at moments when their highly developed sense
of right or wrong was questioned, Monk and Nica did not hesitate.

Nica fought in a war to uphold the importance of freedom; Monk went to prison to spare the life of a friend.

Unable to find Monk, Nica went back to England in 1954 to consider her future. She spent time visiting relatives and trying to sort out the details of her separation from Jules. Her siblings had scattered across the United Kingdom: Victor shuttled between Cambridge and the model eco-village that he had built at Rushbrooke in Suffolk; Miriam had started a family and was devoted to a life in science; Liberty was still in a private hospital, being treated for schizophrenia.

Nica was effectively homeless, unemployed, unemployable and at a loose end. At forty-one, with one hell of a past behind her and five children, she was hardly eligible wife material. Not only were there few options open to her but British society had changed. 'About time too,' Miriam said. The gossamer threads that had held that cosmopolitan, international world together had disintegrated after the Second World War. Nica was capable and determined but had no obvious outlet for her abilities and no way of channelling her energies. As long as she was fighting for the Free French, learning

Monk and Nellie on tour in Britain, 1968.

Nica in London's Stork Club in 1954.

to fly an aeroplane or galloping her horse at the largest fence, Nica could manage her own character. But in 1954 she was facing a void. The initial excitement of moving to New York and immersing herself in the world of jazz had waned. Later she admitted that in the vacuum she turned increasingly to drink. Those who knew her in London at that time remembered Nica in the Stork Club, always a little tight, waiting for the latest star to hit town. My belief is that Monk came along at exactly the right moment.

Hearing that her musical hero was playing in Paris, Nica jumped on the next plane. Two disparate lives were about to collide.

17

Black Bitch, White Bitch

Paris was the perfect location for Monk and Nica's first meeting. The city had lost some of its pre-war sheen but was still the capital of chic. Chanel had reopened her fashion house in 1954, introducing natty little suit jackets and slimline skirts. French movies inspired women to cut off their hair, wear cigarette pants and hooped earrings. There was an aura of tolerant multicultural- ism. Nica's friend Kenny Clarke, the bebop drummer, arrived in 1947: 'There's a difference in the mentality here. People are not afraid to walk around their neighbourhood, to become friends; socially you feel adjusted. As a black man, as a musician – as a person, I've been lucky to be able to live here.' Being a mixed-race couple did not present any problems. Observing the passionate love affair between Juliette Gréco and Miles Davis, Jean-Paul Sartre asked the trumpeter why he didn't marry her and take her back with him to New York. Miles answered, 'Because I love her too much to make her unhappy.' It was, he explained, a question of colour.

Nica flew to Paris with her new friend, the pianist Mary Lou Williams, whom she had recently met with Teddy Wilson. Born

Mary Elfrieda Scruggs in Atlanta, Georgia, Mary Lou was self-taught and by the age of six was helping to support her ten half-brothers and sisters by playing at parties. In 1925, aged only fifteen, she was part of Duke Ellington's Big Band. Nicknamed 'the little piano girl of East Liberty', Mary Lou wrote arrangements and compositions for many jazz greats and recorded over one hundred albums. One of the few women jazz artists to make it in a male-dominated world, Mary Lou and Nica became lifelong friends. Her archive, now at Rutgers University in New Jersey, contains many of Nica's letters, paintings and diary entries. A devout Catholic, Mary Lou never shied away from acting as a moral compass and confidante to her European friend. She saw no harm in introducing Nica to her friend Thelonious Monk.

By the time Monk made it on to the stage in Paris, he had smoked a lot of dope chased down with cognac. The audience had come to hear Claude Luter's Dixieland jazz and music of that ilk. They were not expecting a grunting pianist whose makeshift, under-rehearsed percussion section was out of time with Monk's wild playing. Halfway through the set Monk walked offstage to have another drink before returning to play another tune in his inimitable, discordant, dissonant style. The critics, both French and English, hated it, calling it 'startling and banal' and describing Monk as a 'kind of court jester to modern Jazz'.

Nica remembered the evening quite differently. She was enthralled; Monk surpassed all her expectations. In her opinion, the audience was bowled over. 'He played two tunes – that's all – and walked off and the audience were really grasped by it,' she said on tape. 'In fact they were yelling, "Monk, Monk", and he didn't come back but Gerry Mulligan was waiting to play so that was that.'

From that moment, Nica's life changed. The touchpaper lit when she heard the record ''Round Midnight' burst into flames upon meeting its composer. She had heard her calling with a Duke Ellington composition and now found her mission with a Monk tune. For the next twenty-eight years she would devote her life to

Thelonious Monk, laying her time and love at the musician's feet like a cloth of devotion.

After their first encounter, Nica admitted, 'I needed an interpreter to understand what he was saying at the beginning. He wasn't easy. I didn't know Thelonious's English. We hit it off and hung out for the rest of the time he was in Paris. We had a ball.' No one knows what kind of ball Monk and Nica enjoyed; perhaps they consummated their relationship, perhaps not. For her, Monk was 'the most beautiful man I have ever seen. He was a very large man, but his presence was much larger still. Any time he walked into a room he dominated it. In fact he could be sitting in a chair or lying on a bed, speaking or silent, and he still dominated any room he was in.'

Thelonious's son Toot was convinced that Nica was smitten, telling me: 'I know that your aunt fell in love with my dad, I have no doubt about that. Basically he supplied the emphasis for her to come to America. She followed him here. She didn't know anything about him, but she was profoundly moved by his music and his personality.' Was it really that simple? Toot smiled and then added, 'He was a good-looking cat, she was a hotty.'

Stanley Crouch thought that the attraction was musical. 'There is a certain kind of aristocracy in Monk's music and [the] United States is 3,000 miles away [from Paris] so it actually is possible for somebody from almost as different a background as Monk's to become entranced by his music. You see, there's always a kind of a human magic that can transcend what we know about society and relations and all that. They had that for each other.'

A week after their meeting, Monk returned to New York with a suitcase weighing twenty pounds that contained innumerable French berets, and with a bottle of cognac stuffed in each pocket. He went home to his family and a familiar existence, while Nica travelled to London. Determined to introduce Monk to a wider audience, she hired the Royal Albert Hall, the capital's premier and, at the time, largest concert hall. Holding over five thousand people, it was founded by Prince Albert specifically for the purpose of enlightening the public. Having taken over the entire venue for six Sundays in a row, Nica planned to fly Monk and his chosen backing group from New York to London. 'They were going to be called the Jazz Promenade concerts,' Nica explained nearly twenty years later, and 'they were going to be [so] people could walk around, lie down, sit down, whatever.'

Unfortunately, Nica's enthusiasm ran ahead of her. Monk might not lack a cabaret card for London but he and his colleagues still needed permits. Nica begged the immigration authorities to waive their usual restrictions, ringing every person she knew in government and in high places, but no exception was made. Without the right papers, Monk could not work in Great Britain. The authorities were prepared to consider his case but in the specified time and according to procedure. 'I had to pay for all these services and for nothing! Thelonious was very disappointed too,' Nica said phlegmatically.

Nica left London and returned to New York: she would never live in England again. It's not known whether Monk mentioned this new friend to his wife. But shortly afterwards, the residents of the San Juan district were astonished to look out of their windows and see a huge Rolls-Royce cruise into their midst, driven by a white woman in a fur coat. Toot, then aged five, has never forgotten the day.

> This was not an elegant neighbourhood so when she came rolling up into the block, it was certainly a sight to see – the whole neighbourhood knew that she was there. She acted like the car was the norm. But it wasn't normal for America at all. Everyone else's car was full of all kinds of plastic. This car was all full of wood and leather that you could really smell. She had on this crazy leopard coat. I'll bet you it was ocelot because she wouldn't wear just a leopard, it would have to be something special, something very hip.

What on earth did Nellie Monk make of this vision in a Rolls-Royce? Did she feel threatened or at least bemused? When asked, Nellie said, 'She was a good friend to us and we needed friends.' Toot Monk elaborated on his mother's explanation: 'Somewhere along the way Nellie and Nica had some kind of meeting of the minds. I don't know whether they had words over it or not, but they decided that they were going to take care of him. They shared the load equally. From the time I was about eight or nine my family was me, my mother, my father and my sister and Nica.'

Lorraine Lion Gordon, who ran the Village Vanguard, remembered, 'Nellie would be on his left and on his right the Baroness Pannonica de Koenigswarter with her cigarette holder, blowing smoke into his face. They truly were a ménage à trois. I always marvelled at that.'

Fellow musician and close friend Hampton Hawes describes driving with Monk, Nica and Nellie in the Bentley down Seventh Avenue: 'Monk feeling good, turning round to me to say, "Look at me, man, I've got a black bitch and a white bitch," and then Miles pulling alongside in the Mercedes, calling through the window in his little hoarse voice cut down [by] a throat operation, "Want to race?" Nica nodding, then turning to tell us in her prim British tones: "This time I believe I am going to beat the motherfucker."'

Nica had a piano installed in her suite and Monk spent most days there, practising and working on tunes. She loved watching him compose: 'His concentration was awesome. What was strange was that the melodies seemed to come to him in a flash, but he would spend hour after hour on the bridges, sometimes for days at a time. The inner Thelonious, the true Thelonious, where that incredible music came from, was [on] an altogether different plane to the rest of us.'

While Monk composed, Nica painted and made collages, mainly abstract works, using naptha pens or paint mixed with anything to hand. Monk told her to enter a competition: the annual art contest held at the ACA Gallery in New York. 'I only entered . . . because Thelonious dared me. They took my work absolutely seriously. When they asked me how I obtained my rather unique colours, I told them it was a secret formula, but the truth is that I used somewhat weird ingredients, anything from Scotch to milk to perfume. Anything liquid that happens to be around.' Her canvases sold out quickly but, according to her son Patrick, she spent the next few years trying to buy back her work.

Once darkness fell, Nica and Monk climbed into the Rolls and hit the town, often attending many gigs in a single night. Monk acted as her companion and teacher, introducing Nica to his friends, helping her understand the music. They were an odd couple: Thelonious and Pannonica; the High Priest and the Baroness. The good-looking cat and the hotty.

The jazz scene was intimate, with most clubs based on 52nd Street. On any night it was possible to see Sarah Vaughan, Charlie Parker, Billie Holliday, Art Tatum, Monk, Dizzy and Duke playing within yards of each other. The trombonist Curtis Fuller remembers looking out from the stand at Nica:

> There were many big limos and big stars – Ava Gardner, Frank Sinatra and so forth. They would send notes and try and get you to join their table. But when the Baroness came in and sat at her table, everything stopped. She was way above all of them. When Nica came in the place there is like a big gong going off, boom, and the word would go out that the Baroness is here. Play well, the Baroness is out front. She played the part so well. She could sit there with this thousand-foot cigarette holder and the fur coat with such elegance and you could tell at some part of her life she must have been an all-star beauty.

Late at night, after the concerts had finished, Nica invited musicians back to the Stanhope for dinner. 'We would go there once the clubs had closed,' a musician reminisced. 'We could order anything we wanted: it was steak and champagne all the way.' For Nica, the club was simply the aperitif; the main event often happened later. According to Curtis Fuller, Nica was a 'free spirit' and would lie naked in the bath, smoking and listening to the music. Monk might have been banned from the clubs but at Nica's he was the centre of an ever-changing supergroup of talent. 'All the cats came up,' Nica recalled, citing a list of legends such as Sonny Rollins, Oscar Pettiford, Art Blakey, Bud Powell and Charlie Parker.

The musician Hampton Hawes remembered dropping in on Nica one day and noting that her suite had 'a lot of paintings on funny drapes, a chandelier like an old movie palace, a Steinway concert grand in the corner. I thought, this is where you live if you own Grant's Tomb or Chase Manhattan Bank.' Hawes heard a terrible sound coming from the bedroom. Popping his head around the door, he saw the extraordinary sight of 'a body laid out on a gold bedspread, mud-stained boots sticking out from a ten-thousand-dollar mink coat'. It was only when Nica, finger to her lips, implored him to be quiet that he realised it was Thelonious, taking his afternoon nap.

Monk was used to the dedication of women. That Nica was wealthy and white had its advantages but what mattered most to Monk was that she loved his music. As his son Toot said, 'Nica was there when the critics didn't get it and half the musicians didn't get it but she got it and that was very important for her and very important for him. He loved her for that.' Monk, commenting on his new friend, said, 'She is not judgemental, she is there, she has some money which is sometimes needed. She might be helpful there, but that is not a primary thing. She's got a nice place to stay in. She can drive me places in that Bentley, which I enjoy driving, and she is a funky, nice lady.' Later he added, 'She's a Rothschild, which makes me pretty proud.'

Nica expressed her admiration for Monk in equally simple terms. She told Bruce Ricker:

He was not only unique as a musician; he was also unique as a
man. A strange word comes to mind when I think of him.
Purity. That word seems to fit him like a glove. He was uncompromisingly honest. He abhorred liars and never lied himself. If
the answer to a question meant hurting somebody's feelings, he
would remain silent and his capacity for silence was such that
many people think he never spoke. But when he was in the
mood he could talk non-stop for days on end. His mind was as
sharp as a razor and he was interested in everything from the
flight of a butterfly to politics and higher mathematics. He was
the greatest fun in the world. He would keep one laughing till
one cried.

In many ways, Nica was following in the tradition of Rothschild
women who were used to playing supportive roles to powerful
men. Like her forebears, she could make a real difference to Monk's
life and legitimately bathe in the glow of his success. 'Thelonious
was a performer and it required dedication, sacrifice and sometimes
a little genius to get him to function,' Harry Colomby explained.
'Every fight has corners, and we were the corner people. I was the
official manager, Nellie was his wife, and Nica was his friend.'
    The trombonist Curtis Fuller, who spent a lot of time with Nica
and Monk in the 1950s and 1960s, told me, 'There were no signs
of affection other than, you know, your kiss on the cheek.' When
another musician asked Monk whether he was sleeping with the
Baroness, Monk replied incredulously, 'Man, why would I do that
to my best friend?' The saxophonist Sonny Rollins told me that,
while Nica and Monk were rarely apart, they were also seldom
alone. 'We used to hang out; Monk and Nica would come to my
house and we would go out some place together and drive around
after hours until it was light.'
    In the documentary footage shot by Michael and Christian
Blackwood, the roles of Monk's two women were captured on
celluloid. Nellie, small, birdlike and as neat as a pin, fusses around

Nica and Monk. Stills from Straight, No Chaser.

Monk while he seems, if not out of it, certainly not that rooted in the present. In one scene he lies in bed with his hat on while Nellie hovers, getting his clothes ready. A waiter comes and asks him what he wants to eat and Monk, lying there naked, wearing a hat, hardly reacts. When Monk does get up he moves slowly around the room while his wife tries to help him put on his jacket. Nellie is so tiny that she has to jump up to get the coat on straight. Monk does nothing to help her. In another scene Nellie is trying to sort out tickets at the airport while Monk goofs around behind her, leaning on her shoulder, making faces at the crowd. Later he stands in the middle of the concourse and spins in a circle. Nellie puts up with his antics but her annoyance is palpable. Perhaps the most revealing moment is when Monk is dancing in a room and for no reason suddenly sweeps the ashtray off a side table on to the floor. Almost immediately Nellie's anxious face pokes through the door and looks around. What now, her expression seems to say. What is it this time?

Footage of Nica with Monk reveals a more relaxed relationship. She had the advantage of being neither his wife nor his employee. There are scenes where the two chat and hang out in the basement of a club, talking about history, about what he played that night. All the time Nica looks at him with great tenderness, never taking her eyes off him. 'He was original in his way of life,' Nica said of Monk's habits. 'He would often go for days without sleeping and he was pretty tough to keep up with that way and he just did things the way he liked doing them. Sometimes he would walk backwards instead of forwards or stop for no particular reason and twirl in the street.' Nica, however, respected the Monks' marriage and said that he and Nellie 'adored' each other.

Nellie was relieved that Monk now had somewhere else to go. For three years the family had been cooped up in their tiny apartment. Monk had also begun to display increasingly worrying behavioural traits: he would, as Nica said, stay awake for days at a time and then promptly fall asleep, or fixate on an idea. A cocktail of different drugs exacerbated these highs and lows, some prescribed, some illegal. Nellie – frequently ill, tired, worried about money and anxious for her children – was relieved that her husband had found a new friend who was prepared to drive him around and encourage him to work. Nica recalled several occasions when Nellie rang her, asking for help: 'Come immediately, Thelonious is drinking up the place, I have sent for the police.' By the time Nica reached 63rd Street, Thelonious would be calm. However, as soon as she got all the way back home, Nellie would ring again: 'Thelonious is breaking up a tree outside the Lincoln Towers. He is in his pyjamas.'

Far from being upset or irritated while recounting these stories, Nica, on tape, laughed at the memory. 'I have been in more nuthouses than you would believe. [Laughter] When you got there he would always be the centre of calm. Then he'd say, "I am nuts but every time they check me out they have to let me go so I can't be nuts, can I?"' Nica believed the doctors caused more harm than good. 'You know what they were doing? They were slugging him full of drugs and you can imagine how that would have helped.' At that time no one assumed there was much wrong with Monk: he was simply an eccentric who indulged in substance abuse.

Occasionally when Monk had a gig out of town, Nica and Nellie went too, even sharing a joke over some of his more outlandish behaviour.

One time on a flight to San Francisco, he walked from one end of the plane to the other during the entire trip. And when they started showing the film, he cast a huge shadow on it and then had to duck to get under the screen. Nellie and I were trying to pretend we didn't know him! But about an hour before we were due to arrive he came up to us and said, 'Come on, let's get out of here.'

And Nellie, horrified, said, 'But, Thelonious, we haven't landed yet!'

'Right, shut my mouth!' said Thelonious, and carried on walking.

The concert promoter George Wein, who went on tours with the Monks and Nica, and who knew all three well, is in no doubt about how the relationship worked and where Monk's priorities lay.

Thelonious loved Nellie. One day we were sitting in the tearoom on the way from London to Bristol about three o'clock in the afternoon. The sun was coming in the window and picked up Nellie's face. Thelonious turned and looked at her and said, 'You look like an angel.' It was one of the most beautiful things I saw in my life. Nellie was not a beautiful woman but she did everything for Thelonious. She put up with every single thing, and he appreciated that.

How, I asked Wein, did Nica fit into this ménage?

Thelonious respected quality. He liked the Rolls-Royce. He had the finest suits he could afford. He would put on a show. Hey, this woman was a Rothschild. A baroness, this was a great compliment to Thelonious, and particularly since she loved him and was respectful of Nellie. Nellie loved the Baroness, I mean, Nellie allowed the Baroness to do whatever she wanted to do with Thelonious and they were overwhelmed by the status of baroness. They were very keen on status.

Harry Colomby believed that Nica's life was hugely enriched by this new friendship. 'Thelonious gave her validation. Thelonious really respected who she was and what she had done, where she had come from and her understanding of the art. When Thelonious said, "Hey, she is hip," that would make cats deal with her in a very different way. Cats could not just treat her like a groupie, you know. I think the association with jazz emotionally nourished her.'

Having failed to organise the Royal Albert Hall concerts, Nica focused her efforts on the return of Monk's New York cabaret card. Introduced by New York's Mayor LaGuardia, the card was enforced from Prohibition until 1967 as a way of punishing drug users. 'It was a stone-cold rip-off used by the police to exact bribes,' the drummer Chico Hamilton said. The loss of the card spelled disaster for many careers. Billie Holiday, like Monk, lost her card for much of her career and so there were few opportunities for her to earn money or nurture an audience. Sometimes, with the help of a good lawyer and a decent bribe, cabaret cards could be reinstated earlier than the ban prescribed. Nica tried in 1954, 1955 and 1956 but still failed.

'I didn't set out to be a freedom fighter,' she told me, 'but when I got there [New York] I did see that an awful lot of help was needed.' Her visit to the tiny Monk apartment had been a revelation: Nellie Monk could not offer Nica hospitality as she had trouble putting food on her own family's table. Nica might not have been trained as a lawyer, or as a manager; she might not have been cut out for marriage or motherhood; but finally she had found a purpose and a place where she could be useful.

18

Bird

For a few months, from the end of 1954 until early 1955, the disparate elements of Nica's life united in relative harmony: Jules had been appointed France's plenipotentiary to North America and moved from Mexico to New York with their children. Although Berit, Shaun and Kari lived with their father, the whole family were, at least, in the same city.

As long as Nica was discreet, the Stanhope Hotel tolerated her chosen lifestyle. But Nica, according to the legendary producer Orrin Keepnews, 'was a pretty damn flamboyant woman who didn't give a damn what people thought. She was doing what she wanted to do and she was obviously damned aware of the power and influence that her good financial position gave her and she behaved accordingly.'

The Stanhope was a segregated hotel: black people were allowed in as servants, but not as guests. Nica had no intention of smuggling her friends up to her suite in a service elevator. She insisted that the musicians accompany her openly and that they order whatever they fancied from the bar or on room service. 'The hotel tried to get me out by doubling and tripling the rent and then moving me to smaller apartments,' Nica said. She refused to go.

An added problem for the hotel management was that many of these musicians were also drug addicts. The use of narcotics had become an endemic part of the jazz lifestyle. Some historians blame the plantation owners, who distributed free cocaine to their slaves to make them eat less and work harder. Others allude to the mob's involvement in the drug trade. From the late 1940s the mafia started dumping illegal substances in black communities. 'If you grew up in Harlem in the 1950s and were coming out of high school at three in the afternoon, there is no way you could walk two blocks without somebody offering you drugs,' the jazz historian Gary Giddins told me. In interviews with musicians, including Monk and older generations, the lament was always the same: nobody knew then that it killed you.

The most notorious drug user was Charlie 'Bird' Parker. He and Nica were acquaintances rather than close friends but, due to a series of unfortunate coincidences, his death was to become inextricably linked to Nica's life.

Parker was born in 1920 and raised in Kansas City, Missouri. His absentee father had been a promising pianist and dancer until alcoholism put an end to his career. Parker Snr ended up working as a waiter on the railways while Parker's mother worked nights at the local Western Union office. Young Charlie learned to play saxophone on a rented school instrument but he was thrown out of the school band due to his lack of obvious talent. Spurred on by this rejection, Parker spent three or four years practising fifteen hours a day to ensure that he was never evicted from another band. Handsome, charismatic, enigmatic and thrillingly gifted, Parker inspired a generation of jazz musicians. British saxophonist John Dankworth explained his genius: 'What Charlie Parker did was take popular songs, analyse each chord and create a whole new set of chords around it. It was almost mathematical and yet he touched the heart and the brain at the same time.'

At the age of eighteen, Parker was badly hurt in a car accident and was given morphine as pain relief. From then on, his life was marred by an addiction that blighted his health, his relationships and his music. Tragically, many younger musicians assumed that Parker's heroin use was the secret of his profound ability. Sonny Rollins admitted, 'Charlie Parker was our idol and one of the reasons that we got involved with the type of drug use that we were into.'

Quincy Jones was a teenager when he met his hero Charlie Parker. 'Bird said, let's go buy some weed. I said, great. Anything with Bird. I mean, *anything*: he was the man,' Jones told me, shaking his head in disbelief at his own naivety. 'We went up to Harlem in a cab and he asked how much **money** I had on me. I handed over everything. He said, wait here on this corner – I'll be back. I am standing in the rain for half an hour, forty-five minutes, two hours, until I realised what had happened. It was a painful thing to happen at that age with your idol. I had to walk from 138th street all the way down to 44th Street.' There are many similar stories. Nica knew Parker was a genius but she had also heard that he could charm money out of pockets, spirit rings off fingers and watches from wrists.

Unlike many of his friends and colleagues, Nica, always compassionate, saw the loneliness and torment that plagued Charlie Parker. Many years later she wrote a piece for Ross Russell's book *Bird Lives!*, a collection of essays and memories penned by Parker's friends and colleagues. 'For all the adulation heaped upon him by fans and musicians, Bird was lonely,' she wrote. 'I saw him standing in front of Birdland in the pouring rain and I was horrified and asked him why? And he said he had no place to go. When this happened he'd ride the subways all night. He'd ride a train to the end of the line and when he was ordered out, he would go to another train and ride back.'

When Parker knocked on her door on the night of 12 March 1955, Nica welcomed him in. It was a decision that would launch a hundred conspiracy theories and make Nica a figure of public notoriety and speculation. That evening Parker was supposed to go to Boston for a concert, but he was in a shocking state. He had

A young Charlie Parker

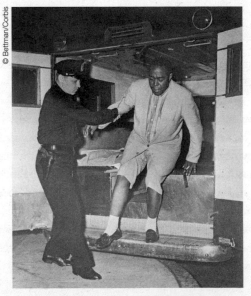

Charlie Parker shortly before his death

recently attempted to kill himself by drinking iodine following the death of his daughter Pree and the departure of his wife Chan.

Nica's friend Ira Gitler had seen him earlier that evening at Birdland. 'I got there very early and I noticed he was taking some little white pills, which, I guessed, were codeine. He was wearing bedroom slippers because he had swollen feet.' Parker stopped off at the Stanhope on his way to the station, knowing that Nica would offer him food, drink and possibly money. Unusually, Nica was at home in the Stanhope that night with her daughter Janka.*

Some believe that Parker had finally stopped using. However, his friend, the drummer Freddie Gruber, whom I tracked down in a suburb of Los Angeles, strongly refutes this claim. 'Three to four days prior to Bird's demise I ran into him on Sheridan Square. I was standing there by that cigar store and I was waiting for a "friend" of George Wallington who we both knew. Now, I was waiting for the same reason that he apparently was there.' Wanting to be absolutely clear what Gruber was saying, I asked whether this was a euphemism for meeting a drug dealer and whether they both scored heroin. Gruber confirmed that this was the case.

In Clint Eastwood's film *Bird*, based on Nica's version of the events, Parker appears at the door to Nica's suite, rain soaked and docile. He lies on her sofa watching television and is sweetly co-operative with the visiting doctor. Common sense suggests the reality was rather different. If Parker was a using addict, he would, over the next three hours, have gone through the unpleasant cycles of withdrawal, including cold turkey. With advanced cirrhosis of the liver and stomach ulcers, Parker must also have been in considerable pain.

Nica was in a difficult situation. The hotel already wanted to evict her. She was in the middle of negotiating the terms of her

---

*Birdland, the landmark jazz club on Broadway, established in 1949, named after Charlie Parker whose nickname was 'Bird'.

separation from Jules and access to her children. Her family tolerated her chosen lifestyle but insisted on discretion. A particularly
intrusive investigative journalist, Walter Winchell, had begun to
feature 'The Baroness' in his columns; his pen was poised, waiting
for a proper scandal to break. Nica knew the dangers of harbour-
ing a sick, drug-addicted musician. Trying to keep Parker's presence
a secret, Nica bypassed the hotel's medical team and arranged for
her personal physician, Dr Freymann, to examine her friend. The
doctor decided Parker must be about sixty (he was actually thirty-
four) and asked him whether he liked to drink. 'An occasional
sherry before dinner,' Parker replied, proving that even if his health
had deserted him, his sense of humour had not. It is not known
what treatment or drugs the doctor prescribed.

On that Saturday night, Nica and Janka propped Parker up in
front of the television. Mother and daughter were giving him large
amounts of water to try and quench his thirst. *The Dorsey Brothers
Stage Show* came on and during the juggling act Parker started to
laugh, then choked and suddenly died. 'It was one in the morning before the ambulance came to carry the body away. One can
imagine all sorts of things alone with death; it's dramatic enough
without special effects,' Nica said later. 'Yet I did think I heard a
clap of thunder as Bird passed away. I convinced myself finally
that I hadn't until I talked it over with my daughter, and she had
heard it too.' The clap of thunder has now passed into jazz
folklore.

Nica was catapulted into notoriety, her name becoming linked
for all time to the death of a brilliant, troubled saxophonist who
was not even a particularly close friend. Reflecting on the event,
Toot said, 'Charlie Parker was lucky that Nica was loving enough
to open up her door so he had some place to die or he would have
died in the street because there wasn't anybody else who was going
to open their door to Charlie Parker.'

Charlie Parker's death was not reported for forty-eight hours.
Nica claims that she kept it secret while she tried to find and warn

his estranged wife Chan. Others claim that those two days were needed for darker and more sinister reasons. Was she hiding evidence? Clearing the apartment of drugs? Giving others time to sort out an alibi? The sceptics ask, for example, why the medical examiner came, unusually, to the hotel room; why the body was shipped to the morgue where it lay, mislabelled, on a slab; why Parker's age was given as fifty-three. 'That's what Charlie told me,' Nica said. 'There was no indication that he was putting me on . . . He seemed quite serious about it.'

Another theory claimed that the delay was to protect her 'lover', Art Blakey, who had got into a fight with Parker over Nica and had shot or punched his rival in the stomach. Even today the rumour mills keep on churning. Recently I received an email from a distinguished American academic whose female friend claimed to be present shortly after Bird's death and, according to her, Nica shot Parker. Why, I asked, had it taken so long for this key witness to come forward and what was Nica's motive? The answer to the first part of my question was left hanging. The answer to the second question was that 'Nica disliked addicts.' More than half a century after the event, the death of Charlie Parker and the involvement of the Baroness are still generating outlandish theories.

Ira Gitler saw Nica and Art Blakey in a club the night after Parker died but before the news had broken. 'The Baroness and Art Blakey walked in and I distinctly remember she had a kind of a little leather container with a strap over her shoulder and inside were two plastic bottles. I think one was gin and one was whisky.' Nica and Blakey did not stay long. The following morning Gitler woke up to the headline, 'Charlie Parker Dies in Baroness's Apartment in the Hotel Stanhope'. 'I thought, wow, she carried herself with a lot of calm for someone who had just gone through this.'

A reporter who regularly scoured the city's morgues broke the news of Parker's death. Once the mislabelled body was correctly identified and the pieces of the jigsaw had been fitted together, the tabloids had a field day. 'The Bird in the Baroness's Boudoir' screamed one headline, another, 'Bop King Dies in Heiress's Flat'. The *New York Times*'s subheading ran: 'A Be-Bop Founder and Top Saxophonist is Stricken in Suite of Baroness'. Most reports painted Nica as the evil vamp: 'Blinded and bedazzled by this luscious, slinky, black haired, jet eyed, Circe of high society, the Yardbird was a fallen sparrow.'

CHARLIE PARKER, JAZZ MASTER, DIES

A Be-Bop Founder and Top Saxophonist Is Stricken in Suite of Baroness

Charlie Parker, one of the founders of progressive jazz, or be-bop, died here last Saturday night.

The news of the death of the noted musician, known as "The Yardbird," spread quickly last night through Tin Pan Alley, where he was affectionately referred to as "The Bird." A virtuoso of the alto saxophone, Mr. Parker was ranked with Duke Ellington, Count Basie and other outstanding Negro musicians.

Mr. Parker had appeared several times in Carnegie Hall and had played in Europe. More than five years ago the Broadway jazz hall at 1678 Broadway was named Birdland in his honor.

Mr. Parker died while watching a television program in the apartment of the Baroness de Koenigswarter in the Hotel Stanhope, 995 Fifth Avenue. He had called last Wednesday on the Baroness on his way to Boston to fill an engagement. The Baroness, who is 40 years old, is the former Kathleen Annie Pannonica Rothschild of the London branch of the international banking family of Rothschild. She and Mr. Parker had been friends for many years.

Disturbed by Mr. Parker's appearance, the Baroness called Dr. Robert Freymann, with offices in the hotel. He urged the musician not to drive to Boston and advised him to enter a hospital immediately. Mr. Parker refused but the Baroness persuaded him to stay in her suite until he recovered.

At 7:30 o'clock Saturday evening Dr. Freymann found Mr. Parker in satisfactory condition. Forty-five minutes later he collapsed and when the physician returned, Mr. Parker was pronounced dead.

Dr. Freymann, who notified the Medical Examiner, attributed death to a heart attack and cirosis of the liver. The body reached the Morgue at Bellevue Hospital at about 2 A. M. Sunday. Last night Chief Medical Examiner Milton Helpern said an autopsy had disclosed death was due to lobar pneumonia.

The police said Mr. Parker was about 53 years old. He lived with his wife Chan at 4 Barrow Street in Greenwich Village. They had three children, a son, who has just entered the Air Force; a daughter 7 and a second son, 5.

Bop King Dies in Heiress' Flat

By RICHARD KENNY and DAN MAHONEY

Jazzdom's "Bop" king, Charlie "The Bird" Parker, 53-year-old saxophonist, died Saturday night in the swank Fifth Ave. apartment of wealthy Baroness Nica Rothschild de Koenigswarter, and has lain unclaimed in Bellevue Hospital morgue ever since, it was learned Monday night.

DR. MILTON HELPERN, New York County Medical Examiner, said an autopsy completed Sunday on the famed jazzband leader showed he had died of lobar pneumonia.

The Baroness—a member of the English wing of the internationally famous House of Rothschild banking family—became Mrs. de Koeingswarter when she married a French diplomat.

Monday night she explained that Parker, "a friend of mine," had been taken ill while visiting her in her suite at the Stanhope Hotel, 995 Fifth Ave., en route to a Boston engagement, and had been treated by the hotel physican.

DR. ROBERT FREYMAN, of 9 E. 79th St., the hotel doctor, said he was summoned to the

Jazz idol, Charlie "Yardbird" Parker, died Saturday of pneumonia in the Fifth Ave. suite of Baroness de Koenigswarter.
(Hearst Photos)

*Following Parker's death in Nica's hotel room,
the newspapers went to town.*

Walter Winchell finally had Nica in his sights: 'We columned about that still married Baroness and her old fashioned Rolls Royce weeks ago – parked in front of midtown places starring Negro stars. A married jazz star died in her hotel apartment.' From that moment on, Nica became Winchell's obsession. Harry Colomby told me, 'Walter Winchell actually pursued her. He persecuted her in his column as a dealer of drugs. Oh, he made her out to be this harlot. He was the guy who literally made or broke people.'

Toot Monk explained, 'Her life became absolute hell. The black cops would stop her, saying, that's the white girl who killed Charlie Parker. The white cops would accuse her of being the woman who hung with black men. She could not win. New York was a very small community fifty years ago. There was not very much chance of the Baroness driving round in a Rolls-Royce not being noticed and people not knowing who she was. Nica paid a very dear price for her kindness.'

One of the most intriguing characters in the Parker affair was the shadowy Dr Robert Freymann. Perhaps the best first-hand account of him came from another great-aunt, this time on my mother's side, the painter Ann Dunn. She spent a lot of time in New York in the 1950s and often visited Dr Freymann's surgery on the Upper East Side.

'You'd have all the grand Park Avenue ladies sitting on one side of the waiting room and the musicians on the other, all waiting for that little injection. We used to call them "happy shots".'

What was in the injection?

'Officially they were vitamin B shots but they cost a fortune and made one feel like a million dollars, so use your imagination!'

Did the shots contain heroin?

'That and other narcotics.'

Did she ever see Nica and Monk in the doctor's waiting room?

'Frequently.'

Lorraine Lion Gordon also spotted Nica and Monk entering Freymann's office.

In Nica's correspondence with Mary Lou Williams, she said she had contracted hepatitis from one of Dr Freymann's dirty needles.

Following his arrest in 1958, the police asked Monk why his veins were scarred with track marks. Nica explained that these were the result of Dr Freymann's vitamin shots.

Dr Freymann was eventually struck off for supplying heroin to addicts.

Was my great-aunt Nica a drug addict? Did she enable her friends to use? These questions haunted my research.

Arriving in New York in the early 1950s, Nica was, at first, unaware of the consequences of addiction. The death of Parker was a terrible wake-up call and after that she tried to come to the aid of her afflicted friends. 'I used to think I could help,' she said later. 'But no one person can. They have to do it alone.'

The months following Parker's death were hard. 'I was thoroughly investigated then by the homicide and narcotics squads,' Nica said with typical insouciance. 'That was the one short period that was rather full.'

Jules, mortified and furious, started divorce proceedings, winning custody of their children. Victor Rothschild flew to New York in an attempt to persuade the Stanhope to let his sister stay on, but failed. 'After Bird died there, they chucked me out,' she said. For Thelonious, Parker's death was an inconvenience that brought the jam sessions to an abrupt end. For Nica, however, a moment of impulsive generosity had left her homeless, husbandless and hounded.

19

Pannonica

After Nica moved to the Bolivar Hotel, she and Monk chose a magnificent Steinway piano for her new suite. 'That's where he wrote "Brilliant Corners", "Bolivar Blues" and "Pannonica". And he would be up there all day long,' she reminisced.

The album *Brilliant Corners* was Monk's musical tribute to his new friend and contained the song 'Pannonica'. Only a few women received the honour of a special Monk dedication: 'Ruby My Dear' was dedicated to his first love, Ruby Richardson; 'Crepuscule with Nellie' was a love song composed for his wife; 'Booboo' was written for his daughter Barbara.

It was the first time Nica had been involved in the creation of an album, witnessing every stage from its composition to the final recording. An obsessive documentarian, she took photographs of Monk at work and recorded the practice sessions on her portable tape recorder. One of her snapshots shows Monk, Sonny Rollins and Al Timothy* rehearsing 'Brilliant Corners'. The sense of

---

*Most records prior to 1948 were pressed on to the highly brittle mixture of shellac, lamp-black and limestone. In their manufacture, gold, glass, copper, wax, nickel and

Monk and Nica, Central Park, 1956.

excitement is palpable. Monk, a cigarette hanging from his mouth, stands in the centre, staring intently at the keys and flanked by his friends. All three are united in the pursuit of a song, by their attempt to capture a musical dream. The composer David Amram was also there but out of shot. 'That was one of the most amazing things I ever heard in my life. They just kept going back and forth, stopping and starting, until they finally got to the end of the tune. Of course Monk knew it already but he was teaching Sonny.'

Monk insisted that the musicians learned the notes by heart. The music was composed in an unusual thirty- rather than thirty-two-bar structure but, when they finally got to the studio, Monk again changed the tempo and rhythm. The producer Orrin Keepnews told me it was a minor miracle that the recording was finished at all. Sonny Rollins kept pace but Oscar Pettiford and Max Roach kept threatening to walk out.

Nica played a vital role, financing some of the rehearsal sessions and even rounding up the musicians. 'It was Nica who called me up,' Sonny Rollins said, 'Nica who came and got me there.' At the time Nica was registered as a manager and licensed by the American Federation of Musicians. Her clients included Horace Silver, Hank Mobley, Sir Charles Thompson and the Jazz Messengers. 'To me,' Nica said, 'a manager should be the errand boy of the musicians. He should do the dirty work. A musician should never have to sit around a booking agent's office and try to sell himself.'

Meanwhile, an ocean away, Miriam was staring down her microscope, or noting the activities of fleas and butterflies. Both sisters had found a fulfilling, engrossing obsession and a world where they could make a difference. Miriam, I suspect, would scoff at any parallels between her and Nica. For Miriam, nothing came close to the miracle of scientific exploration, the thrill of understanding and seeing connections in the natural world. She fought hard to get the academic training required to be a pioneer in her field. She also had to overcome prejudices: some people assumed, because she was a Rothschild, that she could not be serious about work, that she did not need the money, so why should she bother? Others assumed that she could not combine research and motherhood. Only time, dedication and dogged hard work silenced her critics.

Unlike her sister, Nica approached her special subject without discipline or analysis but with equal amounts of passion and enthusiasm. For Nica, understanding the jazz family tree – the myriad relationships and influences handed on like batons between generations of musicians, across oceans and races – was every bit as fascinating as the life cycle of a flea. Both sisters made it their life's work to preserve and publish their findings. Both sisters were seeking the same outcome but in different milieus.

Nica's stay at the Bolivar was short-lived, as the other guests hated the all-night jamming sessions. Nica could not understand their antipathy. 'People complained about the noise, not realising that they were hearing this fantastic music they would never hear again in their lives and I was thrown out of there,' she said, laughing on tape at the memory.

Her next home was a small hotel famous for its literary salon, the Round Table, started by Dorothy Parker and her friends. 'I went to the Algonquin, because they were supposed to be broader-minded and they liked having geniuses there,' Nica recalled. 'But Thelonious turned out to be one genius too far for them.' At the time Nica had arranged for Nellie to have treatment in a private nursing home in Westchester. The Monk children, Toot and Barbara, stayed with relations while Monk moved between the family apartment and Nica's suite at the Algonquin.

Thelonious started walking around the corridors on other floors of the hotel, and he would be wearing a red shirt and shades and carrying a white walking stick in his hands, and he would push open the door [of someone's room] and stick his head in . . . and say, 'Nellie?' All these old ladies who had been living at the Algonquin for about fifty years got the wind up . . . and they started sending for their trunks from the attic. Saying they were cutting out.

Nica laughed while describing her friend's escapades.

I got this very polite call from the manager, saying, gee, sorry, Baroness, but Mr Monk is no longer welcome at the Algonquin. So, well, actually we got around that for a short while by sneaking in when the night manager's back was turned and walking up one flight of stairs and ringing for the elevator from there. But one day the night manager was in the elevator and he came up [with us], so we had to stop that, so I obviously wasn't going to stay there if Thelonious wasn't allowed.

It was increasingly clear that Monk could not be left alone. Behavioural traits once excused as 'eccentricities' were becoming more pronounced. What was harder to unpick was if his behaviour was the result of mental instability or drug abuse. When his mother Barbara lay ravaged by cancer in St Clare's Hospital, Thelonious refused for a long time to see her, reasoning that it would upset him more than it would comfort her. When she died on 14 December 1955, Monk was holed up in a shooting alley with some addict friends and missed the funeral completely. He just made it to the end of the wake.

His equilibrium was further rocked when the family's apartment caught fire and, although no one was hurt, their possessions – including clothes, books, furniture and Monk's music manuscripts, plus his upright piano – were all destroyed. The loss of his music was so devastating to him that Monk never again went anywhere without it.

To make getting around town easier for him, Nica bought Monk a black-and-white Buick. His first (and last) car, he spent hours aimlessly driving it around the city. Nica switched her own car from a Rolls-Royce to a silver S1 Continental Convertible that became known as the Bebop Bentley.

In early 1956, Monk played a well-received concert at the Town Hall, one of the few venues where he could perform without a cabaret card. His album *Brilliant Corners* was released to good reviews. He engaged an eager if inexperienced manager, Harry Colomby, a schoolteacher who had no experience in the music business but was a passionate supporter of Monk as well as an honourable man. Unmotivated by financial rewards, Colomby wisely did not resign from his day job and his endeavours on behalf of his eccentric client bordered, at times, on the heroic.

In spite of Nica's and Colomby's efforts, Monk still failed to get back his licence, so he spent his days composing and hanging out. Finally, when the family apartment had been renovated, the Monks were able to move back into it. To celebrate, Nica rented her friend a Steinway baby grand, an instrument that must have eaten up most of the small living space.

Shortly after Christmas 1956, Monk had his first serious breakdown. Driving through Manhattan in the Buick, he hit a patch of ice and skidded into another car. He got out and stood silently in the middle of the road. The other driver called the police, who left a note on the car: 'Psycho taken to Bellevue.'

Bellevue Psychiatric Hospital was heavily guarded and surrounded by a high fence. It often had more patients than beds but for its inmates it was easier to get checked in than checked out again. It took the combined efforts of Nellie, Nica, Dr Freymann and Harry Colomby, plus affidavits from leading producers, to persuade Bellevue to let him go.

Shortly after Monk's release (without a diagnosis), Nellie collapsed again. This time she needed an operation to remove her thyroid. Monk coped with her absence by working tirelessly on a song, 'Crepuscule with Nellie', a title suggested by Nica.

Victor Rothschild, exasperated by calls from his sister and legal summonses from hotel managers, instructed his agents to find Nica a house. In 1958, they identified the perfect property. It belonged to Josef von Sternberg, Marlene Dietrich's director, who was moving to California.

Kingswood Road, Weehawken, New Jersey. Nica's last home, 1958–88.

Nica's view over the Hudson River.

Kingswood Road is an ordinary suburban street in Weehawken, New Jersey, but number 63 has one of the most stunning urban views in the United States. Poised on a hill, the house looks across the Hudson River to the skyline of Manhattan's West Side and out towards the George Washington Bridge in the south. It is a dramatic sight at any time of day. In the early morning, the sun rises over the back of Wall Street, light catches the great plumed smokestacks and rays glint off the silver water towers crowning every downtown block. In the early dusk – the magic hour, as painters call it – the setting sun bathes the windows in a golden hue and turns the river blood red. After the sun has gone down, the vista changes to an icy blue and when darkness falls at once the whole sky shimmers with a myriad different lights. The huge tower blocks give off an opalescent glow and office windows twinkle like tiny stars. Car lights like red-and-white streaks shoot up the Westside Highway, while flashing neon signs battle with each other to seduce and entrap passing customers.

Compared to the Rothschild properties she had known since birth, Nica's new house was a modest affair: three boxy rooms stacked one on top of the other. One, almost the biggest, was the garage; a galley kitchen led directly off that and beyond it a large sitting room with a huge plate-glass window overlooked Manhattan. Upstairs there was another large bedroom, Nica's, and at the back a smaller room. When her children came to stay, the Bentley was parked in the street and the garage became a bunkroom.

I remember Nica driving me to her house in 1986; few could have forgotten it. Nica liked to maintain eye contact with her passenger at all times while holding the steering wheel with one hand and a cigarette in the other. It was incumbent on other drivers to make way, whatever side of the road Nica was on. Orrin Keepnews told me about a similar experience of his: 'She was of the opinion that it was very rude to talk to somebody without looking at them, except she was driving the car and I was a passenger in the back seat. So it was a very hair-raising conversation and I do not believe I ever rode with her again.'

My overwhelming memory of the house itself was the cats. They were everywhere; the smell was almost overpowering.

In some ways, Nica's house was like an animated version of the private museum that her uncle Walter Rothschild had founded at Tring. Her childhood playground had been the secret magical place where Walter had installed his collection. From floor to ceiling, the walls were lined with glass cases containing stuffed animals from all over the world. Tigers, lions, leopards, gorillas, polar bears, minks, whales, elephants, hummingbirds, ostriches, antelopes, fleas, butterflies: all were on display. The whole of the top floor of one wing was devoted to every type of domesticated dog from a terrier to a Great Dane.

Nica's house heaved with living cats. The ones I saw were the descendants of two valuable pedigree Siamese that had interbred, with abandon, with any passing New Jersey stray. The animals made a huge impression on Thelonious's son Toot. 'The house became this sanctuary for cats and there would be cats in every cupboard. There would be cats in the basement. There would be cats in the garage; there would be cats on the roof. We had a deal where I would count the cats and she would give me 50 cents for counting the cats. I remember I once counted, I think it was 306. That was the most I ever counted.'

Nica treated her cats rather like anyone else, being tolerant and welcoming to all but having her favourites in both human and feline form. Only the special cats, about forty in all, were allowed in her bedroom and she built barriers in flexi-glass to keep the riff-raff out.

'She knew the name of every single cat,' Monk's saxophone player Paul Jeffrey told me. 'All the cats were named after different musicians and she was very caring about these cats. One of her favourites was Cootie, named after Cootie Williams, the jazz musician. But the rest, well, they were multiplying all over the place.' Thelonious christened Nica's new home 'Catville'. Monk's biographer Robin Kelley told me that Monk was not a cat lover. 'He hated them, he absolutely hated them. But he loved her.'

Nica's Bedroom.

Nica's Uncle Walter's collection of stuffed dogs.

I asked the producer Ira Gitler, a frequent visitor to Weehawken, whether Nica's love of actual cats was in any way related to her love of musical cats. In jazz slang, a musician was often called a cat. Gitler laughed but didn't take my question very seriously. 'The term cats in jazz comes from the cat houses of New Orleans where the musicians played in the early days. That's how they started calling each other cats.' Gitler remembered that the only place Nica's feline friends weren't allowed was the Bentley. Nica had a fence built around the car in the garage so the cats could not scratch the paintwork or leather seats.

Nica's love of cats didn't stop at home. On the night I took my father and some friends to meet her, as we left the club she flipped open the trunk of the Bentley to reveal it was full of cat food. 'I stop at certain places on my way home to feed some needy strays,' she explained.

Many will place Nica in a long line of eccentric British animal lovers who prefer their company to that of people. Sometimes I wonder whether Nica's obsessive love of cats was a form of displaced maternal impulse. Although she did not live with her younger children, her letters are full of references to them and her excitement over their visits. One Christmas she wrote about painting the garage in yellow and white and making bunks for the children to sleep in. 'It was the craziest ever,' she wrote to her friend Mary Lou Williams. Toot described the wonder of the mass family Christmas where the Monk family would join Nica's and they would hang out around a tree groaning with presents.

In the spring of 1957, Monk finally regained his cabaret card and the right to play in alcohol-serving New York clubs. Almost immediately he got a gig at the Five Spot Café. Writing at that time, Joyce Johnson, Kerouac's girlfriend, said:

> The best place to end up was the Five Spot, which during the summer had materialised like an overnight miracle in a bar on Second Street and the Bowery, formerly frequented by bums. The new owners had cleaned it up a little, hauled in a piano and

hung posters on the walls advertising Tenth Street gallery open-
ings. The connection with the 'scene' was clear from the
beginning. Here for the price of a beer you could hear Coltrane
or Thelonious Monk.

Nica decided that the piano was not good enough for Monk and
bought the club a new one. The Five Spot paid Monk the quite
princely sum of $600 a week, $225 of which he kept himself and
the rest was divided between his three sidemen, who included the
drummer Roy Haynes.

Although the eighty-year-old has been a professional drummer
since 1945, Roy Haynes was still sprightly and youthful when we
met in 2004. 'When I did start to play with Monk at the Five Spot,
it was Nica who called me up. She was the one who made the deal,'
Haynes told me. 'The money was very slim, but it was great to play
with Monk. We were there for eighteen weeks at a time.'

Roy Haynes has clear memories of Nica and Monk sweeping
into the club every night. Her arrival was preceded momentarily by
a whiff of her favourite perfume, Jean Patou's Joy, a scent powerful enough to cut through any cigarette smoke.

Thelonious was usually very late. We were supposed to start at
nine. Sometimes he would get there eleven or even later with the
Baroness. They would walk in together and go right back into
the kitchen, that was the hangout, and start making hamburg-
ers. Sometimes Monk would come right in there and lie down
on the table and go to sleep. He wouldn't even talk, you know.
Nica was responsible for getting him to the club but getting him
on stage was not easy. When he was ready to wake up and play,
he would come up and play his heart out.

Bundled up against the winter cold in a huge fur coat, Nica was
often surrounded by a group of admirers. She sat in her favourite
spot nearest the stage with a Bible on the table in front of her: the

good book was a flask of whisky in disguise. Apart from the coat and a triple string of the finest pearls, Nica dressed simply, having long since ceased to be bothered with couture or hairdressers. It was not her appearance but her demeanour that most struck Roy Haynes. 'She was always smiling, you know. I will never forget that smile of hers.'

Nica captured a typical night at the club on her tape recorder. Introducing the evening in her inimitable gravelly voice, she says over the general clatter and chatter of the crowd, 'Good evening, everybody, this is Nica's tempo and tonight we are coming to you direct from the Five Spot Café and that beautiful music you hear is the Thelonious Monk quartet, Charlie Rouse on saxophone, Roy Haynes on drums and Ahmed Abdul-Malik on bass.' She pauses and the first strains of her tune, 'Pannonica', float over the ambient noise.

Then Monk starts to speak. 'Hello, everybody, Thelonious Monk here. I'd like to play a little tune I composed not so long ago dedicated to this beautiful lady here. I think her father gave her that name after a butterfly he tried to catch. Don't think he ever caught the butterfly but here's the tune I composed for her, "Pannonica".'

Monk's star was in the ascendant: he was recording and finally getting decent reviews. His manager Harry Colomby knew that there was a lot of ground to make up. 'A Thelonious Monk album would sell ten thousand copies. Forget a million, forget platinum. Jazz was a limited world with a tiny audience. Thelonious Monk was listed in the phone book as: "Monk, Thelonious". Now someone on his level today would be unlisted. Because they were poor, they wanted the phone [to be listed] for jobs.'

Colomby booked Monk to play a gig in Baltimore, Maryland. As the date got nearer, though, Monk's close circle became nervous, because he was having one of his 'mental episodes'. Colomby explained to me that periodically Monk would refuse to sleep for up to five days in a row. During that time he would wander the streets or stare catatonically out of the window, often shuffling from foot to foot, mumbling under his breath. Eventually he would fall into a deep sleep that would last twenty-four hours. Occasionally during an episode he destroyed things, objects rather than people. Once he tried to take a ceiling down in a hotel room. Another time he swept ashtrays off pianos and knocked over furniture.

Paul Jeffrey, Monk's last saxophone player, was frequently asked to watch Monk during one of his episodes. I asked him if he was ever frightened. Jeffrey shook his head. 'The Baroness told me, "He will never hurt you." She was certain so I never worried.'

The only time Monk hurt Nica was falling off stage at the Village Vanguard and landing on his patroness. 'He toppled over from the stage, on top of me, 'cause I was sitting on the table underneath,' she said, roaring with laughter.

Monk had not slept for three days before the job in Baltimore. 'We weren't in a position to cancel a job,' Colomby said. 'It is easy to say now why did we let him go? But we simply could not afford to cancel work. You just had to do it.'

20

Strange Fruit

At eleven o'clock on the morning of Wednesday 15 October, 1958, Nica drove out of New York City and into a whole lot of trouble. She had always, her contemporaries recalled, been a mischief magnet, the kind of child who climbed too high in trees, the sort of young woman who gave her chaperone the slip, the type of wife and mother who thought a regular routine was a death knell rather than an achievement. On this occasion the fortuitous combination of luck, breeding and charm that normally got Nica out of difficulty failed her, and for the first time in her life being white, rich, beautiful, British, well connected, female, titled and even perhaps innocent, counted for nothing. Although the Baroness left New York a free woman she would soon be caught up in a chain of events that would lead to a spectre not only of personal disaster but also of the end of the life she'd chosen, a life for which she'd sacrificed so much.

After a series of delays that morning, Nica pointed her Bentley Convertible downtown and left Manhattan via the Lincoln Tunnel, bound for a jazz club some three hundred miles south-east in Delaware, Maryland. In the back of the car was the young tenor saxophonist Charlie Rouse and in the front seat was Monk. In Clint

*Nica and Monk with her 'Bebop' Bentley outside
the Five Spot Café, New York, 1964.*

Eastwood's storeroom, I found transcripts of interviews with Rouse and Colomby relating to this incident. In the Baltimore archives, the courtroom transcripts still exist and, using these sources, I was able to piece together what happened next.

The atmosphere in the car was tense. The trio had set off late and were unlikely to make Baltimore for a sound check, let alone a rehearsal. Neither the Baroness nor Monk was used to rising before noon and their departure had been further delayed when Monk insisted on trying on several suits and a variety of hats. Nellie, who normally chose his clothes and helped him dress, was unwell. That day Monk was particularly taciturn, not having slept for fifty-two hours. His manager Harry Colomby agonised about cancelling the gig but eventually decided to take the risk on the condition that Nica drove him and never left his side.

Nica understood how much the Baltimore gig meant to Monk. Since the return of his cabaret card in 1957, every concert from that day onwards, however small, represented a precious financial and emotional fillip. He had been off the scene for over seven years, and it was vital to keep him playing and to recapture his lost audience.

Determined to keep Monk's spirits up during the journey, Nica wedged the steering wheel under her right knee and, leaning into the back of the car, pressed the play button on her portable eight-track recorder. She often played back some of his recordings to boost Monk's morale. She chose the track 'Pannonica', played most nights in the Five Spot Café.

'Good evening, everybody,' her distinctive voice reverberated around the car out of the machine.

Twenty years later, in an interview for the documentary *Straight, No Chaser*, Charlie Rouse remembered those few hours clearly.

'Isn't it beautiful?' Nica turned to Rouse who was sitting alone in the back seat.

Realising that he was the only person looking at the oncoming traffic, Rouse whispered urgently, 'Baroness!'

'What?' she replied, still leaning over the seat, trying to adjust the volume.

Rouse gesticulated towards an oncoming truck. Nica wrenched the wheel and the Bentley swerved back to its own side of the road, narrowly avoiding a major collision. To calm her nerves, she took a swig of whisky from a hip flask.

Within half an hour they had left the New Jersey Turnpike for Interstate 295 and the car was cruising comfortably at ninety miles per hour. Nica turned on the lunchtime news. That day CBC Radio reported that in Japan the death toll from Hurricane Ida had risen to 1,200. President Eisenhower was due to address the Senate on reports coming out of the USSR that nuclear tests had been performed at Novaya Zemlya, while BOAC's new service offering passenger flights across the Atlantic was proving to be a smash hit. John Hamilton, the well-loved actor from *Superman*, had died that morning, aged sixty-one. For the fourth week running, the number one hit was Domenico Modugno singing 'Volare'.

They had been driving for just over two hours when Monk spoke for the first time that day.

'I need to stop.'

Monk's prostate problem would increasingly impact on his life and career, making travelling for any distance and eventually sitting at a piano uncomfortable.

'We're only six miles from Wilmington. I know a place there,' Rouse piped up from the back seat.

'Stop,' Monk insisted.

Nica exchanged looks with Rouse in the rear-view mirror. All three understood that finding a suitable place for Monk to use a bathroom wasn't going to be easy. They were west of the Mason-Dixon line, technically in the more emancipated North, but the state's fortunes had been built on agriculture and slavery, so traditionally it sided with the South. Racial prejudice was the norm rather than the exception.

To a casual observer, New Castle was a quaint, unassuming town, red-bricked and clapboarded, with an annual chicken festival and a factory cranking out the finest nylon stockings. However, public whipping and segregated schools had only recently been abolished and racially segregated accommodation and bars were still commonplace. As Nica drove her car down Main Street, she looked in vain for an establishment that would allow Monk to use its facilities. The inhabitants of New Castle stopped and stared. The sight of a Bentley Convertible in itself was a surprise. The sight of this grand European car being driven by a woman in a fur coat was an event. But the sight of a Bentley being driven by a woman in a fur coat with two black men was a spectacle.

It took only a glance to see that the Cherry Corner Soda Shop on 2nd and Cherry Street would not let Monk use its facilities. Hostile white faces stared in outrage at the car. Comegy's Oyster House on 12th looked equally uninviting and only white faces were visible in the Deerhead Hotdog Store, Eddie's Soda Fountain and Peterson's House of Fudge. The only coloured faces at Baker Ben, at Gino's and at the Charcoal Pit on Maryland Avenue were those cleaning the stoop.

Heading out on Route 40, Nica caught sight of the Plaza Motel and pulled off the road. Contemporary postcards reveal a low, orange-roofed building arranged in a horseshoe around a reception area. A sign proclaimed 'All welcome'. Nica ignored the neatly painted parking spaces, headed straight for the front door, mounted the pavement with the Bentley's nearside tyres and, yanking the handbrake up with both hands, came to an abrupt stop right by the entrance. 'She'd park by crossings, in front of fire hydrants, you name it, she ignored the rules,' one frequent, and intrepid, passenger confirmed. Monk, as usual, looked smart in a homburg, a beige suit, black shirt and black pencil tie but, at a little over six foot two and weighing 250 pounds he cut an imposing figure. Getting out of the car, he walked into the motel, past the desk clerk and towards the cloakrooms.

'All he wanted was to use the bathroom,' Rouse later reported. 'He wasn't threatening nobody. Delaware is a little prejudiced, a little backward, so I see what happened next as a racist thing.'

'The average cop down the street seeing a black guy and a white woman would probably be enraged,' Colomby added. 'Even in Greenwich Village at that time, when the older folks used to see the interracial couples, they went nuts.'

Nica and Rouse sat in the car waiting. Every minute that passed spelled trouble.

Rouse spotted the state trooper's car first. It passed the motel a few times, back and forth, like a great white circling its prey, then pulled in about twenty yards down the road. Nica saw a middle-aged man through her rear-view mirror. These were the types that you had to watch out for, musicians later told me, the ones who had missed promotion, who were finally forced to accept that their careers were on a fast track to nowhere and who'd decided social progress was firmly to blame.

Monk had used the bathroom but now he wanted water. He was sweating in the afternoon sun but perfectly calm.

'Water,' he said to the woman at the check-in desk. She could not understand his way of speaking; few could.

'Water,' Monk repeated loudly.

The woman began to feel scared.
'Water.' She rang the police.

Half a century later I read my great-aunt's own account of the events that followed, notated in the transcript of the final appeal:

Q: When if at all did you see Officer Littel drive up in his troop car for the first time on October 15th, 1958?

Nica: I think it was about 1.15 and I saw Officer Littel drive up in his troop car and park a little way in front of me.

Q.   What, if anything, did you observe Officer Littel do after he drove up in his troop car and, if anything, which you also heard him say?

Nica: He got out of his car and came back to my car on the side on which Monk was sitting and asked him to get out.

Q: What, if anything, did Monk do when the officer asked him to get out?

Nica: He didn't do anything. He just stared at Trooper Littel and didn't move.

Q: What conversation, if any, did you have with Trooper Littel at this time?

Nica: After Trooper Littel asked him a second time to get out and he didn't move, I got out of my side of the car and went around the back to Trooper Littel and asked him what was wrong. Because I hadn't seen anything happen, and I told him that Thelonious Monk was a very well-known musician and I was his manager licensed by the American Federation [of] Musicians and we were going to Baltimore for an engagement.

Q: What, if anything, did Trooper Littel reply to you?

Nica: He said, 'All right' and went back to his car.

Putting the Bentley into first gear, Nica flipped the indicator and slowly pulled out on to the highway. The signpost showed how far it was to New York; they were on the right road but facing in the wrong direction. Nica made a U-turn. As they passed the patrol car again, all three noticed that the officer was still on his radio. Moments later they heard the siren. In her rearview mirror Nica saw the patrol car also make a U-turn and speed towards them. Drawing up beside the Bentley, Littel stabbed his finger towards the kerb and on his loudspeaker instructed the Baroness to pull over. No one in the Bentley spoke. This time the troop car parked right in front of the Bentley. The officer got out of the car carrying a pair of handcuffs and yanked open the front passenger door. He tried to cuff Monk but the musician sat on his hands and turned his large frame away from the trooper.

Q: Did there come a time when the musician used a profanity in Trooper Littel's presence?

Nica: It is possible he said, 'What the hell,' or something like that.

Q: What conversation if any did you have with Trooper Littel at this time?

Nica: I said, 'What are you doing this for?' And he said, 'Because he's under arrest.'

Littel straightened up and slowly walked around the car. 'Driver's licence and registration,' he commanded rather than asked and then took the keys out of the ignition before returning to his own vehicle. Rouse, Nica and Monk watched in silence as Littel picked up his handset and radioed for help.

Q: What did you do next?

Nica: I got out of my car, went over to his and pleaded with him to take no further action. I assured him that if I asked Monk, he would get out of the car, if that is what he wanted.

Q: What was the trooper's reply, if any?

Nica: He said, 'He'll get out all right.'

Q: After this conversation what did you do next?

Nica: I returned to my car but by that time there were already other troop cars arriving and lots of troopers got out.

Q: After the other troopers arrived would you describe to His Honour what took place in connection with them and Monk at your car.

Nica: Three or four of them started trying to drag Monk out of the car and he resisted, and they began to hit him with coshes and blackjacks, and I asked them not to do it and be very careful of his hands because he was a pianist.

Rouse later said that at first Nica did ask the troopers to be careful with Monk's hands, but when they ignored her and thunked the leather-covered lead down on to his fingers, she begged them to stop. 'Soon she was screaming and begging, "Protect his hands, please protect his hands."'

Nica: They didn't take any notice and they finally dragged him out of the car, and they were on top of him on the ground, beating him, and they handcuffed him with his hands behind his back and dragged him to Officer Littel's car and tried to get him in the back . . . I went over to a detective and said, please, I don't want him to get hurt any more. Then I went over to my car but Officer Littel approached me and said, 'You are under arrest too.'

Monk lost consciousness, probably following a trooper's use of a beavertail sap with a flat profile. Once his body crumpled the troopers lifted Monk's legs over his head and just closed the door on him. Detective Eckrich agreed to let Nica drive the Bentley to the local courtroom; Rouse was also arrested and transferred to another trooper's car.

Not long after the Baroness and the musicians arrived at the local courthouse, news of the arrest had spread. The troopers told their families to come and see that day's catch. Snotty-nosed kids pressed their faces against the window to get a better look at Monk, who was now conscious but in serious pain. There was nothing the Baroness could do apart from ask repeatedly to use a phone to call her lawyer. Rouse, also handcuffed for good measure, was held in another room.

'What is the charge?' Nica kept asking.

'Can we look in your pocketbook?'

'If you mean, can you search my handbag, then here it is. But can we please get a doctor for Mr Monk. He's sick. Surely you can see he's sick? We'll plead guilty. Let us pay the fine and let us go.'

'We need to search your car.'

'Go ahead.'

Things were about to get significantly worse.

Nica followed the officers outside and sat on the bank, watching. She took out her sketchbook and began to doodle.

Q: How did you happen to have a pad with you?

Nica: I always have a pad with me, and when I am under stress and strain I usually start doodling. That's what I was doing.

Q: At the time the officers took your luggage out of the car, you knew, did you not, that the Indian hemp was in the suitcase.

Nica: Yes.

Q: (continuing): Why, Baroness, did you not refuse, if you had any choice, to let them make these searches?

Nica: I was surrounded by police officers and troopers and detectives, and I was rather frightened. I had asked for my attorney and had been told I couldn't telephone and I was really rather frightened and confused at this time and I

> just didn't think there was any alternative to allowing
> them to search.

Q: Did you believe that you had a choice as to whether you
        could allow them to search or not search?

Nica: No.

Q: No choice?

Nica: No.

Q: (continuing): After you arrived at Judge Hatton's, when,
        if at all, did you ask to use the telephone other than to
        call your lawyer?

Nica: I asked several times. When they found the needle marks
        on Monk, I wanted to call the doctor because I knew the
        doctor could explain the vitamin injections Monk was
        getting.

Monk was not only sweating but had track marks on his arms. It
needed little more to convince the police that they had another
junkie on their hands.

Then they found marijuana in the car, which in those days was
classified as a narcotic; those found in possession faced imprisonment. Fully aware of what she was doing, Nica claimed that the
dope was hers.

Harry Colomby was teaching a class when he was summoned to
the telephone. 'Normally I wouldn't take it but on that occasion . . .' He still remembers the phone call, the absolute despair
that he felt and his lingering incredulity at the injustice of the
system. 'They even impounded the car; the car became a witness.'

Colomby described having to go back to his classroom and hear
the students discuss literature but only being able to think that
Monk would once again forfeit his cabaret card and his livelihood.
Since getting back his licence to perform, Monk had had about fifteen months to build up an audience. 'The response was staggering,
it was great,' Colomby remembered. 'The word was out; it was like

a conversion, yes, that's the word. Because for all those years he'd been an artist who had never had his due in terms of recognition and that was changing. Thelonious was vindicated. Then this happened.'

'But Nica said that the drugs were hers so surely Monk got off?' I asked.

'Yeah, she took the rap, but that didn't mean anything.'

It meant everything to Nica. The consequences for her were appalling. She faced a long prison sentence of up to ten years, a large fine and then, on her release, immediate deportation. Her family had tolerated the death of an infamous, married, drug-addicted musician in her suite, but how would they treat her imprisonment for drugs? Would they cut her off finally and ostracise her? Jules had custody of their children but, up to now, he had allowed Nica limited access. If his former wife was found guilty, would Jules allow her to see their children at all? How many friends and relations would trek to a jail to visit her? If Nica lost the

Nica, seconds after being charged, October 1958.

case, her life with Monk was finished. She was suspended between two worlds, the one that she had rejected and the other that she had come to love. Her future lay in the hands of lawyers and judges, and this time there was nothing that her influential family could do to help.

I wondered why Nica risked so much. Was the explanation simply that she loved Monk and was prepared to give up everything to spare him going to jail? One of her oldest friends, the historian Dan Morgenstern, told me: 'She was prepared to sacrifice herself for him. She did not think twice about it. That was what she was like, the way she looked at things. That was the way she was.'

BARONESS SENTENCED

Gets 3-Year Jail Term, $3,000 Fine in Narcotics Case

WILMINGTON, Del., April 21 (UPI)—Baroness Kathleen Rothschild de Koenigswarter was sentenced to three years in prison today for having $10 worth of marijuana in her car when she was arrested in 1958 with Thelonius Monk, Negro pianist, and another musician.

The 46-year-old mother of five also was fined $3,000 for illegal possession of narcotics. She was released in $10,000 bail after her attorney, Arthur J. Sullivan, said he would appeal to Superior Court.

Mr. Monk and Charles Rouse, also a Negro, were arrested with the baroness but later were released.

Mr. Sullivan said the baroness, who now lives in Weehawken, N. J., served five years with the Free French forces in Africa, Italy and France during World War II.

He said her three younger children live in Paris with their father, the baroness' former husband. The other two children, a son, 23, and a daughter, 21, live in this country.

The New York Times *reports the outcome of Nica's trial.*

21

Blood, Sweat and Tears

Nica was found guilty as charged on 21 April 1959. She was sentenced to three years in prison and fined $3,000. On the day of her release, two policemen would accompany her to the airport and put her on a plane to England. She would be forbidden from returning to America.

Although the Rothschild family could not protect Nica from prison or ignominy, they did engage a top criminal attorney to represent her appeal. Moments after the sentence was passed, her defence lawyer Arthur J. Clark argued passionately for a deferment and retrial. The judge reluctantly agreed to send Nica's case to the Supreme Court, and she was released pending retrial. Victor put up bail of $10,000. Nica was temporarily free but for the next two years the prospect of a prison sentence hung over her.

'Such a bore, I can't be bothered to talk about it,' was Nica's reaction, twenty years later, to a question about the Delaware incident. I didn't, for one second, believe her. 'Such a bore' was exactly the phrase her sister Miriam used when age robbed her of her eyesight. 'Such a bore' was what my grandmother said to describe her diagnosis with cancer. 'Such a bore' is merely a figure of speech used by a generation who were never given the language or permission to express their feelings adequately. I had heard 'such a bore' enough to know that it was a metaphor for fear.

Rather than reject Nica, the Rothschilds made a renewed effort to understand her. 'Everyone got the message . . . they all got to realise what was going on and [that] Thelonious was something important to my life,' Nica said. One of her first visitors was her sister Miriam, who came to New York with her son Charlie, claiming they were 'dying to meet' Thelonious. Nica admitted the visit did not go smoothly. 'I went to get Thelonious from 63rd Street and he was as high as a kite. He got high because he was worried about meeting Miriam and nothing on earth would make him sit down. He never came down to earth the whole time.'

Miriam, Nica said, was 'frankly cool about it and said, "Don't worry, I understand, he is a genius" and all that stuff.' Miriam rarely went back to 'Catville', although the sisters kept in regular contact. Nica and her children would visit Ashton several times over the next twenty years.

Victor tried to impress his sister by making a musical connection with Thelonious, recording his own attempt to play a Monk composition. Victor was delighted with his effort; Monk thought it appallingly amateur and responded by sending back a spoof of Victor's tribute. Nica later said that her brother 'never recovered from Thelonious's impersonation; he almost gave up the ghost. It was hilariously funny, his imitation. I have got that on tape somewhere.'

For the next two years, while the case was waiting to be heard, Nica's family and friends begged her to flee the country to avoid the trial. To be certain of keeping out of jail, she simply had to go back to England and start again. Nica had not fought for freedom in the Second World War to run away now. For her, the case was not really about a few dollars' worth of marijuana; it was what happened when white and black people became friends.

Nica with her children: Janka, Shaun, Berit and Kari in 1957.

I found one of Nica's paintings in Mary Lou Williams's archive at Rutgers University. Although abstract, it depicts two figures hanging from trees in a sea of blood-red gloom. The composition was based on a well-known photograph of the lynching of two young black men, Thomas Shipp and Abram Smith. The same image prompted the Jewish schoolteacher Abel Meeropol to write the song 'Strange Fruit'. Nica's painting was her pictorial protest against racism and against her arrest in Delaware. In the corner she scribbled the words 'Strange Fruit' and the date, October 1958.

I wondered whether there were parallels between the Jewish and the African-American experience of prejudice. Was it possible that Nica understood, through family and even through personal experience, something of what her new-found friends had to endure? I put this question to Miriam.

'It's all the same really. That's how the human race works. The office boy has got to kick the cat. Everybody has got to have something below them that they can either bully or torment or kick. It is just unlucky if you are Jewish because you are one of the easiest things to boot downstairs. The next day it will be the Negroes and the next day it will be something else. The human race always needs something on which to vent its anger at what life is like.'

I asked Quincy Jones whether he could explain the roots of racism and whether there were parallels between the experiences of those two groups. He echoed Miriam's words: 'Yes. It's all part of the same psychological disease. Make yourself feel like a giant by making other people midgets.' Did he think that Nica understood what he and his friends were going through? 'Of course she did.'

Following her arrest in 1958, Nica increased her efforts to help the jazz community. Driving her Bentley into the rougher neighbourhoods, she would park and, leaving the engine running, go in search of a 'cat in trouble'. Wearing her fur coat and pearls, she cut an eccentric figure striding through the drug dens and tenements. Once she spent several days looking for the pianist Bud Powell, who had drunk all her Rothschild wine before heading for the city to score heroin. Nica found him destitute on a street corner but Powell, despite his friends' best efforts, was beyond help. She gave him a bed and food but the musician died from a lethal combination of TB and liver failure due to alcoholism and malnutrition. Nica paid for his funeral in Harlem, where a thousand mourners followed a band playing 'I'll Be Seeing You' and ''Round Midnight'. Thanks to her inheritance, she was able to dignify the deaths of other musician friends such as the pianist Sonny Clark and the tenor player Coleman Hawkins by arranging proper funerals and burial grounds. Sometimes her charity was more practical: Lionel Hampton was one of the musicians she taught to read.

She showed no qualms about using the cachet of her name and title to defend those in need. Her headed notepaper bore a crest and the name 'The Baroness de Koenigswarter' in bold blue ink. If she was writing to a close friend she sometimes printed cat's paws on the paper; for fellow jazz lovers she drew piano keys. When a jazz critic announced that Coleman Hawkins had displayed an alcoholic death wish, she rang her friend Dan Morgenstern who worked at *Downbeat* magazine to insist that he print her rebuttal. Her letter appeared in the next issue: 'On the contrary . . . like his music, it's the kind of sound to make the dead rise up from their graves and begin dancing! It makes you dig that you, yourself, were less alive before you heard it.'

Perhaps wanting attention, or recognition, or just to have some positive press attention, she co-operated fully with Nat Hentoff for an article in *Esquire* published in 1960. 'She used to post little notes through my letter box, asking if I had considered this or that,' Hentoff told me. Published between her arrest in 1958 and before her case went to the Supreme Court in 1962, Hentoff's article is full of personal insights into Nica's background, the end of her marriage and her relationship with Monk and other musicians. Although it contained a few barbed comments, the article served Nica well, showing another side to her, portraying her as naïve and 'goofy' but well meaning.

However, many reviled Nica's behaviour and chosen lifestyle: 'They shouted at her, "nigger lover",' her friend the trombonist Curtis Fuller recalled. 'The Baroness went through quite a bit and we could appreciate what it was like. We would have fought to the death for her if someone insulted or hurt her. She was our pride and she was our light; she gave us a light because she had status.'

Although race relations became easier during the 1960s when love was supposed to be 'free', mixed-race relationships and mixed-race children were unusual. Until the Civil Rights Act in 1968 laws criminalising interracial marriage and allowing racial segregation were enforced in some Southern American states. Nica's daughter

Janka and the drummer Clifford Jarvis gave birth to a mixed-race son, Steven, in 1964. The couple never lived together and Steven grew up with his mother and grandmother in 'Catville'. Attending a school in New York, Steven was, he told me, bullied and victimised because of his mixed-race heritage. On one occasion a black female singer called his grandmother 'an aristocratic misogynistic slut'. Steven was appalled and deeply upset. 'I was so dumbfounded. [It was as if] she sliced me open with a knife. Ever since then I have become sensitive to that, you know, reputation of my grandmother's and I felt really injured by it. I found out that this is not an uncommonly held view.'

I asked the British photographer Val Wilmer, who spent a lot of time in New York in the 1960s, what her experience as a white

© Private Collection

Nica with Charles Mingus in a record store.

woman in the jazz world had been. 'When I first went to New York in 1962 there were many bars where women would not be served on their own, because the implication was that you were a prostitute. White women who mixed with black men were in a very difficult situation because although the jazz world was more liberal, more progressive than other sectors of society, there was still enormous racism and sexism.'

The black journal *The Liberator* published a piece accusing money-hungry agents, club owners and women like the Baroness Pannonica de Koenigswarter of making ruthless demands of hapless musicians. Nica served as a 'bitter insinuation that a rich white woman is the black man's salvation'. Amiri Baraka, the poet and activist formerly known as LeRoi Jones, was equally dismissive. 'She was a wealthy dilettante and a groupie. That is the kindest thing I could say, that she was somebody who had the wherewithal to be where she wanted to be and do what she wanted to do.' A Rothschild relation, hearing that I was writing a book about Nica, wrote, 'She was not even interesting. She just lay in bed and listened to music.'

Nica was pilloried in fiction. The South American writer Julio Cortázar published a collection of short stories containing 'The Pursuer', about a doomed saxophone player by the name of Johnny (Charlie Parker) and a group of hangers-on led by a particularly creepy Marquesa Tica (Baroness Nica) who settles among jazz musicians to boost her own rather vapid life as another groupie. The narrator explains, 'We're a bunch of egotists; under the pretext of watching out for Johnny what we're doing is protecting our idea of him, getting ourselves ready for the pleasure Johnny's going to give us, to reflect the brilliance from the statue we've erected among us all and defend it till the last gasp.' Johnny's girlfriend, a woman called Deedee, singles out the Marquesa character in particular: 'Tica's doing very well,' Deedee said bitterly. 'Of course it's easy for her. She always arrives at the last minute and all she has to do is open her handbag and it's all fixed up.'

Her friend Mary Lou offered Nica the following advice:

People will say unpleasant things through jealousy etc but you must remember that a star is made and everyone wants to meet you as much as they do Duke Ellington or Monk . . . So what are you gonna do about it? You cannot change it . . . so learn to live with it and laugh, the way you do. You are one of the Rothschilds, this makes you a target. The Duponts, Fords, Rocks [Rockefellers] . . . smile and all the greedy rich folks are at each other's necks to keep all the loot in their pockets. You may seem notorious to them but look at them, they are murderers of men's souls. You are very kind to those you love.

The saxophonist and human rights activist Archie Shepp was impressed by Nica's courage.

She was a woman who was ahead of her time. She took a stand when it wasn't popular to do so. Actually she stands as a role model. One of the early feminists who not only served her right to be herself, but to see herself as a person who implemented social change and that social change was possible from her class. By being associated where people like her were never seen and standing up when she saw injustice, she impressed my entire community with a sense of democracy.

Nica was an instinctive rather than a political animal. Avoiding self-reflection or organised causes, she was whimsical and impulsive. If there was a situation where she could help, she waded in regardless of the consequences. There was no attempt to systematise her actions or organise a strategy.

The world was changing while Nica was stuck in a bebop time warp, apparently oblivious to the musical, social and political revolution unfolding around her. Monk's music was no longer new wave; it was old hat. It had been superseded by rock and pop and cool jazz. Monk believed that Miles Davis had sold out rather than

Monk and Nica backstage.

progressed and that new practitioners of jazz such as Ornette Coleman were dismissible. Nica agreed with him: after all, he was her teacher, her guide. Outside of 63 Kingswood Road, society and music was changing. Elvis vied with Chuck Berry and the Beatles took on the beatniks. The Rolling Stones rubbed shoulders with Andy Warhol; Tamla Motown and Phil Spector hogged the airwaves while Frank Stella and Jasper Johns amazed the museums. The election of John F. Kennedy and the clarion call of Martin Luther King promised to erase the stains of political injustice. Men had even landed on the moon.

All this seemed to pass Nica right by. The co-ordinates of her life barely changed: she slept till late and drove into town at night. She was focused on Monk, his music and his mayhem. Whatever was going on outside, Nica's private collection of photographs show that life in 'Catville' hardly changed. In them, the clothes people wore, their hairstyles and wrinkles show the passing of time but otherwise number 63 Kingswood Road seems frozen in the fifties. Nica was the Miss Havisham of bebop.

There was one event she could not ignore: her forthcoming trial at the Supreme Court. The date was eventually set for 15 January 1962. The night before, she wrote the following letter to Mary Lou Williams:

Today is the day upon which my entire future may well depend. At this very moment it may well be being decided. Release, miraculous escape, the chance to start afresh with a clean slate or the onset of inevitable catastrophe, the beginning of the end. I don't mention it to Thelonious or Nellie or anyone else. And now I sit outside St Martin's and wonder which of them has any idea of what I'm going through today. And as for Thelonious, well, his protection is at the root of the whole business and I have never discussed it with him. And I don't think he's really aware of it. He and Nellie have enough problems as it is. I have been sitting here for almost two hours and it is very cold. So now I am going in to light a candle to St Martin.

So there it was: she was facing 'the beginning of the end'. Nica was truly scared and had no one to turn to. She had gone back to Baltimore to stand trial and hear her sentence alone; there were no family members or friends by her side, no one to wave her off as she confronted the possibility of leaving the courtroom only to be sent directly to the clink. 'And now I sit outside St Martin's and wonder which of them has any idea what I'm going through today.'

How extraordinary and heartbreaking that someone whose house was Party Central, a place where others went to have a good time, to eat and make music, should have had to face her darkest hour alone. Where, I wondered, were those people whom she had so generously helped? If found guilty, Nica would go straight from the dock to the jail; then, after serving her term, she would be deported. With no one to turn to in person, she had to write her feelings down. Nica planned to send the letter only if she was found guilty. If set free, she would destroy it.* She had been taught from an early age not to display emotion and not to talk about her feelings. When, as a young woman, she crossed war-torn France, avoided the Nazis and got her children to safety in England, her mother had praised her for 'looking fresh as a daisy'.

Both Monk and Nellie were battling with ill health. Following the Baltimore arrest, Monk had one of his most serious breakdowns and was placed in a mental asylum where he remained for several months. Nellie suffered from recurring stomach pains and had to send her children to stay with her in-laws while she fought to regain her health. At this point I began to wonder about the relationship between Nica and the Monks. Was Nica being used or simply allowing herself to be used? Their relationship, in her hour of need, seemed to be rather one-sided. Perhaps Nica herself had set these distant personal parameters; perhaps the lack of intimacy suited her. The alternative was too painful to contemplate. I did not want to believe that Nica, naive and desperate, was just another groupie, a patsy to be pitied.

The night before Nica's case came to court, she suffered a further setback when, at the last minute, her distinguished trial lawyer, Mr Bennett Williams, failed to appear. She was represented instead by two of his associates who were far less familiar with the case. It was an unusually cold January with snowfalls recorded as far south as Pensacola, Florida, and as far west as Long Beach, California, but the courtroom was crammed with onlookers. Children had been given the day off school and the troopers' wives came dressed in all their finery to see what promised to be a great show: the sentencing

sometimes chromium were used by skilled craftsmen who had to operate machinery to skilfully squeeze the sound into a scratch. It was such an exacting and fiddly

of a British aristocrat who smoked a cigarette in a long holder and drove a fancy European car. As the defendant had already admitted that the narcotics were hers, most assumed the outcome was assured and it was worth taking the day off to enjoy her humiliation.

The judge, the Hon. Andrew Christie, presided over his jury and a packed courtroom and frequently had to call the crowds to order. Despite her admitted guilt, Nica's advocates fought the case on a technicality, arguing that the police had failed to follow the correct procedure. While arresting the defendant, the troopers had searched Nica's handbag and car without her full permission. The judge was forced reluctantly to agree. The courtroom vibrated with disbelief and disappointment.

The case was dismissed. Nica was free.

Later she told Max Gordon, 'Darling, I never dreamed Delaware could be such a mean, uptight little state.'

Although Nica was released and had taken full responsibility for possession of the drugs, Monk still lost his cabaret card. Once again he was banned from the clubs. Nica engaged an attorney to represent Monk to fight, 'blood, sweat and tears', for justice and to repeal the police decision.

22

Gotten Me Crazy

Nica was fifty. Athough linked to Monk via his composition 'Pannonica', she longed for more involvement in his work. She had risked her freedom for this musician but had no official role: he already had a wife and a manager. Nica wanted to be recognised as more than his groupie. At times, Harry Colomby admitted, Nica made his job harder. 'Sometimes she could be an absolute pain in the arse,' he said. 'We'd be trying to get on with work and she would whisper some conspiracy theory in Monk's ear about who was doing what.'

'I really want to do an album cover for him,' she wrote to the producer Ted Macero, as it 'would make up for the disappointment of having had one of my paintings chosen by Charlie Parker for a record that was never made'. When Macero arranged to meet Nica to go through some of her artworks, she failed to keep the appointment. Macero had to choose one of her photographs instead.

Frustrated but undeterred, Nica sent him a rambling and fulsome eulogy about Monk that the producer edited and used as the sleeve notes for Monk's 1963 album, *Criss Cross*. She starts by

Nica and Monk in a recording studio.

comparing Thelonious to Bartók: 'Monk's name is synonymous with "genius"; Thelonious is at his greatest. The only thing which is not easy about *Criss Cross* is to keep your foot from tapping. His greatness lies in the very fact that he transcends all formulae, all well-worn adjectives and clichés; only new vocabulary, perhaps, could suffice. Even if Thelonious' music is precise and mathematical, it is at the same time pure magic.'

I came across other examples of Nica talking about Monk. 'The thing that always shook me up about Thelonious was how he could hear the music around the music,' she told the producer Bruce Ricker in 1988. 'He'd take tunes and make them twenty times more beautiful than they were before, he explored all those possibilities that one never dreamed of.' He was, for her, like Beethoven because in her view he too had the facility, imagination and skill to improvise and play variations on a tune. 'He took things and plumbed depths with them that had never been done before and Thelonious did that with everything he played.'

Even when he performed other people's music, Nica believed that Monk 'saw infinitely more possibilities in them than the people who wrote them'. She said that he 'heard the music all around. It was like the air was just filled with all those different variations and Thelonious just brought them down.'

After many years spent in both a critical and a financial wilderness, living on scraps of critical praise and an irregular income, Monk finally began to receive widespread recognition. 'Now it's Monk's time,' Val Wilmer wrote in 1965. 'Times have been hard for the eccentric genius and the work all but nonexistent. But he's famous now. He appears in the sticks, he wears $150 suits and stays at the best hotels.' Even with success, the pianist had not altered his approach; the world had finally caught up with him and the determined efforts of his supporters, including Nica, began to reap benefits. 'I've been doing it for twenty years,' Monk said in an interview for *Bazaar*. 'Maybe I've turned jazz another way. Maybe I'm a major influence. I don't know. Anyway, my music is my music, on my piano too. That's the criterion of something. Jazz is my adventure. I'm after new chords, new ways of syncopating, new figurations, new runs. How to use notes differently. That's it. Just using notes differently.'

Cult status did not translate into audiences or income. Even in his heyday, Monk wasn't filling large clubs or taking home significant pay cheques. In 1963 his earnings were at an all-time high. Gross receipts for his concerts reached $53,832 and his royalties added up to $22,850. But after the normal deductions for band members, travel, rest and relaxation, Monk took home only $33,055. Successful concerts such as Monk's big band collaboration with Hal Overton sold out to 1,500 people in the Lincoln Center Philharmonic Hall but this was still insignificant compared to the crowds of four thousand screaming fans who turned up to see the Beatles get on a plane. It was also galling that Monk's protégé Miles

Davis could sell at least five times more records than his former teacher.

A huge emotional boost came when *Time* magazine asked to put Monk on their front cover. He was only the fourth jazz musician and one of the few black men to receive this honour. The magazine also devoted a long article and several photographs to his life. One section focuses on his relationship with Nica, whom the writer describes as his 'friend, mascot and champion'. Alongside Monk's statement that he only has eyes for Nellie, he claims that he took Nica on as 'another mother. She gave him rides, rooms to compose and play in, and in 1957, help in getting back his cabaret card.' An accompanying photograph shows Nica gazing lovingly up at Monk.

Time writer Barry Farrell spent several months trailing Monk. Although he had full access to the pianist and conducted 'thirty chats', Farrell managed only to glean a few rather nondescript quotes. Asked what it was like to have such an ecstatic crowd at one concert in Germany, Monk just says, 'These cats are with it.' When Farrell asked Monk if he had any friends in the jazz world, Monk replied, 'I was a friend to lots of musicians but looks like they weren't friends to me.' On occasion Farrell just offers monosyllabic Monk quotations, such as 'Solid' and 'All reet'.

The overriding impression from the article was that Monk was rarely sober, always stoned. 'Every day,' Farrell wrote, 'is a brand new pharmaceutical event for Monk: alcohol, Dexedrine, sleeping potions, whatever is at hand, charge through his bloodstream in baffling combinations.' He acknowledged that Monk seemed a very happy man at times, at other times 'he appears merely mad. He has periods of acute disconnection in which he falls totally mute. He stays up for days on end, prowling around desperately in his rooms, troubling his friends, playing the piano as if jazz were a wearying curse.'

Boris Chaliapin was commissioned to produce the cover portrait of Monk. 'He was a very stiff old guy,' Nica recalled. 'Thelonious

On 29 February 1964, Monk became the fourth jazz musician and one of the few black men to appear on the cover of Time *magazine.*

would go every day and just sit down there and go straight to sleep.' His behaviour, she admitted, had 'gotten me crazy'. She was so annoyed with her friend that one day she shook him awake. When Monk half opened his eyes, Chaliapin caught the moment with a Polaroid camera.

Having been burned before by journalists and jazz writers, Monk was ambivalent about the press. Nica claimed that 'He never wanted that stuff, but he got talked into it.' Monk played up to his gnomic reputation. On one occasion he told a critic that he didn't care why audiences came; all that mattered was that they turned up.

'Isn't that cold and businesslike for a genius to be saying?' the critic asked.

'You have to do business to make money,' Monk retorted.

Asked by Francis Postif whether he came from a musical family, Monk replied, 'I come from a musical family, since my family is the world. And the world is musical, is it not?'

In another interview Leonard Feather asked Monk to rate a record by Art Pepper. 'Ask her,' Monk said, pointing to Nellie.

'It's your opinion I'm asking,' Feather replied.

'You asked for my opinion, I gave you my opinion.'

In his last interview, given in 1971 to Pearl Gonzales in Mexico City, the journalist asked him what he thought the purpose of life was. Monk replied, 'To die.'

'But between life and death there's a lot to do,' Pearl said, and asked Monk to say more.

'You asked a question and that's the answer.'

The interview was over.

As they grew older, Nica's children were spending more time with their mother. She was proud of their knowledge and enthusiasm for the music she loved, saying that they 'were all hip to jazz, they don't need to be told anything'. Nica was particularly fond of Janka, her eldest daughter and closest friend. 'Once we were in Iceland, also with some musicians, and they had a competition recognising people on the records and Janka and I won out of hundreds of countries,' she said proudly. 'Janka knew the sidemen on every record.'

Janka had lived with her mother since she was sixteen; her friends were jazz men and, like Nica, that occasionally got her into trouble. In 1956 Janka travelled by car with Art Blakey, Horace Silver and the band boy Ahmed from Philadelphia to New York after a concert. 'We got in the car and Art started driving,' Horace Silver wrote in his autobiography,

> Before we could get out of Philly, we were stopped by a motor-cycle cop. We weren't speeding or breaking any traffic rules. The cop saw three black men with a white woman, and that was enough for him to stop us. If Art had been cool, the cop might have let us go. But Art was high and acted belligerent and indig-nant. The cop told Art to follow him to the local precinct. He found a loaded gun and a box of shells and a box of Benzedrine tablets in the glove compartment. Art had no permit for the gun. The Benzedrine belonged to Janka, the baroness's daugh-ter. Ahmed had track marks on his arms.

They were all booked and put in cells. Art called Nica, who found a lawyer to get them out, but 'when the lawyer found out that three of us were black, he didn't want to get involved with us. He did get Janka out and left us in jail.' Eventually all four were acquit-ted; Horace Silver wrote, 'Evidently everybody paid off the Judge.' I suspect that 'everybody' meant Nica and that her experience in Wilmington taught her to avoid the judicial system if possible.

Success for a jazz musician meant a gruelling touring schedule. Bands often travelled seven hundred miles overnight to save on hotel bills. Once they arrived in a town, particularly in the South, it was hard to find a place that would serve black musicians.

Quincy Jones told me about one incident in Texas. 'We finished a job at about 12.30 a.m. and we had to drive until almost six o'clock in the morning to find the place where we could eat. We had to send the white driver in first to ask. But someone shouted out, "Look at the church," and there, hanging from the steeple of the biggest church in town, was a rope with an effigy of a black man. Drive on, we said.'

Roy Haynes, the drummer who often played with Monk, told me, 'The only place we could usually stay in those days was the black ghetto. There was no way you could eat or stay on the other side of the tracks. There were no hotels so we had to sleep in stations or by the roadside. If you did get a hotel room, you would sleep in shifts to save money.'

'If you went on the road you had two rents to pay,' Paul Jeffrey, Monk's close friend and last saxophone player, explained. 'There were no benefits because there was no income tax taken out. You just got paid for the job. You weren't working every week. It was just the conditions in the hotels and, you know, when I think about it now, I don't know how I made it. The hopelessness of not being able to function with any sense of real dignity.'

In 1969, the promoter George Wein, who also organised the Newport jazz festivals, took Monk and his band around the world. In addition to appearing on television and radio, and fitting in the odd recording session, Monk, in a period of a few weeks, played in Paris, Caen, Lyons, Nantes and Amiens in France; then in Geneva, Berne, Zurich, Lugano and Basle in Switzerland; in the resort of Lecco, Italy; in Brussels; in Warsaw; in the Scandinavian capitals; in Frankfurt; in Amsterdam; and in London (twice), Manchester and Birmingham. He then flew to Tokyo to play nine concerts in Japan before returning to the USA, where he played on the West Coast, in Minneapolis and at two jazz festivals, followed by another run at the Village Vanguard Club.

Even for a younger, healthier man these tours were punishing, but Monk was in poor shape, in his fifties and ill suited temperamentally to life on the road. He hated being out of New York and it was hard for his protectors to manage his routine away from home. Once, when staying alone in a San Francisco motel, Monk ripped up his room. The manager would not let him leave until Nica had flown to the West Coast and paid for the damage. Another time a club owner refused to pay up as Monk had played the whole set using only his elbows. When asked why, Monk said his choice of style had reflected his appalling plane ride to get there.

According to Nica,* one incident above all others had a disastrous effect on Monk's mental condition. He was playing in a club in Minneapolis in 1965 when a young fan slipped him a tab of acid. 'Even though Monk had strange ways, he was not in the habit of vanishing,' Nica told her old friend Dan Morgenstern. 'He disappeared and then he turned up in Detroit [some 694 miles away] almost a week later.' It was one of many contributory factors to Monk's inexorable decline.

A random series of events further knocked the pianist's constitution: the death from an overdose of his beloved nephew Ronnie; the deaths of friends like Coleman Hawkins, Elmo Hope and Bud Powell; Columbia cancelling his recording contract; trusted collaborators Ben Riley and Charlie Rouse quitting the band; a second fire in the Monk apartment; moreover, he also suffered increasingly from an enlarged prostate that affected every aspect of his life, including performing.

One evening in May 1968, on the eve of a trip to San Francisco, Monk slipped into a coma, the result of stress, exhaustion and a mixture of drugs. After several days he came round and announced in Monkish style, 'Y'all thought I kicked the bucket. Thought I was going to split. Thought I was gonna cut out. Ain't that a bitch.'

process that at least 50 per cent of the discs never made it to the final cutting room. Recording studios were kept at high temperatures to ensure that the wax remained

Nica and Nellie embarked on finding some form of treatment for Monk. Both women were determined to succeed but had completely different strategies. It was in the battle for Monk's health, rather than his love, that the two women finally fell out.

Nellie's answer was to substitute all Monk's food with fruit and vegetable juices. Paul Jeffrey explained how it worked: 'She bought this juicer, believing that if Monk just had juices, that would cure him. I used to go to the Bronx market with Nellie in the morning and haul these big crates of carrots and celery and put them in the back of my car, drive to the apartment and unload these things and, you know. So she could make this juice.' Monk stayed on her cure for months, not getting any better, yet becoming terribly thin. Nica, horrified by his weight loss, used to smuggle food into the couple's apartment. Waiting until Nellie went out, she would appear with plates of steak and potatoes, which a grateful Monk would wolf down.

Nellie's obsession with juicing nearly got the family evicted: neighbours complained bitterly that the noise of the whirring machine kept them up all night. Convinced that she was on the right track, Nellie even hoped to start a juicing business to cure ailing musicians. Desperate to find a way of providing a regular income for her family, she was angry with Monk because of his drug consumption. 'She felt he did himself in as a young man. And might have lived to be ninety-five if he hadn't taken ten million tons of drugs,' Toot Monk told Leslie Gourse.

Again I wondered about Nica and drugs. Was she an enabler or a user? A dabbler or a devotee? My hunch is that although she enjoyed the odd 'happy shot' or joint, she did not display any of the tell-tale signs of addiction. Many of her friends were destroyed by opiates. Monk was almost certainly dependent on drugs; he went on using even though it hurt those close to him, damaged his music and his health. Nica showed the classic signs of co-dependency: obsessively placing Monk's needs and welfare before her own and her family's; putting his freedom and security before her own responsibilities and welfare. If Monk was an addict, Nica was a Monk addict.

Another disastrous trip to San Francisco led to Monk being admitted to the Langley Porter Hospital. Nellie, at her wits' end, signed the papers agreeing to a new medical treatment: electric shock therapy. Nica was passionately against invasive procedures but Nellie was persuaded that this latest cure would help her husband. I tracked down the trainee psychiatrist, Eddie Henderson, who was assigned to Monk's case. In his spare time Henderson was a trumpet player who went on to tour with Miles Davis.

Henderson no longer practises medicine but he still plays music. His detailed descriptions of his childhood and his life on the road with Miles Davis convinced me that his recall was close to perfect.

'In late 1969 I became a resident trainee psychiatrist at Langley Porter Psychiatric Institute, which is part of the University of California in San Francisco,' he explained. 'It was late at night when I was awakened and called downstairs to do an intake.' He immediately recognised Monk, although no one else did, and on the admission form he wrote that the musician was committed by Nellie following a long period of silence and odd behaviour.

The following day, Dr Young, the senior psychologist, asked Monk to take the Rorschach Test, which measures patients' reactions to different-shaped inkblots. Some practitioners believe that this gives an insight into personality traits and emotional responses. Monk, according to Henderson, refused to comment, played with his rings and looked steadfastly at the floor. The doctor showed him another blot and suggested that it looked like a little boy playing the violin in front of his parents. Monk shook his head in wonder as if it was the doctor who was crazy. 'It don't mean nothing, it's an inkblot,' he said. The doctor kept showing Monk various patterns and pressing for different interpretations. Eventually Monk, winking at Henderson, turned to the doctor. 'The little boy is really drunk.'

'Oh really, Mr Monk, why?' Dr Young said.

'Because his mother won't give him no more pussy.' When Dr Young dropped the clipboard, Monk added, 'Just swizzle that.'

Henderson remembered that Monk's speech was often humorous and lucid but suddenly he would become 'uncontactable, absent, as if the bottom had dropped out of the elevator shaft. He was somewhere else.' Tests were run on Monk, using an electroencephalography scan or EEG, to record his brain's spontaneous electrical activity over a short period of twenty to forty minutes. An EEG shows, among other things, the cumulative effect of drugs taken during a patient's lifetime. 'Mr Monk's results spiked to the top.' According to Henderson, this meant his brain had been damaged.

Monk was diagnosed as 'Schizophrenic, unclassified' and prescribed the strong anti-psychotic drug thorazine, which he had, in fact, been prescribed on previous occasions. Eddie Henderson explained that a small amount, 100 milligrams, would make the average person drowsy, while the highest dose they had ever given a patient was 3,500 milligrams. Within a week, Monk was on the highest dose but it was having little impact. As electric shock treatment doubles the effect of the drug, Monk was put in a straitjacket and strapped to a table. A probe was put into his mouth, he closed his eyes while electrodes were held to his temples and bolts of electricity were blasted through his brain. It is not exactly understood how the treatment works but in some cases it seems to alleviate depression. Even today, ECT (or electroconvulsive therapy, as it is now known) is a controversial treatment. Little was known then about precisely how it affected neurological balance. Henderson told me it 'scrambles the brain cells' and that afterwards, in many cases, the patients were 'not really the same any more'.

While Monk was a patient at Langley he was allowed out to play a gig under Henderson's supervision. The trainee psychiatrist implored Monk not to drink, let alone take any other mood-altering substances, as he was already on heavy medication. The

Monk in 1968, filming Straight, No Chaser.

moment Monk arrived at the club, he ordered a triple Jack Daniel's, chased down with three beers. Then he managed to score a gram of coke. Splitting the packet in half, he snorted the whole lot up each nostril. 'By this time he is sweating and his suit looks like he has jumped in a pool. Perspiration is just dropping all over him,' Henderson recalled. 'He gets on the bandstand. He is dancing, playing with the ring. He sits down and pushes the keys far enough down not to make a sound. He did not make one sound the whole night.' Later, when Henderson took Monk back to the hospital, the pianist said, 'That was a good set.'

Following his release from Langley Porter, Nellie and Harry Colomby decided that a spell on the sunny West Coast would be good for the family and tried to set Monk up with a contract to record some advertising jingles. Monk insisted on returning to his beloved New York. Unfortunately Nellie had put their furniture into storage following the last fire. Their apartment was not yet restored. With Nica's help the Monks rented an apartment in Lincoln Towers, a place Monk never liked. Wanting his old place and his old table back, Monk went to his friend Charlie Rouse's apartment, pushed past Charlie's wife and demanded, 'Where is my furniture, do you have my furniture?'

I find glimpses of my great-aunt in the footage shot by Michael and Christian Blackwood in 1968. In one scene she and Monk are driving through the streets of New York to catch a set at a club by their friend Lionel Hampton. Nica drives in her normal reckless way, turning to talk to the cameraman in the back seat or sideways to address Monk.

Later, presumably the same night, the couple hang out backstage at another venue. I replay the footage again and again, spooling backwards and forwards, trying to figure out what Nica is think-ing. She is fifty-four now and looks it. Her face is puffy and those exquisite features are lost. Her hair has grown long and is badly cut. She wears a black skirt and an unflattering striped top. By the end of the evening she's quite drunk and has to bite down hard on her long cigarette holder to keep it from falling. Again and again, she asks Monk what tracks he will play. Again and again, he grunts and looks elsewhere, having a little dance, exchanging a half-sentence here and there with a friend. Nica sits down heavily on the stairs and looks adoringly at him. She always looks adoringly at him.

Nica tells Monk that she has bought him a present.

'A million dollars?' he says hopefully.

'No, a marker pen for you to sign autographs.'

'I don't like to carry a pen, you know that,' Monk says, taking off the top. She can't find a blank piece of paper so he tries out his new pen on a paper napkin. The material tears. Nica laughs.

'Is it silver?' Monk asks, examining the pen.

'Yes. Here is a piece of paper.' Nica points to a pad on the table. Monk leans over and scribbles something.

'Do you know what that says?' he asks. 'If you can get someone to sign that, you will flip out. Flip for good.'

They talk about Nica's family and how rich they are, although she claims to be a poor relation. She is not wealthy by comparison with most Rothschilds, but rich, of course, by comparison to most of the people in the room.

Monk turns to the camera. 'I don't want to be without money no more. That's over,' he says earnestly, taking some folded bills out of his pocket and waving them around. One of his entourage gestures to Monk's heavy rings, saying he would prefer the jewellery to the cash. Monk agrees, pointing to a black opal, his birthstone, that is worth at least $1,000, set between cut diamonds. Leaning forward, Nica gently touches his forehead, his brain.

'All you need is this,' she says lovingly.

'Ha,' Monk grunts, as if unconvinced.

Nica brings out some pictures of her cats, saying that she has lost count of how many she has after reaching 106. Monk rolls his eyes at the camera; he at least is not the mad one in this scene.

23

Luvya

Monk's mental health deteriorated rapidly during the 1970s. In 1971 he fell into a catatonic depression and was admitted to the Beth Isracl Hospital. Following his release, he joined George Wein's Giants of Jazz tour in 1972. It was a gruelling schedule: two concerts per night in sixteen cities over a period of twenty-two days. Rare bootleg concert footage, shot in Berlin at that time, shows Monk – thin, sweaty, his goatee beard greying and wispy – bent over a piano, knocking out a tune with little enthusiasm. His body seems to have shrunk inside his suit. His large gold rings slip around on his fingers and perspiration drips steadily from his temples on to the piano keys.

One of the debilitating side effects of Monk's prostate problem was incontinence. 'He had a problem of containment that brought lack of control and that was too bad, because he was very embarrassed,' George Wein said, remembering an incident from the tour. 'He was a very proud man, Thelonious. He always dressed impeccably. He bought fine suits and he never looked shabby in any way.' While Thelonious was at home the incontinence was easier to manage but, on the road, never knowing where the tour bus would stop or what the facilities would be like made a difficult situation almost intolerable.

When he arrived back in New York, his friend Paul Jeffrey had to help Monk off the plane. 'He could hardly walk, he was that weak.' Monk took most of December 1971 and January 1972 off before returning to work. He told friends he had to get out: he was driven mad by the constant whirring of Nellie's juicer.

The seriousness of Monk's situation was made clear to Nica in 1972. 'We were driving home from New York when he suddenly said to me, "I am seriously ill."' Monk's admission spurred Nica into action. 'That is when I started looking for doctors and trying to get the thing worked out.' She devoted the next ten years to trying to find a cure. Listening now to a tape of Nica describing Monk's illnesses, I can hear the quiet desperation in her voice. She consulted doctors across Europe and America but still failed to find an effective treatment or a convincing diagnosis. 'I wish I could tell you what [it was],' she said in low tones; Monk had 'a terrible illness. He was desperately tired. He may have been in pain [but] he would never have said: that is the terrible thing about him. I am sure he was in pain,' Nica said, her voice breaking slightly through the stiff-upper-lip British delivery. 'He had convulsions. He had cirrhosis of the liver . . . high blood pressure . . . borderline diabetes: I have papers up to the ceiling about what was wrong [with him].'

In January 1972, Nica placed Monk under the supervision of a new group of doctors at the Gracie Square Hospital. This led to a significant change in the direction of his treatment. Taking charge of the process, Nica was determined that Monk should not undergo the newfangled 'talking cure', which she thought 'ridiculous: all that happened was the psychiatrist had to go to *their* psychiatrist. You know, he tore them out.' She was equally adamant that the doctors avoid electric shock treatment and heavy tranquillisers, insisting on a gentler, more holistic approach.

Miriam, who was trying, simultaneously, to find a cure for their sister Liberty, influenced Nica here. Like their father Charles and

Monk himself, Liberty had been diagnosed with schizophrenia. The early lives of both Nica and Miriam had been dominated by the constant presence of someone affected by extreme mood disorders. Now the two sisters found themselves, once again, in the orbit of mental illness. Perhaps this time they could make a difference. Their brother Victor, loathing any display of vulnerability and instability, turned his back on the problem while Miriam and Nica searched desperately for the answer. Miriam went on to set up the Schizophrenia Research Fund, still operational today, which tries to identify the biological causes of the disease.

Miriam commissioned a series of microcellular tests on Liberty that showed she also had coeliac disease and could be helped if she followed a special diet that did not contain plant proteins. Acting on Miriam's advice, Nica also ordered a comprehensive profile of Monk's biochemical imbalances at a minute cellular level, testing the quantities and variances in the body's store of vitamins, minerals, amino acids and essential fatty acids. The results, she hoped, could pinpoint a treatment aimed at alleviating his symptoms. The new doctors' first recommendation was that Monk be taken off thorazine and placed on lithium. Getting the right dose was vital: his liver couldn't cope with too much salt. It was also strongly advised that he stay away from narcotics and alcohol, but, according to his friend and sideman Paul Jeffrey, Monk was never able to resist the odd line of cocaine chased down by a stiff scotch.

Tests showed that Monk's system was overloaded with copper and lacked zinc. The doctors tried to counteract this by giving him mega-vitamins and extra zinc, but the levels never returned to normal. Other tests revealed that Monk had mould in his urine. Miriam advised her sister to explore Far Eastern medicine, which takes dampness in the body's chi or energy seriously. Nica hired Chinese acupuncturists and acupressurists to help treat Monk.

Above all, the Rothschild sisters believed that a sufferer should be cared for at home, free from the pressures of work and allowed to follow their own idiosyncratic routine. Although Liberty's beha-viour was often unpredictable, Miriam insisted that she should be allowed to come and go as she pleased. Liberty spent her last years at Ashton and would sometimes wander around the house, sit down at the piano or interrupt a conversation. She was never made to feel uncomfortable or unwanted.

Towards the end of her life, Nica was asked if she had any regrets. I expected her to reflect on being separated from her chil-dren. 'Regrets? Yes!' Nica replied. 'A real strong one: that I somehow didn't find the right doctor for Thelonious. That is my regret, my only regret.'

Monk was engaged to do a series of concerts at the Village Gate in January 1972. The saxophone player Paul Jeffrey became Monk's helper. 'I used to go to Monk's house and get him ready for the job and bring him down to the club. After the job was over I would bring Monk home. It was a bitterly cold evening and Nica, who sat at her usual table watching Monk, offered to drop Monk home and then take me to the train station.'

Jeffrey remembers driving back to Monk's apartment in Nica's Bentley as snow fell on the streets of New York, blanketing the city in white-muffled silence. 'We reached his apartment block, but Monk would not get out of the car. Nica kept turning the heat on and then she got to turn the heat off so the car would not overheat. This went on to about six o'clock in the morning. At that time I lived in Coney Island, which was the last stop on the subway, so eventually I said, well, I am going home, and left them there.'

Monk finally got out of Nica's car and went into his apartment. Perhaps the whirring juicer was the catalyst but the next day he rang Nica to ask her to collect him and his stuff. When Nica arrived, Nellie started to shout at them both, unable to believe that her hus-band intended to go and live with another woman. Who could blame her? Eventually Nica took charge. Taking Monk by the arm, she said, 'Come on, Thelonious, let's get the fuck out of here.'

Nica called Paul Jeffrey the next afternoon. 'The Baroness said, "You don't have to worry about getting Monk from Nellie's apartment any more because he is with me and I will bring him." And that was the last time that Monk stayed at Nellie's apartment.'

For the first few years after Monk moved out of the family home, Nellie went to Weehawken to cook for her husband and spend time with him, but as the years went by her visits began to tail off. When in 1976 Mary Lou Williams requested some publicity photographs of Monk, Nica wrote back, saying that she'd ask 'when or if I see Nellie (she has no telephone). Her visits are few and far between.' Nica had never learned to cook. A Miss D did her basic housekeeping and she had a cleaner, Gracie, but there was never much apart from cat food in the kitchen, so Nica ate at the clubs. Monk was given the upstairs bedroom and for a time it seemed as if his life might continue in a state of easy semi-retirement.

Monk played at a reunion concert at Newport in New York in July 1975 and did two gigs in 1976, the first at Carnegie Hall in March and his swansong at Bradley's on 4 July. Nica says that from 1972 onwards he hardly touched the piano but he would play ping-pong or Peggity with her grandson Steven. The last published recording, 'Newport in New York', was made on 3 July 1975 at the Philharmonic Hall and the last ever recording made by Nica on her reel-to-reel tape recorder was ''Round Midnight'.

One of the mysteries of jazz history is why Monk stopped playing and retired to his bed. Nica described Monk's final years as 'very frustrating. It was like he was not here when he was here. Imagine someone lying in the bed like that. It was like he knew he was going to die almost in this position that people are put in their coffins. And there would be days on end where he wouldn't speak at all. And I would take in his food, get him to take his pills. I could usually get some reaction from him but almost nobody else could.'

Paul Jeffrey, who remained close to Monk right up until his death in 1982, said: 'When you asked Monk [about his inactivity],

Monk said, "I have retired." That makes perfect sense to me. Baseball players retire, you know. People always feel that musicians have to continue to play when maybe their prowess has diminished. In other words, you never retire in music. Well, some musicians live long enough so that they are not able to play at the level. He just decided he didn't want to play any more.'

Monk's son Toot offered a medical explanation: 'My father had had a prostate operation and had his prostate gland removed in, about, I don't know, it must have been about 1973 or '74 and, as a result of that, eliminating was a hassle. Now everybody thought he stopped playing because he lost the fire, or he stopped playing because he became uninterested, or he stopped playing because he was too spaced out from too many stints in the loony bin. It was none of those things. It was simply that he was uncomfortable, you see.'

Hearing these theories made Nica uncharacteristically angry. 'Thelonious only stopped playing when it became a physical impossibility for him: nothing else could ever have stopped him. There was a wrong biochemical imbalance [in his blood] and he was desperately ill during the last years. He wanted more than anything to get well and that [was why] he cooperated with the doctors a hundred per cent and they tried everything but nothing worked.'

Nica never gave up hope of finding a cure. Writing to Mary Lou in 1977, she expressed great excitement: 'I have a line on a new doctor for T . . . he is just about the greatest expert there is on biochemical imbalances (which is precisely what T is suffering from). I am not telling ANYONE (including T) about this at the moment but I want YOU to PLEASE say a prayer for us that WILL be able to help. Luvya!' Two years later she writes to Mary Lou about another expert from Princeton and someone who gives Thelonious shiatsu: 'T is being as good as gold, keeping strictly to his diet, taking all the pills prescribed for him every day.' In a letter to a cousin in 1981, Nica is still talking with enthusiasm about finding yet another practitioner who might be able to help.

© Ben Martin/Time & Life Images/Getty Images

Nica and Monk captured for the Time *magazine article,*
published in February 1964.

Once she and Paul Jeffrey tried to pique his interest by asking young musicians to come and play outside Monk's window. This got no response. On another occasion she asked pianist Joel Forrester to play outside Monk's room. This time, Monk slammed his bedroom door shut.

Monk's old producer and friend Orrin Keepnews visited the pianist at Weehawken in the late 1970s. 'Monk, are you touching the piano at all these days?' Keepnews asked. 'He said, "No I'm not." And I said, "Do you want to get back to playing?" and Monk said, "No I don't." And I said, "Would you be interested in my coming out and visiting you and talking about the old days?" And he said, "No I wouldn't."'

Barry Harris, the pianist, who also lived with Nica and Monk, commented that Orrin was lucky to get 'complete sentences out of Monk. To most people he just says "No" or nothing.'

When my uncle Amschel went to spend an afternoon with Nica in New York, he described Monk lying as if dead on his bed, his hands in the prayer position, not saying a word and not moving as the world went on around him. Sometimes Nica's family might come to help but often she was alone with Monk and the cats. 'I used to play him records a lot, he liked that,' she recalled, remembering one particular autumn afternoon. 'I saw him get up. I was in the big room playing records and I saw him go from his bed to the bathroom [and I] heard this terrible crash and so I rushed in and he had fallen inside the bathroom and the door opens in, it is very small. His feet were against the door and I couldn't open the door. There was no way to get in to him. So I got the ambulance people and they had to get him out of there.'

Eddie Henderson also went to visit Monk and Nica at that time.

The Baroness was sitting in the living room with a cigarette holder surrounded by seventy-five cats. She said, 'Oh hello, doctor, Mr Monk is upstairs.' Mr Monk was sitting in that big room with the piano, looking at the skyline of New York City, fully dressed with a little thin tie and stingy-brim hat. He didn't look at me but he said, 'Hey, doc, how you doing?' I said, 'What you doing, Mr Monk?' He said, 'I'm waiting for a phone call.' He was just looking up at the ceiling and ironically, about ten seconds later, the phone rang. He picked it up. Now he listened, didn't say hello. He just listened. About twenty or twenty-five seconds later, that's a long time, he hung up and said, 'That wasn't it.'

His old friend Amiri Baraka also visited Monk at home. Like Nica, he was convinced that Monk was still fully cognisant. When Baraka asked the pianist what was going on, Monk replied, 'Everything, man. Every googleplex of a second.' Nica said Monk's favourite pastime was standing in front of the huge glass window, looking out at the Manhattan skyline. Sometimes, she said, Monk would conduct the weather. 'He could make the clouds change direction, I don't know if you knew that? People up the road here keep pigeons. Thelonious would stand at the window and make them change direction; I have seen him actually do it. He could make a cloud turn back.'

From 1972 onwards Nica refused to leave Monk's side for the next eight years. Then in 1980 an old friend of the family turned ninety and she decided to go to Europe for his birthday. Describing the moment she went to say goodbye to Monk, Nica admitted.

I am not a crier. I can count the times in my life when I have cried. When I went to say goodbye to Thelonious he was so upset that I could not stop crying. I remember Thelonious saying, it is all right, I will be here when you get back. I am not going anywhere, I will be here. It was my first trip on Concorde and I cried the whole way to England. I must have soaked hundreds of hankies. It was almost like I knew and I said my farewell to him then.

Thelonious was right: he was there when Nica returned and he lived for nearly two more years. Then, on 5 February 1982, he suffered a massive heart attack at Weehawken. Nica called an ambulance and went with him to Englewood Hospital where he lay in a coma for twelve days. Nica, Nellie and her family took it in turns to sit with him. Thelonious died aged sixty-four on 17 February in Nellie's arms. Nica was at home across the river.

At Monk's funeral, Nica and Nellie sat side by side in the front row of the church. Musicians, friends and family filed past to pay their last respects to the two matriarchs and then to Thelonious who lay in an open casket lined with white silk. As usual, he was immaculately dressed in a grey three-piece suit with a stripy tie and matching handkerchief poking out of his breast pocket. His large hands were clasped together and his face, slightly puffy and waxy in death, looked composed and peaceful. Unusually he was hatless. Nica, wearing her pearls, a heavy fur coat and crimson lipstick, looked straight ahead, her face expressionless.

Any sang-froid evaporated when Nica found out that her Bentley would not lead the funeral cortège. Having looked after the pianist for so long, she did not want, at this vital public moment, to be marginalised. Nica kicked up such a fuss that Nellie, Toot and Boo-Boo (Barbara) Monk climbed out of the family limo and into the Bebop Bentley. The procession made its way past Monk's favourite haunts before heading out to Ferncliff Cemetery in Hartsdale, some twenty-five miles away.

Less than a mile from Hartsdale, Nica's car broke down. The Monk family got back into the hired limousine and Nica was left with the car on the side of the road, while the procession continued without her. It was an ignominious, humiliating and sad end to that chapter of her life.

24

'Round Midnight

Nica was sixty-nine, soon to be a great-grandmother, and her life, free from caring for Monk, was at another crossroads. She could have gone home to a cottage on the estate at Ashton and lived with her sisters, or joined her daughter Janka who had emigrated to Israel. Instead she stayed on in Weehawken, sharing the house with the pianist Barry Harris and all those cats.

Her routine hardly changed. Nica spent most of the day in bed surrounded by paperwork, books and magazines and cats. Her daily mission was to complete *The Times* crossword. She remained a night bird and seemed happier as dusk fell. One evening she and I arranged to meet. 'Let's meet at twelve,' she suggested.

'Just before lunch?' I asked: after all she was my great-aunt and already rather an old lady.

'No! Twelve midnight!' she roared.

I asked her grandson Steven if he called her Granny or another nickname. Without hesitating, he said, 'Bye-Bye.'

Why?

'Because I would run into her room and make a noise and soon she would laugh and say, bye-bye.'

Nica in a New York jazz club in 1988.

During 1984, Nica had radiation treatment for cancer but said music was the best therapy. It must have worked, for she kicked cancer as well as the hepatitis caught, as claimed by Nica, from her doctor's dirty needles. The Nica I came to know a few years later lived much the same as she had thirty years earlier: it was Monkless but she was still an avid music follower. When I called her up on arriving in New York, she would laugh, say hello and then immediately fill me in on the news. It was never anything personal or revelatory, just unbridled excitement about what was happening musically: so-and-so is playing at this or that club. 'It'll be a hoot. Let's meet there.' Then, typical of many Rothschilds, she would hang up without bothering to say goodbye.

Nica continued to keep in touch with her British family. In England there were family reunions in 1968, 1969 and 1973, as well as others when family members passed through New York. In the archives at Waddesdon I found many references to Nica in family letters. I remember one large meeting at Ashton on 6 May 1986 when Miriam invited Nica, her children, Rabbi Julia Neuberger and myself to lunch. There were no introductions at Liberty Hall: everyone just piled in, disparate characters united by their not so disparate genes.

In a letter written to a Rothschild cousin on 21 June 1986, Miriam apologises for bringing Nica to a family function. 'I hope that the idea of adding Nica to your dinner with my brother did not prove disastrous. Nica was keen to see you and since Thelonious died she has been very lonely and ill and very much wanted to see every member of the family before going back.' Following the event, Nica wrote to the cousin, apologising for arriving on 'all fours': she had recently fallen down and hurt herself. Soon afterwards she returned to New York on the *QE2* with her daughter Berit, only to crack a rib once she got home: she had been trying to climb on to her roof to get a better view of the Tall Ships Race.

In 1986 Nica appeared in two films. Clint Eastwood's *Bird* was a fictional account of the life of Charlie Parker based partially on Nica's memories. *Straight, No Chaser* was a documentary that mixed old archive of Monk and Nica with recent shots of Kingswood Road and Monk's funeral. Nica took her children to meet Clint Eastwood at Nica's Bar in the Stanhope Hotel. She loved the irony that the place that had once thrown her on to the streets was now honouring her memory. After the encounter Nica wrote to her friend Victor Metz in Paris: 'Clint Eastwood seems to be REMARKABLY cool but I doubt I will like the way my "role" is played. He sent me a picture of the actress and I thought she looked like a constipated horse!!!'

Quincy Jones saw Nica at the première: 'She was with Barry Harris and we had a nice dinner after we saw the film. Streisand was my date that night. When we came out we had a limousine and twenty guys in two cars chasing us up Madison Avenue. Crazy.' What did Nica make of all this? 'She was hip, she was cool.'

In November 1988, Nica was admitted to hospital for heart surgery. It was a straightforward procedure and she was expected to remain there for a few days. One of her last visitors was the pianist Joel Forrester. 'Nica looked parchment white lying in her bed. She was covered up and was all by herself. She explained to me that she was incapable of reading and she couldn't see me very well and yet she was fully conscious. There was no television for her to look at, you know, had she wanted to. I said, "Nica, what are you doing all day?" She answered, "Picking over a lifetime of memories."'

Nica was expected to make a full recovery, but her body, weakened by age, hard living, hepatitis, a few bad car crashes and a bout of cancer, gave up. At 5.03 p.m. on 30 November 1988, Nica died. She was seventy-four. The cause of death was given as heart failure during a triple aorta coronary bypass.

In her will, Nica left $750,000. She had complained of penury but it turned out to be relative. I thought about her tired old clothes, the frayed carpets, the lack of food and decent wine in the house, and realised that these were choices. The only luxuries Nica had wanted were her car, her Steinway piano and her ping-pong table. Everything else was functional. Only the Bentley was a crowd stopper. I wondered whether it was a coincidence that the one thing that cost a lot of money, a flash car, was an escape vehicle. Once she offered to sell her car to Thelonious for $19,000.

'Nineteen thousand dollars!' screamed Monk. 'For that I can buy a home with four bedrooms, living room, kitchen and garage.'

'Of course you can,' Nica replied, 'but where would it take you?'

Nica left one last request: that her family cremate her body, hire a boat and scatter her ashes on the Hudson River near 'Catville'. The timing was very important: it had to be done 'round midnight.

Epilogue

In 2008, twenty years after Nica died, I go back to Tring Park, the family's former home. The train from Euston is packed with commuters, their noses in newspapers, briefcases wedged on laps: a far cry from Nica's childhood experience of taking this journey on a private train in Pullman coaches. Although the family had lived at Tring from 1872 to 1935, this period occupies a brief episode in the town's long history. However, walking up the High Street, I spot tell-tale signs of the Rothschilds: their Five-Arrow crest stamped on some buildings, a Rothschild Dining Room in the local inn. Walter's gentle spirit lives on in the museum. During the war, Rothschild's Bank used the house as its head-quarters, but since 1945 it has been home to a school for the performing arts.

Only the park itself remains in family hands. Although it has been sliced in two by the busy A41, a huge swathe is preserved as part of Charles Rothschild's wildlife scheme. A passionate advocate of preserving areas of natural habitat for wild flowers, animals and insects, Nica's father left a legacy that would found the British conservation movement.

These days, the kangaroos, zebras, emus and cassowaries have gone, replaced by walkers, their dogs and their children. The oddest wild animals are roe deer or muntjac. When Nica was little, local children swarmed around the gates, hoping to catch one of the gold sovereigns that her grandfather Natty Rothschild liked to throw from his carriage window. Only a handful of Tring inhabitants today remember those days or the family. Even Walter's museum has been rebranded as an offshoot of the Natural History Museum.

The once-formal main hall at Tring is almost unrecognisable. The grand furniture was sold, the potted palms and paintings removed. A barre is fixed to the wall and the room is now a practice area for ballet dancers. I wish that Nica could have seen the place transformed by a swirling mass of white tutus. In the former smoking room, younger dancers practise the English National Ballet's Christmas performance of *The Nutcracker*. Dressed up as mice, presents and toy soldiers, they career into each other, shrieking with laughter. The old grass courts are now covered by a marquee and I watch a class of modern jazz: teenage girls in leotards doing a routine to music written years after Nica's and Monk's deaths.

At the top of the grand main stairs, down the end of a corridor, I find Nica's old room. It is smallish and wood-panelled; the fireplace has been boarded up and the walls are covered with the contemporary flotsam and jetsam of teenage life – posters of boy bands, fashion models and furry animals. It was from this window that Nica and her siblings would strain to hear their father returning, his arrival announced by the crunch of the horses' hooves on the gravel. It was from this vantage point that they caught sight of a newfangled thing called a biplane. I stand, imagining the mornings when the children were woken by the sound of their nurses drawing their baths and by maids laying fires in their bedroom grates.

A shrill siren calling the hungry to lunch interrupts my reverie. Immediately the house shakes as four hundred hungry students charge down stairs and corridors, bound for the dining hall in the basement. Nica would have been amazed to see what is on offer: curries, pasta, sandwiches, roasts, exotic fruits and vegetables – a far cry from her childhood staple diet of fish and eggs.

The only remaining artefact from that life is in the basement, outside what was once the butler's pantry and is now the teachers' staffroom. Hanging there is a long row of bells with names underneath: Lady Rothschild's bedroom, Lady Rothschild's sitting room, Lord Rothschild's bedroom, children's nursery and the smoking room.

As a tribute to my great-aunt, I ask a pupil at the school to sing Thelonious Monk's 'Pannonica' in the main hall. Students appear from different classrooms and dorms to listen as the words ring out around the building. I like to think Nica would have been pleased. Perhaps she is coming home in a musical form.

Leaving the school, I walk down the lane to Walter's museum. It has hardly changed: every nook and cranny is still crammed with his collection of taxidermy. In glass cases or suspended from the ceiling are many of the species he discovered and others named in his honour. Walter's work was not widely appreciated during his lifetime, particularly by his family who wrote him off as an eccentric spendthrift with strange habits. It wasn't until his niece Miriam wrote his biography *Dear Lord Rothschild* that his reputation was reconsidered and his colossal contribution to the study of natural history finally acknowledged.

Will Nica be recognised in the Rothschild family pantheon of high achievers? Like Walter, she leaves a legacy of names. Hers are not a Galápagos finch or an improbable fly but a roster of songs. 'Pannonica' is only one: others include 'Nica's Dream', 'Nica's Tempo', 'Nica Steps Out', 'Thelonica', 'Bolivar Blues', 'Cats in the Belfry', 'Blues for Nica', 'Tonica' and other special dedication pieces written by friends whom she helped.

Using her position and inheritance, Nica played a part in nurturing a generation of struggling musicians. She made her sliver of a great fortune go a little further. She made a difference. In return she received the one thing she lacked and desperately missed during her childhood: friendship.

For Nica, though, it was all about being near the 'eighth wonder of the world', Thelonious Monk. While he would have composed and succeeded without her, she nevertheless took great pride in their association and in the part she played to create the right milieu for him to work in. She had not been able to save her own father from his illness, nor her relations from the Holocaust, nor protect her friends from prejudice, but Nica was able to dignify one man's last years and provide her beloved Thelonious with a place of warm, cafe respite.

A friend teased me recently: 'You'll never finish this book, because you can't bear to let her go.' He is nearly right. My bookshelves and study drawers are full of my efforts to get to know and understand Nica: seventeen box and lever-arch files; a documentary feature film; a radio programme; books where she fleetingly appears; other books about her family and friends where she mysteriously does not; records dedicated to her; albums she loved; newspaper clippings; photographs; letters from or about her; a family tree; a tiny moth; stacks of notes, emails and correspondence from strangers – a paper-trail of endeavour.

It was my younger self's question that drove me on: did Nica prove that one can escape from one's past? Superficially, of course, she changed everything about herself: her creed, country, class and culture. She created a life outside her family's system in a world that few could understand. She dared to be different. Twenty years on, my older self sees that total escape is impossible. Our lives, as Miriam said, are shaped long before we are born; tendrils of DNA, ancestral history and behavioural traits are embedded into every part of our being. Nica was tied to her family, in practical terms via the umbilical cord of money and emotionally through shared experience. She could never escape from those who truly understood her; I believe she never wanted to. Nica said that we Rothschilds are a 'weird' lot but a close one. I see that.

I am finally letting this project go. I imagine all the stuff – the research so carefully collated and collected, the myriad bits of paper – fluttering away in the wind. I imagine Pannonica's meandering flight path, haphazard, strong, undisciplined, determined and random. Monk's butterfly, my moth, is released.

If she were here now, she would pretend to hate all this fuss, all this reflection. I know exactly what my great-aunt Nica would say: have a drink, stop being such a bore. 'Shh, Hannah, just listen to the music. Just listen to the music.'

A Selection of Songs Written for or Inspired by Nica

'Blues for Nica' – Kenny Drew
'Bolivar Blues' – Thelonious Monk
'Cats in My Belfry' – Barry Harris
'Coming on the Hudson' – Thelonious Monk
'Inca' – Barry Harris
'Little Butterfly' – Thelonious Monk and Jon Hendricks
'Nica' – Sonny Clark
'Nica's Day' – Wayne Horvitz
'Nica's Dream' – Horace Silver
'Nica's Dream' – Dee Dee Bridgwater (Dee Dee added lyrics to Silver's song)
'Nica Steps Out' – Freddie Redd
'Nica's Tempo' – Gigi Gryce
'Pannonica' – Donald Byrd
'Pannonica' – Doug Watkins
'Pannonica' – Thelonious Monk
'Poor Butterfly' – Sonny Rollins
'Thelonica' – Tommy Flanagan
'Theme for Nica' – Eddie Thompson
'Tonica' – Kenny Dorham
'Weehawken Mad Pad' – Art Blakey

Acknowledgements

Over the last twenty years, during this project's metamorphosis from an idea to a radio programme to a documentary feature film and now this biography, many colleagues, friends and relations have been an incredible help. I am immensely grateful for their guidance and expertise.

Wherever possible, I have relied on contemporary witnesses to explain and describe events and people. I am not a jazz critic or historian, a social commentator or an academic; what I bring to this project is a sense of wonder, a desire to tell other people's stories, a need to understand my own, and a determination to celebrate our similarities rather than our differences.

The musicians, many of whom were Nica's friends, have been particularly generous and non-judgemental, taking time to explain the rudiments of jazz and the ramifications of living and working in that culture. Spending time with these highly articulate, intelligent people has helped me understand why Nica felt 'warmed' by their friendship and enthralled by their music. Toot Monk, Sonny Rollins, Paul Jeffrey and Quincy Jones were particularly enlightening.

My family has been consistently encouraging and supportive. Great-aunt Miriam was and remains a source of inspiration. My father, Jacob, has always encouraged his children to work hard, seize opportunities and explore every avenue. My mother Serena, a devoted bibliophile, helped me to love books. It would be hard to imagine a week without the loving friendship of my sister Emmy. My cousin Evelyn helped me to understand schizophrenia and my younger cousins urged me to exorcise some family ghosts.

I am especially grateful to Nica's grandson Steven de Koenigswarter who has inherited his grandmother's spirit and kindness.

Filmmakers, producers, photographers and archivists often go unthanked and unrecognised. Without the Blackwood brothers, the BBC, Charlotte Zwerin, Bruce Ricker, Clint Eastwood, Melanie Aspey and Jill Geber and others, much of this sort of history would be lost and certainly less redolent.

At every stage, kind but exacting critics have commented on my progress. Thanks to my silent friend for his encouragement and insight, Rudith Buenconsejo for keeping the home fires burning, and Linda Drew for keeping the walls intact. The following helped craft the radio and television programmes: Nick Fraser, Robert McNab, Walter Stabb, David Perry, Anthony Wall, Lucy Hunot, Natalie Howe and Isabella Steele.

Rosie Boycott, Mairead Lewin, Rupert Smith, Laura Beatty, Philip Astor, David Miller and William Seighart were wise and meticulous readers. Bella Pollen and Justine Picardie were particularly helpful on structure and layering. Virago has been a wonderful home for this book and Lennie Goodings its great cheerleader and editor.

Finally I have to thank my utterly glorious, supportive and inspirational daughters, Nell, Clemency and Rose, who have lived through every stage of this project and who remind me on a daily basis what is important and true.

Interviews

I am very grateful to the following people for letting me record their experiences, memories and knowledge.

Family

Nica de Koenigswarter
Steven de Koenigswarter
Miriam Rothschild
Victor Rothschild
Jacob Rothschild
Miranda Rothschild

Emmy Freeman-Atwood
Rosemary Serys
Evelyn de Rothschild
Amschel Rothschild
Barbara Ghika (née Hutchinson, later Mrs Victor Rothschild)

Musicians

John Altman
Jimmy Cobb
John Dankworth
Fab Five Freddie
Joel Forrester
Curtis Fuller
Benny Golson
Freddie Gruber
Chico Hamilton
Herbie Hancock
Roy Haynes
Eddie Henderson
Russ Henderson

Jon Hendricks
Jools Holland
Paul Jeffrey
Quincy Jones
Humphrey Lyttleton
Marion McPartland
Toot Monk
Calvin Newborn
Ben Riley
Sonny Rollins
Cedar Walton
Butch Warren

Producers

Jean Bach
Michael Blackwood
Clint Eastwood
Ahmet Ertegun
Ira Gitler

Orrin Keepnews
Bruce Ricker
George Wein
Charlotte Zwerin

Critics, Historians, Writers

Amiri Baraka
Stanley Crouch
Gary Giddins
Nat Henroff
David Kastin
Robin Kelly
Jimmy Moreton
Dan Morgenstern

Ted Pankin
Ross Russell
Phil Schapp
Keith Shadwick
Pippa Shirley
Richard Williams
Val Wilmer

Others

Harry Colomby
Mrs Gutteridge
Phoebe Jacobs
Robert Kraft

Victor Metz
Gaden Robinson
Frank Richardson

Bibliography

Nica

'L'Extraordinaire Destin de la Baronne du Jazz', *Le Journal du Dimanche*, 18 December 1988

Forbes, Malcolm with Jeff Bloch, 'Baroness Pannonica de Koenigswarter', in their *Women who Made a Difference* (New York: Simon & Schuster, 1990)

Hentoff, Nat, 'The Jazz Baroness', *Esquire*, October 1960

Kastin, David, *Nica's Dream: The Life and Legend of the Jazz Baroness* (New York: W. W. Norton, 2011)

Keepnews, Peter, 'Rouse & Nica', *DownBeat*, April 1989

Koenigswarter, Jules de, *Savoir dire non* (published privately, 1976)

Koenigswarter, Nica de, 'A Remembrance of Monk', *Daily Challenge*, 22 December 1986

——————, *Three Wishes: An Intimate Look at Jazz Greats* (New York: Abrams Image, 2008)

Massingberd, Hugh (ed.), *The Daily Telegraph Book of Obituaries: A Celebration of Eccentric Lives* (London: Macmillan, 1995)

Piacentino, Giuseppe, 'Nica, Bentley and Bebop', *Musica Jazz*, February 1989

Singer, Barry, 'The Baroness of Jazz', *New York Times*, 17 October 2008

Traberg, Ebbe, 'Nica, o el Sueño de Nica', *Revista de Occidente*, 93, February 1989

Zafra, Jessica, 'The Baroness of Jazz', *The National*, 29 May 2008

Rothschilds

Ayer, Jules, *Century of Finance, 1804–1904: The London House of Rothschild* (London: Neel, 1905)

Capdebiele, François, 'Female Rothschilds and their issue', unpublished MS, RAL (n.d.)

Cohen, Lucy, *Lady de Rothschild and her Daughters, 1821–1931* (London: John Murray, 1935)

Cowles, Virginia, *The Rothschilds: A Family of Fortune* (London: Weidenfeld & Nicolson, 1979)

Davis, Richard, *The English Rothschilds* (London: Collins, 1983)

Ferguson, Niall, *The World's Banker: The History of the House of Rothschild* (London: Weidenfeld & Nicolson, 1998)

Holmes, Colin, *Anti-Semitism in British Society, 1876–1939* (London: Edward Arnold, 1979)

Ireland, George, *Plutocrats: A Rothschild Inheritance* (London: John Murray, 2007)

Leslie-Melville, Betty and Jock Leslie-Melville, *Raising Daisy Rothschild* (New York: Simon & Schuster, 1977)

Morton, Frederic, *The Rothschilds* (New York: Secker & Warburg, 1962)

Morton, Fredric, *The Rothschilds: Portrait of a Dynasty* (New York: Kodansha America, 1998)

Rothschild, Mrs James de, *The Rothschilds at Waddesdon Manor* (London: Collins, 1979)

Rose, Kenneth, *Elusive Rothschild: The Life of Victor, Third Baron* (London: Weidenfeld & Nicolson, 2003)

Roth, Cecil, *The Magnificent Rothschilds* (London: Robert Hale, 1939)

Rothschild, Miriam, *Dear Lord Rothschild: Birds, Butterflies and History* (Glenside: Balaban, 1983)

Rothschild, Miriam, *Nathaniel Charles Rothschild, 1877–1923* (privately printed, 1979)

Rothschild, Monique de, *Personal Memoires* (privately printed)

Rothschild, Lord (Victor), *Meditations of a Broomstick* (London: Collins, 1977)

Rothschild, Lord (Victor), *Rothschild Family Tree: 1450–1973* (privately printed, 1981)

Rothschild, Lord (Victor), *The Shadow of a Great Man* (London: New Court, 1982)

Schama, Simon, *Two Rothschilds and the Land of Israel* (London: Collins, 1978)

White, Jerry, *Rothschild Buildings: Life in an East End Tenement Block, 1887–1920* (London: Routledge & Kegan Paul, 1980)

Wilson, Derek A., *Rothschild: A Story of Wealth and Power* (London: André Deutsch, 1986)

Wilson, Derek, *Rothschild* (London: André Deutsch, 1988)

Woodhouse, Barry, *Tring: A Pictorial History* (Chichester: Phillimore, 1996)

Jazz

Alexander, Michael, *Jazz Age Jews* (Princeton: Princeton University Press, 2001)

Alkyer, Frank (ed.), *DownBeat: Sixty Years of Jazz* (Milwaukee: Hal Leonard, 1994)

——————— and Ed Enright (eds), *DownBeat: The Great Jazz Interviews – A 75th Anniversary Anthology* (Milwaukee: Hal Leonard, 2009)

Balliett, Whitney, *Collected Works: A Journal of Jazz 1954–2001* (New York: St Martin's Griffin, 2002)

Berendt, Joachim E., 'A Note on Monk', *Jazz Monthly*, 2/4, 1956

Blumenthal, Bob, *Jazz: An Introduction to the History and Legends behind America's Music* (London: Harper Paperbacks, 2007)

Buin, Yves, *Thelonious Monk* (Paris: P.O.L., 1988)

Carr, Ian, Digby Fairweather and Brian Priestley, *Jazz: The Rough Guide* (London: Rough Guides, 1995)

Chilton, John, *The Song of the Hawk: The Life and Recordings of Coleman Hawkins* (Ann Arbor: University of Michigan Press, 1990)

Crow, Bill, *Jazz Anecdotes* (Oxford: Oxford University Press, 1993)

Dahl, Linda, *Morning Glory: A Biography of Mary Lou Williams* (Berkeley: University of California Press, 1999)

Davis, Miles with Quincy Troupe, *Miles: The Autobiography* (New York: Picador, 1990)

——————— , *Miles: The Autobiography* (New York: Touchstone, 1989)

De Wilde, Laurent, *Monk* (Paris: Editions Gallimard, 1996)

Deffaa, Chip, *Jazz Veterans: A Portrait Gallery* (Fort Bragg: Cypress House Press, 1996)

Dyer, Geoff, *But Beautiful: A Book About Jazz* (London: Abacus, 1998)

Farrell, Barry, 'The Loneliest Monk', *Time*, 28 February 1964

Feather, Leonard and Ira Gitler, *The Biographical Encyclopaedia of Jazz* (New York: Oxford University Press, 1999)

Fishman, Steve, John Homans and Adam Moss (eds), *New York Stories: Landmark Writing from Four Decades of New York Magazine* (New York: Random House, 2008)

Giddins, Gary, *Satchmo: The Genius of Louis Armstrong* (New York: Da Capo Press, 2011)

—————, *Visions of Jazz: The First Century* (New York: Oxford University Press, 1998)

————— and Scott DeVeaux, *Jazz* (New York: W. W. Norton, 2009)

Gillespie, Dizzy with Al Fraser, *To Be, or Not ... To Bop* (New York: Doubleday, 1979)

Gitler, Ira, *The Masters of Bebop: A Listener's Guide* (New York: Da Capo Press, 2001)

—————, *Swing to Bop: An Oral History of the Transition in Jazz in the 1940s* (New York: Oxford University Press, 1985)

Goldberg, Joe, *Jazz Masters of the 50s* (New York: Macmillan, 1965)

Goldsher, Alan, *Hard Bop Academy: The Sidemen of Art Blakey and the Jazz Messengers* (Milwaukee: Hal Leonard, 2008)

Gordon, Lois and Alan Gordon, *American Chronicle: Year by Year through the Twentieth Century* (New York: Yale University Press, 1999)

Gordon, Lorraine and Barry Singer, *Alive at the Village Vanguard: My Life In and Out of Jazz Time* (Milwaukee: Hal Leonard, 2006)

Gordon, Max, *Live at the Village Vanguard* (New York: St. Martin's Press, 1980)

Gottlieb, Robert (ed.), *Reading Jazz: A Gathering of Autobiography, Reportage, and Criticism from 1919 to Now* (New York: Vintage, 1999)

Gourse, Leslie, *Art Blakey: Jazz Messenger* (New York: Schirmer, 2002)

—————, *Straight, No Chaser: The Life and Genius of Thelonious Monk* (New York: Schirmer, 1997)

Hajdu, David, *Lush Life: A Biography of Billy Strayhorn* (London: Granta, 1998)

Hawes, Hampton with Don Asher, *Raise Up Off Me: A Portrait of Hampton Hawes* (New York: Thunder's Mouth Press, 2001)

Heath, Jimmy and Joseph McLaren, *I Walked with Giants: The Autobiography of Jimmy Heath* (Philadelphia: Temple University Press, 2010)

Hentoff, Nat, 'The Private Word of Thelonious Monk', *Esquire*, April 1960
——————, *At the Jazz Band Ball: Sixty Years on the Jazz Scene* (Berkeley: University of California Press, 2010)
——————, *Boston Boy: Growing Up with Jazz and Other Rebellious Passions* (Philadelphia: Paul Dry Books, 2001)
——————, *Listen to the Stories: Nat Hentoff on Jazz and Country Music* (New York: Perennial, 1996)
——————, *The Jazz Life* (New York: Da Capo Press, 1978)
——————, *The Nat Hentoff Reader* (Cambridge: Da Capo Press, 2001)
Hobsbawm, Eric, *Uncommon People: Resistance, Rebellion, and Jazz* (New York: New Press, 1998)
Johnson, Joyce, *Minor Characters: A Beat Memoir* (New York: Methuen, 2006)
Keepnews, Orrin, *Thelonious Monk: The Complete Riverside Recordings* (liner notes, 1986)
Kelley, Robin D. G., *Thelonious Monk: The Life and Times of an American Original* (New York: Free Press, 2009)
Kerouac, Jack, *On the Road* (1957; London: Penguin Classics, 2007)
Kotlowitz, Robert, 'Monk Talk', *Harper's Magazine*, 223, September 1961
Lee, David, *The Battle of the Five Spot: Ornette Coleman and the New York Jazz Field* (Toronto: Mercury Press, 2006)
London Brown, Frank, 'Magnificent Monk of Music', *Ebony*, 14, May 1959
Morrison, Toni, *Jazz* (1987; New York: Vintage, 2001)
Nisenson, Eric, *'Round About Midnight: A Portrait of Miles Davis* (New York: Da Capo Press, 1996)
——————, *Open Sky: Sonny Rollins and his world of Improvisation* (Cambridge: Da Capo Press, 2000)
Ondaatje, Michael, *Coming Through Slaughter* (1976; London: Bloomsbury, 2004)
Ponzio, Jacques and François Postif, *Blue Monk: Un portrait de Thelonious* (Arles: Actes Sud, 1995)
Priestley, Brian, *Mingus: A Critical Biography* (New York: Da Capo Press, 1984)
Reisner, Robert (ed.), *Bird: The Legend of Charlie Parker* (New York: Da Capo Press, 1975)
Rose, Phyllis, *Jazz Cleopatra: Josephine Baker in Her Time* (New York: Vintage, 1991)
Russell, Ross, *Bird Lives! The High Life and Hard Times of Charlie (Yardbird) Parker* (New York: Da Capo, 1996)

Shapiro, Harry, *Waiting for the Man: The Story of Drugs and Popular Music* (London: Helter Skelter Publishing, 1999)

Shapiro, Nat and Nat Hentoff, *Hear Me Talkin' to Ya: The Story of Jazz by the Men Who Made It* (New York: Dover, 1955)

Shearing, George with Alyn Shipton, *Lullaby of Birdland: The Autobiography of George Shearing* (New York: Continuum, 2004)

Sidran, Ben, *Talking Jazz: An Oral History* (New York: Da Capo Press, 1995)

Silver, Horace (ed. Phil Pastras), *Let's Get to the Nitty Gritty: The Autobiography of Horace Silver* (Berkeley: University of California Press, 2007)

Simosko, Vladimir, *Artie Shaw: A Musical Biography and Discography* (Lanham: Scarecrow Press, 2000)

Solis, Gabriel, *Monk's Music: Thelonious Monk and Jazz History in the Making* (Berkeley: University of California Press, 2007)

Spellman, A. B., *Four Lives in the Bebop Business: Ornette Coleman, Herbie Nichols, Jackie McLean, Cecil Taylor* (New York: Limelight Editions, 1985)

Spencer, Fredrick J., *Jazz and Death: Medical Profiles of Jazz Greats* (Jackson: University Press of Mississippi, 2002)

Storr, Anthony, *Music and the Mind* (London: Harper Collins, 1997)

Teachout, Terry, *Pops: A Life of Louis Armstrong* (New York: Harcourt, 2010)

Terkel, Studs, *Giants of Jazz* (New York: New Press, 2002)

van der Bliek, Rob (ed.), *The Thelonious Monk Reader* (Oxford: Oxford University Press, 2001)

Wakefield, Dan, *New York in the Fifties* (New York: St. Martin's Griffin, 1992)

Williams, Martin, *Jazz Masters in Transition: 1957–1969* (New York: Macmillan, 1970)

Williams, Richard, *Long Distance Call: Writings on Music* (London: Aurum, 2000)

——————, *The Blue Moment: Miles Davis's* Kind of Blue *and the Remaking of Modern Music* (London: Faber and Faber, 2009)

Woideck, Carl (ed.), *The Charlie Parker Companion: Six Decades of Commentary* (New York: Schirmer, 1998)

Wolfe, Tom, *The Electric Kool-Aid Acid Test* (1968; New York: Black Swan, 1989)

——————, *The Kandy-Kolored Tangerine-Flake Streamline Baby* (1965; New York: Vintage, 2005)

Documentaries and Film Footage

Jazz

'The Thelonious Monk Quartet', *Jazz 625* (BBC, 1965)
'The Thelonious Monk Quartet', *Jazz 625* (BBC, 1966)
Monk in Oslo (dir. Harald Heide-Steen, Jr., 1966)
Monk (dir. Michael Blackwood, 1968)
Monk in Europe (dir. Michael Blackwood, 1968)
Monk in Berlin (1973)
Thelonious Monk: Straight, No Chaser (dir. Charlotte Zwerin, 1988)
Het Monk Kwartet
Jazz Icons: Thelonious Monk Live in '66 (TdK, 2006)
Masters of American Music: Thelonious Monk – American Composer (dir. Matthew Sieg, 2009)
Solo Piano in Berlin '69: Monk Plays Ellington (DVD Jazz Shots, 2010)
Masters of American Music: Thelonious Monk – American Composer (dir. Matthew Sieg, 2010)
'The Sound of Jazz', *Seven Lively Arts* (CBS, 1957)
Jazz Pour Tous! (dir. Serge Leroy and Paul Roland, 1964)
'Hawk at the Town Hall', *Jazz 625* (BBC, 1964)
'Duke Ellington in Concert', *Jazz 625* (BBC, 1964)
Ellington in Europe (BBC, 1965)
Ellington in Europe 2 (BBC, 1965)
'Teddy Wilson', *Jazz at the Philharmonic* (BBC, 1967)
'Miles Davis Quintet', *Jazz Scene at Ronnie Scott's* (BBC, 1969)

'Johnny Dankworth', *Jazz Scene at Ronnie Scott's* (BBC, 1969)
Jazz from Montreux (BBC, 1977)
Last of the Blue Devils: The Kansas City Jazz Story (dir. Bruce Ricker, 1979)
Let's Get Lost (dir. Bruce Weber, 1988)
Slim Gaillard's Civilisation (dir. Anthony Wall, 1988)
'Dizzy Gillespie', *Jazz 625* (BBC, restored version 1990)
Jazz (dir. Ken Burns, 2000)
Norman Granz Presents: Improvisation – Charlie Parker, Ella Fitzgerald and More (DVD Eagle Rock, 2007)

Rothschild Family

The House of Rothschild (dir. Alfred L. Werker, 1934)
Die Rothschilds: Aktien auf Waterloo (dir. Erich Waschneck, 1940)
'Debutantes', *Tonight* (BBC, 1962)
A Rothschild and His Red Gold (BBC, 1974)
David Dimbleby Interviews Miriam Rothschild (BBC, 1982)
'Lord Rothschild', *The Levin Interviews* (BBC, 1984)
'Miriam Rothschild', *Women of Our Century* (BBC, date?)
Mastermind (BBC, 21 May 1989)

Race and Contemporary History

Panorama 161: Carnegie Course (BBC)
'Romance is Dead, Long Live Romance: Marjorie Proops', *One Pair of Eyes* (BBC)
A Study of Educational Inequalities in Southern California (National Archives and Records Administration, 1936)
The World at War (FDR Presidential Library, 1942)
The Negro Soldier (National Archives and Records Administration, 1945)
The Plantation System in Southern Life (Coronet Instructional Films, 1950)
The Home Economics Story (Iowa State Teachers' College, 1951)
Our Cities Must Fight (US Federal Civil Defense Administration, 1951)
Third Avenue El (Carson Davidson, 1955)
The Dynamic American City (Chamber of Commerce of the United States, 1956)
Palmour Street (Georgia Department of Public Health, 1957)
Eye to Eye: London to New York – A Tale of Two Cities (BBC, 1957)

In the Suburbs (Redbook Magazine, 1957)
The Black and White Minstrel Show (BBC, 28 January 1961)
'Some of my Best Friends are White', *Man Alive* (BBC, 1966)
'The Friendly Invasion', parts 1 to 3, *Omnibus* (BBC, 1975)
Britain in the Thirties (BBC, 1983)

Selected Feature Films

Productions in which Thelonious Monk, or his music, appear

Jazz on a Summer's Day (dir. Aram Avakian and Bert Stern, 1959)
Les liaisons dangereuses (dir. Roger Vadim, 1959)
Heads (dir. Peter Gidal, 1969)
The Homecoming (dir. Peter Hall, 1973)
Lenny (dir. Bob Fosse, 1974)
The Marseille Contract (dir. Robert Parrish, 1974)
Sven Klangs Kvintett (dir. Stellan Olsson, 1976)
'Round Midnight (dir. Bertrand Tavernier, 1986)
A Great Day in Harlem (dir. Jean Bach, 1994)

Archives and Libraries

Barbara Ghika Archive
The Rothschild Archive, Waddesdon Manor
The Rothschild Archive, N. M. Rothschild & Sons, London
Miriam Rothschild Archive
Nica de Koenigswarter Archive
BBC Archive
British Library
Colindale Newspaper Archive
David Redfern Library
Downbeat magazine
Esquire magazine
Express Group
Gaston Eve
General Register Office, UK
George Wein Archive
Hudson County Superior Court
Jazz Archive at Duke University, library.duke.edu/Rubenstein/collections/jazzindex.html
Library of Congress
London Library
Marcus Harrison Archive
National Records and Records Administration
New York County Supreme Court
New Yorker magazine
New York Times

Pathé News
Prelinger Archives, www.archive.org/details/prelinger
The Times
Time magazine
TS Monk Archive
William P. Gottlieb Collection, Music Division, Library of Congress
Wilmington Superior Court

Index